SANTA INES HERMOSA
The Journal of the Padre's Niece

by

Mamie Goulet Abbott
with a foreword by
Mabel Otis Booth

Third edition introduction by

Fr. Robert A. Barbato, ofm cap.
Pastor, Mission Santa Ines

Illustrations
by
Nicholas S. Firfires

OLIVE PRESS PUBLICATIONS

Printed in the United States of America

 OLIVE PRESS PUBLICATIONS
P.O. BOX 99
LOS OLIVOS, CALIFORNIA 93441
805/ 688-2445

TO ALL GUESTS
WHO CAME TO SANTA INES

"Hospes, pulsanti tibi se mea janua pandet,
    tu tua pulsanti pectore pande Deo."

"Guest, as to thy knocking my door opens to thee,
    so do thou open to God, knocking at thy heart."

CONTENTS

INTRODUCTION TO THE THIRD EDITION

September 17, 2002

The California Missions have held a fascination for many people over the years. When I was in fourth grade my class visited Mission San Fernando as part of our study of California History, and I learned to share in this fascination. Being named pastor of one of the Missions, Mission Santa Ines, 19th of the chain, in 1997, was something of a dream come true, but it also taught me quickly the reality that working at a Mission today is not quite stepping into the idyllic world of *Ramona*. Not only was I caretaker of a historical treasure, but pastor of a living community. The fact is that the history of the Missions and their people did not stop with secularization and decay in the 1840s. The Missions continued, and still continue today, to be complex places, which try to bring the reality of faith into contact with daily life.

This is why Mamie Goulet Abbott's book has always captivated me. Here is a chronicle of life at a real Mission not in the time of the *padres* and the *indios*, but in the turbulent days of the early 20th century. Here we find not the story of missionaries who travelled from Spain, but of a young woman who travelled from Minnesota (still a long journey in those days) to help her uncle, Fr. Alexander Buckler, continue the life of the Mission called "the hidden gem." As you read these pages, you will see that their life at Mission Santa Ines was not always much easier than that of the earlier inhabitants.

We owe a great debt to Fr. Buckler and his intrepid niece. Along with the Chumash who built Mission Santa Ines and the padres who ran it, they are an integral part of the history and development of this place. The present parishioners owe them a debt for continuing the atmosphere of prayer, hospitality, and charity that are still hallmarks of Mission Santa Ines today. The people of California owe them a debt for helping to preserve this landmark and keeping it available as a living part of our state's history. We all owe Mamie Goulet a special debt for recording a precious part of the history of the Mission and entertaining us with the exciting tales of her time here.

I am no less fascinated with the California Missions today than I was in fourth grade. I hope that those who read this reproduction of Mamie Goulet Abbot's memories will find that the later history of the Missions is no less fascinating than the earlier. As Mission Santa Ines prepares to mark its bicentennial in the year 2004, I pray that all its parishioners, the community of the Santa Ynez Valley, and all its visitors as well will not only appreciate the Mission's past, but also gladly accept their part in its future.

Fr. Robert A. Barbato, ofm cap.
Pastor, Mission Santa Ines (1997-2001)

FOREWORD
By Mabel Otis Booth

Mrs. Abbott's history has been long in the making for it is the record of accumulated experience. Historical facts form little part of it, but there is poetry in its pages and over and above all a deep devotion to an idea and an exalted performance of duty.

The evocation of the past, of the days of "long ago and far away," is not alone the province of the historian but of the poet. To impart to cold prose the beauty and the art of other times means to have an understanding of those things which lie behind the tabulated events of an historical era.

The dignity and grandeur of spirit that pervades the life of peoples who live somewhat apart from the larger world marks the early days of California life, a dignity which is reflected in this narrative of Mrs. Abbott's life with her uncle, the Padre, in the primitive surroundings of life in Santa Ines Mission. The labors of two inspired people, without money or trained skill, to restore the splendid old Mission to something of its early beauty are a great evidence of that finest of all courage, the courage to face day after day a life devoid of comfort, filled with every hardship, yet met with joyousness and hope.

INTRODUCTION

In January 1932 the Rev. Zephyrin Engelhardt O.F.M., loving and distinguished historian of the California Missions and missionaries, wrote to Mrs. Abbott, then Miss Mamie Goulet, as follows:

"Brave Heroine of Mission Santa Ines: It was generous and in a measure heroic to agree to that hard life at Santa Ines but you saved the Mission with your uncle. I want to make that stand out. It was well that I preceded you and Father Buckler by several months otherwise what I have to say would be interpreted as ungenerous boosting of you two at the expense of predecessors."

A little over two months later Father Engelhardt died at the old Santa Barbara Mission, but not before his *Mission Santa Ines Virgen Y Martir, and its Ecclesiastical Seminary* had been published.

Over a period of some years Father Engelhardt had turned to Miss Goulet for information. In one of his many letters to her he wrote: "It is all so graphic and touchingly beautiful that I would print it as it was. I wish it all in your own words first person. It is too graphic and beautiful to have it lost for history."

Now twenty years later Mamie Goulet Abbott's journal and reminiscences of her life at Santa Ines 1904-1924 appear in these pages.

Women from the beginning of time have astounded masculine strength by their resourcefulness, practicality and daring in the face of rugged difficulties. Mamie Abbott had other virtues, a selfless quality that dedicated itself whole-heartedly and with affection to the task at hand. This intensely human, unaffected and unpretentious journal tells the story of how she, the Padre's niece, restored the historic Santa Ines Mission from a dusty ruin to a noble chapel and convent.

There is no outward sign that this is a religious book. It has a wry and dry sense of humor which breaks through endless difficulties and frustrations like the sun, and like the sun warms the heart of the reader; but as we read on and become more and more aware of the herculean task, the disasters which befell the Mission, the loneliness, the lack of help from hands or pocketbooks, we know full well that only faith made manifest in deeds accomplished the task.

Although this journal adds a modest chapter to the fascinating history of California of another day, it is not preeminently an historical document in the commonly accepted understanding of that phrase. It is the record of what one woman did for her uncle, the Padre, and the Mission they both loved. Although walls were built and rubble removed there were other amiable and loving duties performed. Mrs. Abbott records that in one year she served over six hundred meals to the "Wandering Willies," the tramps who were never turned away. To give honor its due, it should be acknowledged that many of these lost souls remained to help in the reconstruction of the Mission. Certainly one of the highlights of the journal is the picture painted of these tramps who in restoring the Mission often restored themselves.

Mrs. Abbott discovered a number of old and priceless vestments, some of them dating to the 15th and 16th centuries. Her service of heart and hand continued as she meticulously mended and restored these vestments so that they might again be used in the solemn services of the church.

To those of us who have been privileged to read the manuscript in advance of publication, comes a common reaction. The story of the restoration of Santa Ines as told by the house-keeper, an exact and inspired description of Mrs. Abbott's duties, is not only the story of rebuilt walls, bell towers, mended vestments and so on, but the story of a Mission by the side of the road which gave loving hospitality to all who came knocking at its door. No one was sent empty away.

Father Engelhardt, who encouraged Mrs. Abbott to write her memories of Santa Ines, should have the last word.

Father Buckler "introduced his all around assistant, Miss Mary L. Goulet, who had arrived on September 21st, 1904. 'Can this comely but frail looking young lady be equal to the difficulties she will encounter?' was our mental comment. In less than a week this maiden of 23 years had proven her mettle. After that we had no more misgivings as to her courage and ability. Ere long we found her a well trained and noble hearted lady who went about her duties conscientiously, energetically yet gently, silently yet cheerfully, asking no curious questions, but looking after the needs with solicitude and having everything in neat and orderly condition. Truly the pastor of the Mission Santa Ines had acquired a jewel."

". . . . What happened thereafter we have asked faithful Miss Goulet to report in her own way."

Note. Quotations from Father Engelhardt are taken from letters to Mrs. Abbott or from Father Engelhardt's *Mission Santa Ines.*

NOTE

Santa Ynez Valley. which was named after the Old Mission Santa Ines in Solvang, is properly spelled with a "Y." The Old Mission records and signs refer to "Santa Ines," using the Latin spelling of the Saint's name.

Both "Ines" and "Ynez" are correct, but the latter is usually applied to the valley, while the Mission uses the former.

In English, "Ines" or "Ynez" means "Agnes." Thus both the Mission and the Valley were named after the martyred young saint who lived in Rome in 304.

DATES FOR SANTA INES MISSION

Exploration for Mission Site.. 1796

Order of Viceroy Iturrigaray establishing Mission.........Feb. 1803

Established (19th Mission) by Fr. Estaban Tapis, Sept. 17 1804

Partly destroyed by earthquake.................................Dec. 21 1812

Present Church begun 1815

Present Church dedicated..July 4 1817

Indian revolt ....Feb. 21 1824

Secularrization ("Confiscation")... 1836
    (Valued at that time at $62,876.00)

College founded 1844

Mission lands rented out by government to private parties 1845

Mission and lands sold (for $7,000.00)....................July 15 1846
    (Title later on declared invalid and property returned
    to Church)

Mission and College abandoned... 1850

Period of "Vandalism"..1850 to 1882

Mission and lands leased to private parties.............1882 to 1898

Work of Restoration begun... 1904

xvi

ACKNOWLEDGEMENT

This book was designed and prepared for publication by the editors of the Sunwise Press, 899 Coast Highway, Montecito, Santa Barbara, California. It was printed for the editors by Schauer Printing Studio, Inc. The type used is ten point Baskerville.

The manuscript was read for corrections by Ronald and Dorothy Scofield and by Mrs. Winthrop Sargent.

The manuscript was typed by Mrs. Ethel B. Drew and by Mrs. Vera Cooper.

The introduction is by Leighton Rollins.

Miss Mildred B. Moody designed the cover of the book. It is based upon one of the old vestments of Santa Ines Mission.

The editors wish to express their gratitude to Miss Harriett J. Moody and Miss Wilma C. Moody for many helpful suggestions, and to Mr. and Mrs. Ronald D. Scofield who read the manuscript.

The title of the book, "Santa Ines Hermosa," is taken from an old Spanish hymn traditionally sung at the Mission.

Photograph of Santa Ines. View looking southwest at Santa Ines by Ralph Arnold, U.S. Geological Survey, Washington, D.C.

Portrait photograph of Father Buckler by Clarence Mattei.

Self-photograph of Mamie Goulet.

Photograph of Santa Ines Mission Bells by Fritz Walker (Knight of the Road).

xvii

THE PADRE'S APPOINTMENT

In the later part of July nineteen hundred and four, the good Padre Alejandro Buckler received his appointment as pastor of the Santa Ines Mission, one of California's historic landmarks. He could not say that he was elated over the appointment, or that he was very enthusiastic about his new charge. Coming to California from the middle west, a Mission church would be a new experience to him. He had seen the San Gabriel Mission and the ruins of the San Diego Mission. He wondered what the Santa Ines Mission would be like.

A few days later found him aboard the Southern Pacific railway train leaving Los Angeles for Gaviota, a railway station on the ocean front, one hundred and thirty miles north of Los Angeles. There connection would be made with the Gaviota-Los Olivos stage. This would take him over the Santa Ynez range of mountains into the sleepy valley bearing the same name, and to his new home, new duties and new environment.

It was late afternoon when, tired and dusty from the long ride of eighteen miles over rough roads, sitting on a dilapidated seat of the stage with its cushion worn down to the bare springs, he finally reached his destination, the Mission.

"Here we are at the Mission," cried out the stage driver as he thrust his battered whip into its socket on the dashboard, and letting himself down from his high seat proceeded to unload Padre's trunk and suit-cases.

1

The Padre was speechless. Was this the Santa Ines Mission? Was this the place to which he was assigned?

The stage driver dropped the trunk and suit-cases on the creaking board floor of this once beautiful arched colonnade, climbed back to his high seat on the stage, and with a parting glance at the Padre and a gee-daap to the horses soon disappeared from sight.

The Padre stood for a moment, dazed, the isolation and desolation of the place creeping over him. He gazed around. A peaceful and lovely mountain setting, he thought, but how could anyone live in such a place? This unique and massive structure was a ruin. Stooping, he picked up his two suit-cases and walked through the big open front door into a large spacious room, with a big open fireplace in the opposite wall, devoid of any furniture save a few rickety chairs. It was dark and gloomy looking in the late afternoon light and had a strong musty odor.

Presently, through the door of an adjoining room, a woman appeared, large, robust, and with an inquiring look upon her face.

"I am Padre Alejandro sent to take charge of the Mission. I did not expect to find anyone here," said the Padre.

"Yes, my husband and I live here."

"So," said the Padre.

"Yes, we came from Ar'zone, and when we come 'long here and no one was alivin' in the place, we thought 'twould be a good place to stay the winter. So here we be."

"So," again said the Padre.

"You will be wantin' something to eat I reckon. Did you come far?"

"Not so very far but I think I will want something to eat if I stay," said the Padre, not altogether sure in his own mind that he would stay.

"We're long way from a hotel or store, but my husband drives to Sant'nez now and then for provis'ns. We're jus' plain folk an' live simple, and if you will pay for the meat and 'taters, I'll be glad to give you meals."

To say that the offer was novel to the Padre would be putting it mildly. He was hungry, there seemed no way out of the situation, so he acquiesced. He then excused himself by saying he wished to take a walk about the place before it grew too dark.

Padre went first to the chapel. He was surprised and pleased as he walked inside and up the center aisle to the sanctuary. The walls of the body of the church were whitewashed but the walls of the sanctuary were covered with Indian fresco paintings. In soft greens, reds, yellows and browns, they were done to imitate marble panels. The decorations on the beams represented trailing vines and leaves and were carried out along the sides and facings. The painting was blended into the altar itself. The two-step wood shelves on either side of the tabernacle and wood candlesticks were also done in marble imitation. An exquisite oil painting of the Good Shepherd adorned the tabernacle door, and a most interesting oil painting in floral design, tacked on a frame, was used as an antipendium covering the space below the altar table. Above the altar in a fluted-shell niche Santa Ines, sweet and graceful, looked on in silent approval.

"It is very beautiful. God give me strength to make it whole," Padre said aloud as he stood before the altar.

Retracing his steps through the front door, he walked down the long colonnade towards the end of the building. All rooms facing the colonnade opened onto it and, as he proceeded, sad sights greeted him everywhere: windows broken, doors battered, cobwebs and filth lurking in every corner and crevice. In two rooms that had neither doors nor windows left and very little roof, chickens were going to roost. In another was an incubator, and countless little chicks huddled here and there in the debris. Just outside this room, under the arched colonnade, was a bed spring and mattress supported by dry-goods boxes, and used by this apparently shiftless and indifferent couple who were squatting at the Mission for the coming winter.

Going on and around the building to the back, he found another colonnade as in the front, but more dilapidated, a part of it fallen down, and the remainder, about to fall, was braced here and there to hold it together. A part of the building was completely torn down, leaving a mass of crumbling adobe that had almost melted away into dust from which it originally came.

It was a sorry sight and Padre was at a loss to know what to do. To remain under present conditions seemed utterly impossible, and there were no funds available to better them. "Even in its ruins it has a kind of grandeur," he thought, "and must have been a wonderful place of activity in the days of its glory." Then, through the fancy of an active mind, he found himself making plans to rebuild the structure as a monument to that glorious past.

He returned to the large front room and on through to another back of it, looking for that great solace, that mediator between an unappreciative world and dissatisfied man, a good dinner. He found a simple but good meal awaiting him. Cooking on a battered and rusty stove set up in one of the roofless rooms, the good-natured woman had exercised her best wits to prepare savory dishes. She introduced her husband, a tall, angular man with sharp features and a thin high voice, who had little to say, but musingly listened to his wife carry on conversations with the Padre.

Besides the Mission were four places, or stations, of which the Padre was to take charge: Lompoc, a distance of twenty three miles, Los Alamos, sixteen miles, Sisquoc, twenty-six miles, and Las Cruces, about fifteen miles away. These he would have to reach by various routes, either by long tiresome trips with horse and buggy, or roundabout ways by stage and railway trains.

He would give one Sunday each month to services at the Mission, one to Lompoc, one to Los Alamos, another to Sisquoc, and in such months as had a fifth Sunday, he would go to Las Cruces. All these places outside the Mission had little frame churches except Las Cruces. There Padre would have to read Mass in the village schoolhouse, and for that reason had to take along all the equipment for use in the service.

There were days when Padre would sit hours basking in the warm autumn sun on the front veranda, dreaming and planning for the restoration to usefulness of this now so neglected structure. Previous to coming to California he had spent a year in Europe where he had visited great cathedrals and churches. This happy experience had a stimulating effect on his earnest desires to restore Santa Ines Mission.

When days had grown into weeks, and weeks had waxed into more than two months, Padre became fully determined to put the dream of his plans into real operation. So far he had just worried along trying to make up his mind whether to remain and face the huge task, or give up and ask his Bishop to release him from the assignment. It was at this point that I received a long, long letter telling of his assignment. It was a graphic word picture of the Mission, its ruined condition, its magnificent and picturesque mountain setting, and its possibilities. It was then Padre extended to me, his niece, a pressing invitation to come to California to assist him in the task of making his dream become a reality.

MY TRIP TO CALIFORNIA

When I received Padre's letter I was beside myself with joy. What a thrilling trip I would have! The thoughts of going West, to California, the land of which I had heard so much, made my young heart leap!

I looked up from my letter. My mother's face seemed pale and wistful. Her deep blue eyes were looking straight into mine. I was seized with an indescribable feeling of love for her and I longed to enfold her into my strong arms and keep her there.

"How soon do you want to go?" my mother asked in her soft, well modulated voice.

"Oh any time, Mother. I presume the sooner I can go the better," I replied, still thrilling with the thought of seeing California, not knowing what was in store for me in that wonder land beyond the high Rockies.

Father Zephyrin Engelhardt wrote in his "Mission Santa Ines":

"The condition of the vestments convinced Father Buckler that he could not singlehanded cope with the difficulties encountered. Feminine hands, directed by a capable head and a stout heart devoid of all thought of self, would be needed, not merely for housekeeping but as an assistant in the general restoration. Where could such a person be found? He resolved to appeal to his niece in far away Minnesota. He was asking a great sacrifice, indeed. The young woman would have to renounce all worldly prospects, and bury herself in the solitude of the Mission structures, and think of nothing but work, work. . . . . There was dearth of almost everything, yet no store nearer than the town of Santa Ynez four miles distant. The Father described the situation and left the decision to the niece, who promptly and heroically consented to leave her home in order to assist her uncle in the great undertaking.

"The cheerful news from his generous niece put Father

6

Buckler into a happy mood which he communicated to us in the following letter:

" 'Santa Ines Mission, California, Aug. 31, 1904.—Dear Reverend Father: How I enjoyed your missive! Gladly do I place myself at your service. You are welcome at any time. Unfortunately, there are so many question marks in the way that it is proper to explain to you the whole condition of things here. I arrived at the Mission on July 22nd, and encountered solitude, ruin and abomination of desolation everywhere. . . . . Dirt and neglect stare at me all around. There is a lack of linens, kitchen utensils, etc. My housekeeper, my niece, will appear on October 1st. Then we shall start to clean out the house, purify the interior of the church, and procure the articles necessary for housekeeping. . . . . After November 1st, Rev. Father, you may come at any time, because by that date I hope to be in a position to harbor a priest. As it is, I am a sort of hermit, and a tertiary of St. Francis, half a Franciscan also.

Your devoted

Alexander Buckler'."

There were busy days that followed the receiving of Padre's letter, both for myself and for my mother. Hours were spent in sewing, mending, remodeling and creating all sorts of pretty and fluffy things to wear in that fancied fairyland in California. My mother was a very clever seamstress and took great pride and joy in making up many of her children's garments.

As the days slipped by and the date for my departure grew near, I would often find myself looking into my mother's sweet face. I had never seen so many lines of care upon it. To soften the pangs of our parting I would say to her, "Mother, it will be harder for me to leave you than it will be for you to have me go. You will still have the rest of the family with you while I shall be going alone."

"Yes, dear child, although I shall miss you very much I am glad of your opportunity to go and to have the trip which will mean so much to you."

Mother was a widow, Father having died when I was still quite young, and, being the eldest of her children, I probably was, to a measure, some help and comfort to my grief stricken mother in sharing the many burdens that arise in the household of a large family.

September the fifteenth, the date for my departure had come. My trunk and suit-cases, filled to their full capacity, were strapped and labeled, waiting for the expressman to convey them to the station. There had been a stream of friends to say "good bye" and to wish me Godspeed on my journey. My mother remained calm and placid. No one knew the suffering of her mother-heart at the realization that now her children were grown up and eventually she would be called upon to part with them from her fireside.

The evening meal was a quiet one with everybody doing his best to make conversation without saying that which was uppermost in mind and heart. "We must not tarry or we will be late for the train," I said, as we arose from the dinner table, and slipping my arm around my mother's waist proceeded towards my room for my wraps. It was to be the last visit to my room and I lingered long with a yearning for communion with all that had come into my life during my tender years of its occupancy. I put on my hat and coat with deliberation, meanwhile surveying the room and all its furnishings, until I felt the very pictures on the walls were giving their silent benediction. Taking a last loving glance in their direction I walked out, silently, to the waiting carriage.

At the station we had a few minutes of waiting. My heart beat so loud I thought all about me must hear it. I reassured my mother of my love for her and for my brothers and sisters, promising ever to keep the light of hope for an early visit to them or from them.

The toot - toot - t-o-o-t of the big engine gave its last signal. I bade farewell to all that had been nearest and dearest to me in the large twin cities of the Middle West. Striving hard to stay the lumps that persistently came to my throat and blinking away the tears I waved a last "good bye" with my handkerchief. The train rumbled softly and slowly out of the station, taking me to a new home, new surroundings, but to the same good Padre, of that I was sure.

All the world was dark without. Many of the passengers were retiring. I sat, thoughtful and unmindful of what was taking place about me, until the colored porter had pulled down and made up all the berths save mine. Suddenly I realized it was very late and immediately I too retired, not to sleep, for sleep did not come to me before I had given vent to tears and pent up feelings that had been restrained for so long.

The long journey was a pleasant one as each day brought its interesting diversions and experiences. The first day a change of trains was made at Omaha, Nebraska, which gave the passengers a couple of hours stop-over and an opportunity to see something of that city. Thus far the scenery, mostly wide open prairie which looked very desolate in its gray-brown autumnal colors, had not been very interesting or attractive.

On the morning of the second day more prairie, and the sun rose over the plains looking as pale and colorless as the prairie itself. At about eleven the train arrived at Colorado Springs, Colorado, where Pike's Peak can be seen in the near distance. I recalled my early geography days with a vivid picture of the peak in my mind. A cousin lived there and met the train so we could have a visit together during the twenty minute stop-over. I was delighted to see him and it gave me a feeling that I was still in touch with some one I knew.

Later in the day the scenery, more hilly or mountainous with color in both rock and soil, began to be more interesting. Again my geography came to mind as we were going through the Royal Gorge, that wonder of nature's wonders, with the Arkansas River running and tumbling all the way through it. The train followed the river first on one side and then on the other, crossing and re-crossing the stream and picking its way around the sharp curves and narrow bottom of the Gorge. The immensely high, rugged, and rocky walls on either side gave one the feeling of being imprisoned and the possibility of being held up by bandits. The highly vivid coloring in the grotesque rock formation turned to grim blackness as night came on, and I wished to be out of it. The porter turned on the lights. My eyes ached and my neck seemed to be twisted out of place from the craning all day long to view the scenery. I retired early.

On the third day fellow passengers were getting acquainted. One of the passengers, an elderly gentleman, died of heart failure—probably owing to the altitude at which our train was traveling. This caused considerable commotion until the body was removed from the train at the next principal station.

Most of this day was spent going through Utah. The scenery was interesting. The rugged mountains in their rocky formation of countless hues were beautiful. Vegetation was sparse and scattered. Mines and quarries here and there along the way, gave signs of habitation.

Like most young people on their first long trip of importance, I kept a diary. Nothing was omitted that had any excuse for being or happening. Also, I wrote long letters every day, full of all that I saw as I traveled, to assure my mother that all was well and that I thought of her often.

A forty minute stop was made at beautiful Salt Lake City. Everybody got out of the train, walked up and down the long platform, got a glimpse of the world-renowned Mormon Temple, and breathed the exhilarating salt air which sweeps in from the Lake a short distance away. It was about nine o'clock that evening when the train proceeded to cross the Lake, a distance of nearly forty miles, over a newly constructed bridge. Will I, or any of the passengers, ever forget that trip over the Lake? What a thrilling experience it was, traveling on a train with water all around us, giving the feeling of being in mid-ocean. A magical and bewitching full moon in a clear sky looked down on the Lake, which was calm and smooth, reflecting that fiery red moon—truly enhancing a fairyland dream. It was the third day the bridge was put into use and the train traveled very slowly over it. Workmen were stationed at intervals all along the way to see that all went well. The time was an hour and twenty minutes in crossing, much too short, I thought, on such a sublime night. The hands of my watch pointed to twelve o'clock before the spell of that charm was sufficiently diminished for me to think of retiring for the night.

On the morning of the fourth day the train was laboring through long stretches of Nevada desert. The fine sand sifted into the car until everything was dusty, dirty and grimy. The heat was oppressive and everybody looked bored. After some time, however, the train arrived at Truckee, a little mining town at an elevation of five thousand eight hundred and twenty feet above sea level. Here the air was invigorating and many of the passengers stepped out to get a breath of it. Here too, we learned that the first section of our transcontinental train, which was traveling just ahead of us, had met with an accident. Going on a side track, the train ran into a box car, killing the engineer and fireman. This caused us some delay.

Our section of the train added two locomotives to help it over the high Sierras, which now loomed before us in their indescribable, and almost unbelievable, beauty of scenery. The passengers brightened and again showed interest. I let the spirit of romance woo my fancy as the engines, puffing and snorting, wound their way round and round. Up and up we climbed, in and out of many tunnels, through miles and miles of snow sheds and emerged into more beautiful canyons than before. The stately dark pine and fir trees all laden with fleecy white snow, and little water streams dancing down the mountain sides at every turn, made it a veritable dream of a winter fairyland. Many legends exist of the wild passes of those rough mountains, of their deep canyons and dizzy trails.

As night came on the trees, mountain tops and huge boulders became nothing more than faint outlines against a sky that was overcast in thin fog, the full moon scarcely visible through its dense blue-gray. Sleep came as the train hurried down into the valley.

On the morning of the fifth day I looked out and thought, "I am really in California at last."

The westward trip ended at the Oakland Pier. There I boarded a south-bound train. The scenery held little interest for me until, in the late afternoon, we reached the long trail up the Santa Margarita mountains.

Always in after years in my journeys to and from San Francisco, while living at the Santa Ines Mission, I would live over that first trip over this most absorbing and picturesque Santa Margarita grade. It had so impressed me with its loveliness.

As evening came on, the Pacific Ocean was sighted and soon we were following its shore all the way into Santa Barbara. How perfectly thrilling it was to see the ocean for the first time. The sun, which looked larger than any sun I had ever seen, was just setting. Its long bright rays painted the calm waters in all the indescribable shades of reds, blues and orchids, from the horizon to the very edge of the shore; truly an intoxicating sight. I put my head out of the window that I might breathe in some of its charm and magic and salty freshness. Unfortunately, all too soon the mantle of night wrapped itself around the earth and the dream of another day had passed on.

It was fifteen minutes past nine o'clock when we reached Santa Barbara. An elderly gentleman, his daughter and I were the only passengers to get off. The porter hurriedly gathered up our suit-cases as the train slowed down and with a thud dropped them on the creaking boards of the depot platform. The engine gave a few short puffs and sped on its way into the darkness of the night.

There was a waiting carriage for the elderly gentleman and his daughter, so they too disappeared into the night. We had arrived on a special train which the town bus did not meet, neither did the station agent wait for it. His office looked dark and forbidding as I stood there, a stranger in a strange land, setting foot on California soil for the first time. I stood for a moment too dazed and bewildered to think or move. It seemed a long way to the pale glimmering lights of the village, and an eternity to collect myself sufficiently to pick up my suit-case and small bag. I started off at a brisk pace over a board walk that was poorly lighted by lamp posts a block or more apart. The trees and shrubs and dark alleyways seemed to hide strange creatures as I hurried past them, not daring to look in their direction.

A night's stop-over in Santa Barbara was necessary to make connections the following day with the Gaviota-Los Olivos stage that would take me over the mountain to the Mission. Padre had recommended the Mascarel Hotel for my stay. When I saw a man coming towards me I stopped to ask directions to reach it.

"You long way from hotel," he replied to my inquiry.

"Are there any street cars?" I asked.

"Si Señora, street car on State Street every half hour. Shall I carry suit-case for you?"

"That would be very nice," I said, after some hesitation. With my heart thumping, my knees trembling and my eyes casting side glances at the man, we walked nine or ten blocks to the hotel.

"What do I owe you?" I asked, as the man deposited my suit-case in the hotel lobby.

"Nothing, Señora," the man replied as he made a courtly bow.

I insisted, and dropping some coins in his blue denim jumper pocket, I thanked him. Gladly would I drop more coins in that jumper pocket were I to meet that man again, so grateful I felt for the kind assistance of that perfect stranger.

I registered, and, escorted by the proprietor, walked up a long flight of stairs and down a narrow hall to room number one.

It was a hot, stuffy room opening out on a balcony that faced State Street, the main thoroughfare of the village. There was a window facing the side street and down below it the Salvation Army of four or five members was singing hymns and giving testimonials. Being very weary I retired immediately.

No sooner had I turned out the light in the gas jet than I heard voices on the balcony· Two women, evidently chambermaids out to get a breath of fresh air, were airing their views about California. For about half an hour I was forced to listen to them denouncing the State, its climate, its methods of advertising for Eastern tourists, and its discouraging opportunities for securing employment. Finally they agreed that if they ever got money enough for their fares back home they would take the first train going out. "We will be a long time getting our fares working at a dollar and a half a week," was their parting remark as they passed my window and disappeared.

For the second time since setting foot on this new land my spirits had been dampened. I gave my pillow a few vigorous pokes to inject some coolness into it, and wished I had not heard the conversation.

MY ARRIVAL AT THE MISSION

At twelve thirty in the afternoon of the sixth day of my
journey I stepped off of the Southern Pacific train at Gaviota.
Heavens! What a place, I thought, as I gazed around, the
big gray ocean on one side and high towering mountains on
the other. The small station building and a few freight cars
on a siding were the only signs of life. Awaiting me was the
Gaviota-Los Olivos stage, the same rough riding coach the Padre
had taken some weeks before.

The heat was intense and the stage crowded. A tall, slender,
clean-shaven man, wearing a long black coat that reminded you
of a village minister, climbed on the high seat beside the driver.
A middle-aged woman, a keen-eyed, nattily dressed drummer
and myself occupied the second seat. Our small bags and
trappings filled every bit of space around our feet. The back
seat and end of the coach was piled high with our suit-cases,
express parcels and mail sacks.

The drummer, as is usual with drummers, was very talkative.
Satisfying his curiosity, by pertinent questions, he then made
fun of my being a tenderfoot in California to our fellow passengers. He found me unresponsive and more interested in the
scenery than in his small idle talk, so turned his attentions to the
middle-aged woman who chatted and laughed with him as we
jogged along.

15

Mr. John Waugh, the stage driver, had a kindly face. He was past threescore years and almost toothless, but age had not diminished his long patriarchal beard. He called attention to points of interest along the way, and told at great length of the "flustration" of General Fremont and his Army as we were going through the Gaviota Pass. He brought his horses to a full stop so that I, the tenderfoot, might crane my neck out of the canvas covered coach to view the huge rock, which overhung the road. At that very spot the enemy lay in wait for the General and his Army, all of which meant little or nothing to me at that time. I will say in passing that I am now the proud possessor of a sword which belonged to one of General Fremont's soldiers. It was found on the San Marcos Pass where Benjamin Foxen led the army safely into Santa Barbara.

At Las Cruces, a little wayside place, a change of horses was made at a stable maintained for that purpose. The stage was drawn by four horses. With fresh horses kicking up the powder dust we went up the long Nojoqui grade, and then down through the beautiful Alisal Rancho. The road, which was nothing more than a wagon trail in most places, was lined on both sides with dark green oaks and graceful sycamores in their autumnal browns and gold. The streams, most of them dry at that season, had no bridges for crossing. With the wooden brakes grinding against the wheels, the stage went down to the very bottom of these streams. The horses picked their way around big rocks, over white gravel and clambered up their banks. One stream, however, had a ribbon of clear cool water running. We crossed it at a very picturesque and shaded spot. As we approached it the driver very obligingly stopped his horses and, stepping down from his high seat, loosened their reins so that they could put their noses down into the water and refresh themselves. Then, taking a tin cup from a nail on the dashboard and filling it from the silvery stream, he offered it to the passengers. Champagne never tasted better than did that ice cold water on that long, dry, dusty ride, and no one questioned the sanitary use of the one tin cup by all the passengers!

One could read all this in a story book, but to actually live it! Oh what a thrill I was getting out of it!

The thing that really impressed me most was seeing the countless hundreds of ground squirrels all over the fields and hillsides running in all directions to get off the road as we drove along. The roadsides were simply honeycombed with their ground holes into which they ran for shelter. I voiced my astonishment and called them gophers. Coming from Minnesota, known as the gopher state, I naturally took them to be gophers. They differed in that they were a bit larger and had a bushy tail instead of the short smooth tail of the Minnesota gopher. The alert drummer was quick to make sport of my ignorance and told all sorts of impossible stories about them to the amusement of the passengers.

"There's the Mission," the driver announced as we rounded a corner and came out into an open space.

"Yes, there's the Mission," the drummer repeated. Stretching and craning my neck in all directions I saw nothing but a small ranch house with its out-buildings and what appeared to me to be the ruins of a dejected and forgotten fort with crumbling walls scarcely discernible against the sun-parched landscape of the valley. Not wishing to expose my ignorance to the jests of the drummer I pretended that I saw the Mission. In fact I did see it, but how was I to know that the mass of ruins was really the Mission, and the place which was to be my home? Not till the stage driver had driven his horses from the main highway into the lane that led to the ruins and stopped abruptly in front of them was I convinced that it was the Mission indeed.

The feeling that came over me as the driver descended from his high seat to help me off the stage can never adequately be put into print. I had suddenly lost my power of speech and could only stare in amazement.

For days I had anticipated a noisy, happy meeting full of jests and joyous laughter to take place on my arrival. Instead, as I descended from the coach I saw coming out of a door under the arches, Padre, wearing a long cream-colored duster that came down well below his knees. In the late afternoon's gray light he looked for all the world like a ghost of the ruin's dead.

He came towards me, hands outstretched. As I placed my hands in his, tears came into his eyes. He swallowed hard, then, as if to defy his past fears said, "I knew you would come." Immediately his face brightened. I regained my power of speech and, as arm in arm we walked through the big front door, the fancied noisy, joyful chatter began.

In order that the reader may better understand my description of things as I found them it may not be amiss to give a brief sketch of the life there before Padre was put in charge. In 1882, by permission of the Bishop of the diocese, a family by the name of Donahue went to the Mission to live. They established themselves in the ruins as well as they could, making such repairs as was absolutely necessary to keep them dry and under cover during the rainy seasons. The Father in charge of services at the Mission was at that time living at the College some three miles away.

In 1891, Father Fred Lack was put in charge, and, with his sister, established himself at the Mission. The Donahue family remained till 1898. Father Lack was a kindly man of quiet, unassuming and simple tastes. Satisfied with conditions as he found them he made little effort to do anything more than to keep the few rooms, which he and his sister occupied, in fairly good condition. The unoccupied portion was left to the severe treatment of the weather. A great lover of flowers, he spent much of his spare time in his garden back of the convento. In 1903, leaving the Mission in a sad state, they, with a few household furnishings, moved to Arroyo Grande to take charge of the little frame church there.

Father Thomas King was then appointed to the vacancy. Being a young man and not particularly interested in the Mission, he found it hard to adjust himself to conditions. As a consequence he spent most of his time at Lompoc and Los Alamos, where he also had charge. It was during this time that the Yankee couple, squatters from Arizona, came along and started their chicken raising business in the ruins of what was left of the Mission.

At this most discouraging, disheartening, and pathetic point Padre Alexander Buckler was appointed by his Bishop, the most Reverend Thomas Conaty, to become pastor and guardian of what was left of this once beautiful and prosperous historical structure.

When the excitement, joy and chatter of our meeting had subsided, Padre led me through the five most livable rooms of the building and expressed the hope that I would have patience to bear with him until conditions could be improved.

"Are you hungry?" he suddenly asked, as we came to a large room with a rusty, battered and smelling coal oil stove sitting in the middle of it.

"Not very," I replied, dismissing the fact that I had not tasted food since breakfast in Santa Barbara.

There was a pot on the stove and the burner under it was lighted.

"This is to be our supper, with some crackers," said Padre, as he lifted the pot cover and invited me to have a peek at the boiling meat. "I bought it this morning from the butcher who peddles it from house to house," he continued. He had long since given up buying meat and potatoes as his share in the meals with the Yankee couple.

To one side, against the wall, was a table covered with soiled dishes—all sorts of odds and ends, mostly heavy china, cracked, chipped or partly broken and unfit for use. There were some rusty pots and saucepans, a most uninviting jumble of things thrown together. Next to the only window in the room was a wall closet with four shelves, where a few more pieces of kitchen-ware rested. On a bench near the stove was a bucket half full of water which had been brought up from the river a quarter of a mile away. The floor was of uneven black asphaltum and had a hole in the center of the room. Padre cautioned me not to step into it and explained that he had tried to fill it with broken glass and small rocks in order to keep squirrels or skunks from coming up through it.

We laughed and joked as I picked out the most inviting pieces of china, washed them and dished out our humble meal of broth, boiled beef and crackers.

The meal over, drugged by the fatigue of the long journey, I was anxious to retire early. With a lighted candle in my hand I retired to a large square room. It too had the black asphaltum floor and only one window, which faced the garden back of the building. There was an old fashioned wooden bed with a mattress, quilt and one pillow on it, a dresser with marble top that had a dejected look from the loss of one of its castors, and on which I set my candle, and a washstand also with marble top, near the head of the bed. Against the wall stood a long bench covered with all sorts of junk, odds and ends of things that Padre had gathered about the place, all covered with rust and dirt. Lying around it was more rubbish looking for all the world like things fished out of a village dump.

I put my suit-case on the washstand, and out of it pulled two nightgowns, one to wear and the other to wrap around the one pillow on the bed. Padre had explained that the only two sheets and one pillow-case that he found had been on his own bed since his arrival many weeks before. The room felt chilly and had a strong musty odor. It was altogether dismal. I added my big wool coat to the one quilt as I shuddered, more from nervous fatigue than cold, and, battling with mixed feelings of the joy of seeing Padre and my disappointment about the Mission, I gave a prayerful sigh and went to bed. I tucked the quilt and coat gingerly about me and tried to forget—everything.

"O dear, what was that?" I was being serenaded as screech owls and bats winged back and forth past my shadeless window. I was not exactly timid about the place but I was not comfortable. In my efforts to find sleep, I counted sheep, repeated the Lord's Prayer, and mentally went over every word of Padre's letter in which he had asked me to come, his enumeration of the difficulties we would encounter and his hope that I would be courageous. Try as I might, sleep would not come. Many times I lit my candle, rubbed my eyes and tried to find just what it was that was making night life so miserable for me. At first I saw nothing, then I did see something, small insects hopping or flying in all directions as I flashed the light of my candle on the bedclothes. I stood up and gave the quilt and coat a good shaking, hoping to free myself of the pesky things. After a whole night of vigilance and futile efforts to capture one of the disturbers for closer observation, I arose with neck and arms looking as if I were afflicted with chicken pox. Then and there I made up my mind that this was no place for me. I could not possibly stay and would tell Padre so that very morning.

"Good morning, Mamie. Did you have a good night?" Padre called out cheerily from the end of the piazza, as I appeared at the big front door in search of him. He was taking his morning's constitutional, pacing up and down the corridor in the early morning sun.

"Good morning, Daddy," I replied, using the nickname I had for him, and swallowing hard, said I had not slept at all. "Something in the bedclothes," I began—

"Fleas," he laughed. "California is full of them." He then told me that in the long watches of the night he had battled with them, and on one occasion caught and counted ninety-eight and put them out of existence by dropping them in a cup of coal oil.

I did not have the heart to tell him that I could not stay. Instead I screwed up my courage and said, "Never mind, we will get rid of them when I begin to clean up the house."

With knit brow I went to the so called kitchen, hoping that in some mysterious way, during the night, food would have found its way there. But no, only left overs of the boiled meat and crackers were visible. I had just lighted the oil burner under the pot of meat when Padre appeared with a quart jar of milk in his hands.

"Miss Donahue, the school teacher, brought this," he said. "That solves our breakfast problem," I added, as I removed the meat pot from the fire and heated the milk instead. Warm milk and crackers made us each a bowl of warm breakfast, and left the meat for another meal later in the day.

Apparently Padre was happy, and he did his best to be encouraging. We talked of plans to better conditions as he took me about the place and pointed out possibilities here and there as we rambled around the building.

In the back yard, or garden, the weeds had choked out all flowers and shrubs save a few bushes of pampas grass and several varieties of cactus. We were reminded of the cacti as we picked our way in the tall dry grass and brushed up against them here and there, or stumbled over boulders that formed their beds.

"What is that, Padre?" I asked, as I looked at a large box with wire screen sides dangling from a limb of the lone pepper tree.

"That, Mamie, is a meat safe."

"A meat safe? What's that?"

"A meat safe is a box in which to keep meat, or any other food, out in the open. Here it is shady and cool. It keeps food fresh. Its screen sides let in the air and keep out the insects and flies," he explained.

Continuing our ramble we came to what used to be Father Lack's greenhouse, a glass house in which he spent so many happy and interesting hours with his beloved flowers. How very sad it looked, its roof sagging, its windows battered, wood boxes that once held rare plants rotting and mingling with the soil they held. Spiders had worked long and industriously, undisturbed. Their fine lacy web formed a perfect screen in the open doorway and we decided to peer in through its delicate meshes rather than to disturb it by walking through.

The Yankee couple occupied the south end of the convento, the part that was almost in total ruins, which they had picked as the best suited to their chicken raising business. I did not wish to encounter them so viewed that portion of the building from the garden.

We again went through the rooms Padre had shown me the previous evening, and now saw them in the bright midday light. I found little to say as I looked around. I could see nothing but grim, long hours of hard work for both of us if we were ever to bring order out of all this chaos. I could see no comforts whatever in the large, spacious rooms with their high ceilings and uneven asphaltum floors. The few pieces of furniture, chairs, tables, beds, dressers, washstands and rough board benches all covered with dust and dirt, all in need of some repairs, parts broken and missing on nearly every piece, gave a most disheartening and dejected look as they stood at all angles about the rooms. The dozen or more pieces of coarse, heavy china in their cracked and chipped condition made the preparation of our meals anything but a delight. Not one clean, decent thing in that whole building was found.

The loss of sleep, the meager meals, and the appalling condition of the place made it almost impossible for me to keep up my spirits as the day wore on. Late that afternoon the stage coach brought my trunk, which had been left at Gaviota the previous day. I could hardly swallow the big lump that rose to my throat as the coach-driver, with Padre's help, dropped the trunk on the black asphaltum floor of my room. Lingering after them, I brushed away two big tears that involuntarily came to my eyes.

Early the following day Padre walked to the small village of Santa Ynez, four miles away, to purchase some groceries. He returned with his pockets and small bag full to overflowing with packages of coffee, sugar, salt, crackers, canned salmon and milk. These and the meat we bought from the butcher twice a week, as he made his house-to-house calls, took care of us for several days.

The weather was hot, dry and enervating. I felt as if I could never get sufficient rest, and continued to go about dazed and listless. There were no tools of any kind, not even a broom to do some much needed sweeping, and brushing away of some of the cobwebs that decorated every nook and corner, or hung in long festoons from the huge beams of the high ceilings in every room.

During those first trying days much of our time was spent on the front piazza, making plans to improve conditions, and if possible make the place habitable. There were no funds available and our only hope for betterment lay in our own hard work in cleaning up the place and repairing such things as doors that were battered, with locks and hinges missing, windows that sagged in their frames with cracked or missing panes. Furniture could be made useful with a few nails and a little glue, then freshened with some paint or varnish. An endless number of things could be done but all would take time.

It was almost painfully quiet as we sat there basking in the warmth of an autumn sun. The owls and bats, having spent themselves during the night, found many a hiding place to shelter them during the day. Numerous squirrels noiselessly played in a pile of roof tiling that once adorned the convento, and now lay in a huge heap partly buried in dry grass in front of the Mission. Now and then a lizard came out of hiding to take a squint at us and quickly disappeared. Small insects buzzed and droned in the stillness, as we talked on in low monotones.

A picket fence surrounded an old garden in front of the convento's remaining ten arches. The once beautiful, luxuriant garden contained a couple of rose bushes fighting for existence in the hard adobe soil, and a large century plant that had recently bloomed. The blossom's tall, dry stalk, heavy with seed, had toppled over to one side, forming a weird silhouette against the clear blue sky as we gazed out through one of the arches.

Looking beyond the garden the scenery was superb. To the left lay a dry grass-colored range of mountains and to the right a range covered with dark green oaks. These ranges met and melted into a hazy orchid blue and gray in the far distance directly in front of the Mission. The Santa Ynez River wound its way around the curves of the tree-covered mountains. The autumnal yellow, gold, and brown of the poplars and cotton-woods that lined its banks formed a lovely fringe to the dark green range and gave color to the vast panorama.

There were no houses in sight. The only signs of habitation were a few cows and horses. Now and then these followed a trail leading to a row of tall eucalyptus trees on a small elevation in the foreground, seeking shelter in the cool shade.

All this was peaceful and beautiful to look upon by day, but when the purple black haze and darkening shades of night crept on, the isolation and desolation of the place were appalling and frightening. Everything seemed so large, so immense and massive, that it made one feel very small and insignificant in the midst of it all.

SMOKED MEALS ON AN OLD CAST IRON STOVE

Among our first visitors were Mr. and Mrs. Peter Hanly from a neighboring ranch. Both were Irish, he keen witted with a mischievous twinkle in his eyes, and she of an affable disposition and a big generous heart. On this occasion she brought a large loaf of bread for the Padre. If you have ever, for a whole week, substituted insipid, tasteless, dry crackers for fluffy, moist and tasty home-made bread you will appreciate just what that loaf of bread meant to us. When our visitors had departed we treated ourselves to generous slices of the luscious white bread without butter, jam, or any other trimmings.

It was a very pleasant visit that we had with our neighbors, and before they left all arrangements were made for a trip to Santa Ynez to do some much needed shopping. I made a long list of things and when Mr. Hanly appeared the following day, I buoyantly climbed the spring wagon and sat on the high seat beside him. The drive was beautiful, with the horses going full speed up and down grades and winding around such short curves that at times they seemed ready to leap off the road and down the precipices many feet below. The mountain wagon trails were all new and wonderful to me.

Although I had been told that Santa Ynez was a very small village, I was especially disappointed in its general merchandise stores, two of which the village boasted. My list was considerably shortened when I found that their stocks were very limited. However, at one store where Mr. Hanly's daughter acted as clerk I did manage to procure staples such as flour, sugar, bacon, butter and eggs. Also, I found soap, lye, washing powder, brooms, scrubbing brushes, mops and various articles so necessary in good housekeeping.

Needless to say there were long, busy days that followed this trip to the village. When the day ended and night came there were red and rough hands, usually a torn fingernail, a bruised

26

finger or deep cut or scratch to be doctored. The brain too was often weary from making plans and meeting problems.

During our first year at the Mission Padre had no conveyance of his own to transport him to the outlying districts where he held services. He made the trips by stage and railroad trains in round-about ways. Sometimes Mr. Hanly, or Ed. Donahue, accommodating neighbors, took him with horse and buggy. Lompoc being the largest of his outposts, Padre usually planned to get whatever we needed from there. As a consequence we sometimes had to wait a long time for a few nails, a hinge, a tool or anything that was necessary in the progress of our making the place habitable. However, all this had its good points, for it taught us the art of patience and perseverance.

One fine day I worked up my courage to face the ire of the industrious spiders and break through their lacy screen web at the greenhouse. I had espied a cast iron stove there and wished to make a closer inspection of it. I was, by now, thoroughly disgusted with the smelly oil cook stove. No matter how much I had cleaned, soaked, and scraped, it still was very unsatisfactory, and the thought that the stove in the greenhouse might be put into use egged me on to investigate. It had evidently been used to heat the greenhouse, and was very rusty. One lid was missing and a corner of its top near the stove-pipe was broken, but this in no way would interfere with cooking, I thought, as I made my inspection. As for the missing lid, I could keep the iron teakettle over that opening when not otherwise in use. I was jubilant over the find until Padre was told about my intention to use it. He looked dismayed and said, "My child, there is no chimney or flue anywhere in any of the rooms where we could install the stove."

I thought for a brief moment. "They say that it is summer the year around in California. Couldn't we set it up out of doors, somewhere near the house?"

"Perhaps we could if you think it is good enough," Padre replied, not wishing to discourage me.

"I could use it to bake bread. The oven seems to be in good condition and that would be a great help," I assured him.

It was a long way from the greenhouse to the convento but we tugged, lifted, pulled and shoved the old, heavy iron stove until we finally got it where we wanted it under the arches on the west side of the convento.

After that we had the usual wait until Padre took his monthly trip to Lompoc by buggy and procured the lengths of stove pipe and stove blacking, to put it in working condition. Eventually all was accomplished and the stove served our purpose for nearly two years. We had many a smoked meal when the stove refused to draw or the wind blew in the wrong direction, but what matter? We were working hard and appetites were good.

OUR FIRST ENCOUNTER WITH A MISSION GHOST

Do you believe in ghosts? I do. I've never actually seen one, but who ever has? You may see their forms or shadows, hear their moans and feel their presence in dark and weird places, yet never see the ghosts themselves. They never hurt or molest you as long as you are not scared, but should you become panicky, woe unto you!

In the evening of the eighth day after my arrival Padre and I sat in the big front room and listened to the pattering of the season's first rain. Softly and gently it came, like sweet music from a distance. The small coal oil lamp was burning on the mantel, casting its yellow light around the bare room. The front double doors were wide open and we could smell that delicious, pungent odor which comes when rain wets the soil for the first time at the end of a long dry summer. We had never seen a country so dry and parched and in need of moisture as was this valley.

At about nine o'clock, as we sat there rejoicing and commenting on the benefits of the rain, we heard horse's hoofs on the driveway and presently a man appeared at the door.

"Good evening, Father," he said as he walked into the room.

"Good evening," Padre replied as he stood up to greet his visitor.

"I am William Fabing," the man continued. "My brother, who lives in Lompoc, is very ill and I wish to take you there to see him if you will go."

"Certainly I will go," said Padre, and, turning to me, asked that I get the lantern, which we used in the kitchen, and light him on his way into the church where he had to get the necessities for the sick call.

Strange as it may seem, I had not as yet seen the interior of the church. After going through room after room in the convento part of the building, only to find each one just a bit more deplorable than the others, my curiosity had lost much of its enthusiasm. Padre was a very early riser and read his daily Mass no later than five o'clock, and thus far I had been too weary for early rising and had not attended the morning services.

My hands trembled a little as I lit the lantern and thought of going into the church in the darkness of the night. Somehow, the place was beginning to get on my nerves, not that I feared anything in particular, but I felt a dread of encountering new and unexpected things. However, it was no time for personal feelings and so I went right along.

Mr. Fabing followed us as far as the chapel doors, removed the long two by four inch timber that barred the double doors and kept them closed, and returned to his carriage to await the Padre.

The interior of the church was intensely dark and silent, with a musty odor that was almost suffocating. I carried the lantern low that we might the better see our way, its dim light scarcely penetrating the darkness more than two or three feet ahead of us. Our footsteps resounded on the brick tile flooring as we walked briskly up the aisle towards the altar. When we reached the center of the church we were startled by an indescribable piercing screech that traveled from one end of the building to the other. It seemed to penetrate the very walls of that awful, silent church, and ended with a terrific thud in the choir loft, which left us all but paralyzed.

That frightful, terrifying noise resounding through the large empty building in the darkness of the night had to be experienced to be appreciated. When the noise subsided the situation became more gruesome with the sound of what seemed to be chains rattling overhead. We stood there in the middle of the church, rooted to the spot, too frightened to utter a sound, just listening to it all. I clutched the handle of the lantern tightly with one hand and the sleeve of Padre's coat with the other to steady my nerves until the sound had completely died out.

"What do you suppose that was?" Padre managed to ask when he had regained his power of speech.

"I don't know," I replied, scarcely able to breathe. "But let us hurry to get the things and get out of here."

We walked up the rest of the way to the sanctuary, where Padre got what he needed, and back to the front doors in silence. We put the long two by four timber back into place, and with a "Don't worry, Mamie, everything will be all right and I'll hurry back," Padre climbed into the waiting carriage and was driven into the rain and darkness of the night.

The Mission was an ideal retreat for ghosts. One could feel their presence in so many dark corners of its ruins. Seemingly, they held their nightly meetings in the garrets of both the chapel and the convento, and in the cemetery adjoining the chapel. Right in the rooms too, when the lights were out and everything was still, they would prance forth boldly and sometimes noisily, under cover of darkness.

Lompoc, as I have previously stated, is twenty-three miles from the Mission. The carriage which took Padre on this sick call was an open one, and the only protection the two men had for the three hours or more of hard driving was their rain coats.

I felt sorry for them as I stood there a moment, the gentle rain kissing my hair, my fingernails digging into the palm of my hand, as I still tightly held the lantern. Suddenly I felt that just behind me, in the darkness, the ghosts with their long arms and long crooked fingers were reaching out towards me. Ooo — oo.

Yes, I was sure they were. In defiance, I threw my head up in the air and hurried into the house, keeping just one pace ahead of them. I closed the front doors and bolted them with a long timber similar to the one used on the church doors, except that it was used on the inside instead of outside and afforded protection. I then put out the light of the lamp on the mantel, and with the lantern made my way through two large rooms to my bedroom. The noise of my footsteps on the bare asphaltum floors frightened me almost into a run, such was the condition of my nerves by that time.

No matter how precautious or elusive ghosts may be one can always trace down their antics if gone into deeply enough.

Padre returned early the following morning. During the long trip to Lompoc and back he had had much time to ponder over the puzzling event of the previous evening. When the sun streamed through the south windows and afforded good light in the chapel, we went over the grounds of our visit of the night before, to discover if possible the baffling, mysterious performance of our nocturnal visitor. After a very careful survey, and much conjecture, we finally arrived at this conclusion: A brown owl, which we called the Mission owl, must have been perched on the sanctuary lamp which was suspended from the ceiling by a long chain. As we came up the aisle the lantern light must have disturbed and frightened it, and, with an indescribable, inimitable, unearthly screech it flew from the lamp the whole length of the church and out through an opening in the choir loft that led to the bell tower. The door to this opening was of thick heavy boards. Padre remembered that it had but one hinge by which it hung at a rakish angle. The owl in its frenzied haste to get out must have missed making the sharp turn into the opening and struck the door in such a way that it broke loose from its one hinge, and K-plunk fell the door onto the loft's plank floor with that terrifying, loud thud that frightened us almost into insensibility. There were two chandeliers, elaborately decorated with glass prisms, and like the sanctuary lamp suspended from the ceiling with long chains. These were in the owl's path of flight and were struck by it, leaving the prisms striking each other and producing sounds that resembled the rattling of chains which we heard when the big noise of the fallen door had died down.

"It really wasn't anything to be frightened about," said Padre.

ALONE AT THE MISSION

Some three weeks after my arrival at the Mission Padre was called on an official trip to San Diego. The trip was long, tedious and tiresome in those days. He left the Mission at 9:30 a. m. by stage for Gaviota, where he took the train to Los Angeles. At Los Angeles he had to remain for the night as there was no connection for San Diego until the next day.

When Padre announced that he would be away from home for five days my heart skipped a beat. I realized that I would be alone with the owls, bats and a little puppy in the midst of desolate ruins. However, being one of a large family, I was not pampered or spoiled so accepted the fact without comment.

On the evening of the first day it occurred to me that Padre's bedroom was the only room in the place that could be locked. I decided to use it during his absence. It was the first room next to the chapel facing the front veranda. The only light was from a glass door leading onto the veranda. I recall tacking a piece of cloth over the glass. I moved a small cot from the living room into Padre's room and, locking myself in, I retired for the night and forgot the rest of the world until dawn.

At daybreak, on hearing noises made by the puppy on the veranda, I was prompted to get up and peer through a small hole in the cloth that covered the glass in the door. Right under the window was a man rolling up his blanket in preparation for leaving. The puppy was having a good time pulling and chewing at the corners of the blanket. Rather than resenting it the man seemed to be enjoying the antics. On departing through the garden gate he was careful to see that the puppy remained inside. This man, evidently a wayfarer, had spent the night on the veranda under the shelter of the arches. He was so kind and friendly toward the dog that I was not in the least frightened. The following night, wondering if the man would return, I found

34

myself listening to noises that might indicate the spreading of a blanket on the veranda. Nothing happened.

My earliest recollection of a real tramp coming to the Mission was one evening at dusk. A small middle-aged man with piercing black eyes, wearing a full beard and long bushy hair, neatly dressed, appeared at the big, wide-open front door. "Is Father Buckler at home?" he inquired as I came forward to see who the stranger might be.

"No," I replied, and before I could say anything further he added, "Oh, this is the day he goes to Lompoc." It was Saturday and Padre had left that afternoon for Lompoc where he was to remain for Sunday service. Feeling certain that the man was one of Padre's parishioners I asked him if he wished to see Padre about a sick call. "No-o" he replied, looking puzzled, and lifting his hat scratched his shaggy head. "But perhaps you can help me."

By this time the man had stepped inside the large reception room and seated himself in one of the few chairs that adorned the room. He then proceeded to tell me a long story about having a wife in Santa Barbara who was very ill. He needed a little money so that he could join her. He wanted to borrow it and would surely send it back as soon as he got there. He could walk as far as Gaviota if I would give him the fare on the train from Gaviota to Santa Barbara, the fare at that time being one dollar.

Somehow, his story did not hang together very well. He looked at me sharply and searchingly while he told it. I began to realize I was being "stung" for the dollar. I did not like the idea of being "stung" but I was in the huge building alone with this stranger and I knew I must keep my wits. I knew, too that I must not antagonize this man. As naturally as I could, without a tremor of fear in my voice, I said, "Padre has left me a few pieces of small change and if it will help I will gladly give them to you." Without waiting for an answer I went to the kitchen and from the household box which I kept in one of the cupboards I counted seventy-five cents in five and ten cent pieces. I was being "stung" and was getting back at the man by not giving him the amount he wanted. As I held the change out to him he arose and quickly and greedily took it from my hand and put it into his trouser pocket, staring at me while he did so.

"I'm sorry this is all I can give you," I said, by way of disguising the fear that was creeping over me. He paid no attention to my statement and, looking at a little cupboard with glass doors where religious articles were on display, he said, "I'm not a Catholic but my wife is. Give me one of those rosaries you have there; I want to take it to her." This was in such a commanding tone that I truly became alarmed.

I backed towards the cupboard, so as not to lose sight of the man, took out a rosary and handed it to him. He took it and, like the coins, slipped it into his trouser pocket.

It was growing dark. The man made no move to go, just sat there and stared while I kept up a conversation to hide my fears. Gradually I edged my way towards the front door and stepped outside. By way of getting him out of the house I invited him to come and look at some potted cacti that were in bloom and a great novelty to me.

Reluctantly he came out but showed little interest in the plants. Again cautiously, I backed towards the open door and excusing myself under the plea that I had something to do, I closed the door between us.

It was almost dark by now. The man stood on the porch staring into space for a long time, evidently forgetful of his haste to reach a sick wife in Santa Barbara. The last I saw of him before the darkness obliterated all things from view was his standing in front of the bell tower looking as if he were undecided as to what to do. I had a feeling that he wanted a place to stay for the night. Perhaps he found it in the tall grass back of the bell tower, or he may have returned to sleep on the front veranda under the arches. Verily not a pleasant situation for me and all I could do was to retire without a light so as not to disclose my whereabouts in the big building.

I have a faint recollection of saying my prayers a bit more fervently and beseeching my guardian angel to be more vigilant in my behalf that night. The bats flitted, the owls hooted and the crickets carried on their ceaseless chorus while I kept one ear cocked for any unusual sound. Finally, sleep won out. When I awakened the sun was shining brightly and there was no trace of the strange visitor of the previous evening.

How the tramp knew Padre's name and the day he went to Lompoc remained a mystery. Perhaps he had stopped at some ranch and gathered the information. Too, he must have forgotten that he borrowed the seventy-five cents; at least he never returned it. Fearing that Padre would be worried about my staying alone when he had to be away from the Mission, I did not tell him about the incident.

EXPLORING THE SACRISTY AND CHAPEL

On Sunday following Padre's return from San Diego, services of the Mass were at the Mission. The day previous Padre asked me to go to the sacristy with him to look over the vestments and linens, and whatever was there for use in the service. He also suggested that I put fresh linens on the altar. "There has been no change of altar linens since I came three months ago," he explained.

The sacristy, a large room back of the chancel, had one window which was set high above the heavy door. This door, crudely carved and hung with hand wrought iron hinges, opened out into the courtyard back of the convento. We entered the sacristy by this door, leaving it open so as to afford more light. The sun, streaming through it and the window above, gave a soft pink glow to the room that was very pleasing. The strong musty odor that prevailed everywhere in the building gave one the feeling of being in another world.

The furniture of this room consisted of a long hand carved bench, a sort of wardrobe with primitive carvings on its two heavy doors, the hinges of which were hand wrought and very crude looking. In this wardrobe were flower vases, artificial flowers, some wood carved candlesticks, a small supply of candles and incense, and a few other items usually found in a sacristy. The third piece of furniture was a huge chest of drawers, about four feet deep, the same in height and perhaps nine or ten feet in length.

If I was transported into another world by the pungent, penetrating odor of the place, I certainly felt in an exotic atmosphere when we opened the huge drawers of this wonderful old chest. We pulled out vestment after vestment and their accompanying stoles, maniples, veils and burses; cope after cope, antependiums and an endless number of other pieces with which I was not familiar.

All these had once been very beautiful; their materials impressed me as something very exquisite in texture and coloring. But it was not until some time later when I undertook to restore them and to study their history that I realized their true worth. At this time I saw nothing but a huge pile of dilapidated, threadbare, ragged vestments· From the whole mass there was not one set of vestments that did not need repairing. All were shoved into the drawers with no regard to keeping the sets together. Finally we selected what appeared to be the best set and laid it aside for use on the morrow.

Then there were the linens, consisting of the albs, the surplices, the altar cloths and all the smaller pieces used about the altar. All of these were of the nicest linens exquisitely sewn by hand but now turned to a mellow yellow for want of care. Out of this crumpled and tangled collection, squeezed into the big drawers of the huge chest, I found nothing with which to freshen the altar.

The chapel, with its creamy white walls in the subdued light, was charming. The sanctuary, with its quaint Indian frescoes of soft reds, greens, blues and yellows was most fascinating. The hand carved wood statuary, the old oil paintings in their quiet tones, the pews of redwood without stain or varnish, blending and melting into the brick red of the tiles in the floor, all gave an atmosphere of quiet dignity and restful peace.

It was only upon closer scrutiny that the illusion, or deception, disappeared. There were two panes of glass missing from the windows. This afforded the owls free access to the chapel where they found the heavy frames of the large oil paintings and the wood statuary convenient places upon which to roost, leaving them pathetically disfigured with their filth and dirt. Some of the pews, too, were spattered and soiled from their droppings. Surely not a very pretty subject to write about, but true nevertheless.

Sunday came, and as I remember about fifteen people came for Mass. Some came in buggies, some in spring wagons and others came on horseback. Self-consciously I walked up the aisle and chose a seat in about the center of the church, feeling that all eyes were on the newcomer. Not having as yet unpacked my trunk, I wore my traveling suit which was a bit worse for the wear. That too added to my discomfort. As I looked up at the altar I saw that the lace on the alb Padre was wearing was torn and the vestment had rags hanging from its lining. So altogether instead of being impressed and inspired by the simple service, I found myself distraught and depressed in spirit.

When the service was over I returned to the house just as Padre was hurriedly going through the back door with the revolver in his hand. I was frightened and could not imagine what was happening. Watching him go back into the sacristy, I did not dare follow him. The gun went off. What could it mean? I felt weak. Soon he came out carrying a long snake by the tail. He smiled when he saw how frightened I was. He then related how, during the service he had seen the snake stretched full length against the wall next to the sacristy door, and how he had kept his eye on it for fear of its coming too close for comfort. That accounted for his almost breaking into a run as he left the sanctuary after Mass. Evidently the snake had come up through the broken floor, only to have its life ended with a pistol shot.

That was Padre's snake story. Mine took place the following day, when, late in the afternoon, I went to the dining room. The sun was casting its beams through the windows on the deep recesses of the adobe wall. There stretched out about four feet in length in one of the recesses was an impudent snake taking a sun bath. It did not move as I came quite near to take a closer look, and to make sure that I was not mistaken, or walking in my sleep, I ran for a broom, gave it a few little pushes and it crawled away through a broken window pane, dropped on the ground outside in the corridor and disappeared in the debris near by.

As the days wore on the isolation and desolation of the place loomed larger and larger. The hope of bringing order receded as we encountered difficulties and delays at every turn. Torn with pity for Padre and a longing to return home to mother I found it harder and harder to hold back the tears.

On Nov. 19, less than a month after my arrival, we were to have our first house guest — The Rev. Zephyrin Engelhardt, O.F.M., Historian from Santa Barbara Mission. He wished to peruse the register and records of Santa Ines and acquaint himself with conditions there. His historical works about the California Missions which he has since published need no introduction.

That indeed was a trying time for me. The poor cooking facilities, the scarcity of bedclothes and table linens, the few pieces of presentable china were all things that caused me uneasiness.

"Do not worry about it. The Father is used to missionary life and will understand," was Padre's ever encouraging statement. Nevertheless he too realized that we had to make our guest reasonably comfortable.

In preparation we moved our kitchen equipment from the room facing the front of the convento to one facing the back, and fixed up the front room for our guest. The hole in the floor had been filled with adobe mud, trampled, smoothed and dried until it was almost as hard as the asphaltum in the rest of the floor, and was insect proof. After thoroughly cleaning the room we put in a bed, a dresser, a washstand, which we repaired as well as we could, and a large, bulky mission table which I had to scrape, scrub and clean when Padre insisted it would be just the thing for the Father to use in his perusing of the big parchment books.

The Father Historian was agreeably surprised to find so much of the old original church furnishings, in spite of the condition of the building. Besides perusing the books, he went over all the grounds, taking notes, measurements and making drawings. A quarter of a mile from the Mission he visited the ruins of the old grinding mill and the ruins of the College three miles farther on.

He stayed until November 24th and was so agreeable and delightful that we forgot all about not having all the modern conveniences. If a meal was smoky or a bit late he knew that it was the fault of the old cast-iron stove and not mine. He would very kindly laugh and joke it off and make me forget that all was not as it should be.

For several years after this first visit, Father Engelhardt came to the Mission to assist Padre in the services of Holy Week and Easter Sunday. Through these little visits we became well acquainted and very fond of Father Historian and looked forward, from one visit to another, with great anticipation to having him with us.

I little dreamed at that time that we were making history and that twenty-eight years later I would be asked, by the Reverend Father, to contribute in writing a part of the history for which he now was gathering material.

AN INDIAN FUNERAL

The first funeral I was destined to witness at the Mission, and in California, was that of Usebia, the wife of Capitán José Dolores Solares. It was late in the afternoon when Capitán himself brought the news of his wife's death to Padre and came to make the necessary arrangements for the funeral service and burial. It was their first meeting.

"Mi esposa she die. Mi want Padre bury him," Capitán said in a soft even tone and without emotion. He did not speak much English and Padre had not yet mastered the Spanish language. However, all the necessary information was secured except the age of the deceased. The Indians, we discovered, seldom knew their age and Padre invariably had to resort to the old leather bound parchment Baptismal Register for the information.

The following morning three of Capitán's compadres came to dig the grave in the Mission's Campo Santo which adjoins the Chapel. Late in the afternoon of that day the funeral took place. Fernandito, of whom you shall hear more later, arrived in advance of the funeral procession so as to toll the bell as soon as the cortege made its appearance over the small hill on the road leading to the Mission. Particularly, I think, he wanted to make sure that the right tombas were to be used on which the coffin was to be placed. There was a new Padre at the Mission who perhaps did not know the custom of using the tombas and he was leaving nothing to chance.

There were three low tables, or tombas, that could be placed one upon the other giving three different heights. "The height of the tomba to be used was determined according to the social status of the deceased," Fernandito officiously explained, as he placed three tombas one upon the other for the wife of Capitán José. Capitán José was Chief of the Zanja de Cota Indian Reservation inhabitants and the passing of his wife was not to be taken lightly by her kinsfolk.

43

The cortege consisted of seven or eight nondescript vehicles all filled to capacity with men, women and children. Heading the procession was a light spring wagon, in the rear of which the exceedingly inexpensive coffin was placed. As I stood, where curiosity had taken me, at the end of the corridor, I noticed that Capitán occupied the seat next to the driver of the wagon. There apparently were no picked pall-bearers. The men just lent a hand in carrying the coffin into the Church, and again after the service into the cemetery, Capitán not excluded. Not only did he act as pall-bearer but after the short prayers at the graveside he manipulated one end of one of the straps that lowered the body of his wife to her last resting place.

How barbaric, I thought, as from a respectful distance I looked upon the simple scene. Then quickly I turned away, went to the chapel to put out the candle lights which had been used in the service and returned to the house. There I tried to reason out that after all perhaps it was commendable for Capitán to do all these things for his wife — the very last he could do to express his love and devotion to her.

No sooner had Padre left the cemetery when the Indian mourners broke out in the most audible, mournful, wailing and moaning I have ever heard. On and on, and on and on they wailed and moaned. At times they let out the most piercing shrieks as if to out-do one another in their noise making. They remained in the cemetery and kept up their weird lamentations until dark. Their horses, tied to the fence rails across the road in front of the Mission, awaited their owners in dejected impatience.

Then all was quiet; the mourners, with grim silent stoicism, stalked across the road and climbed into their conveyances and went their way to the Reservation and home.

The doleful wailing, the destitution of the participants and the utter simplicity in which the funeral was carried out cast a pall of gloom and haunted me for days. It was only in retrospect of after-years that I appreciated the beauty of the custom and of the Indian culture. Reasoning convinced me that it was all sincere. Out there in the solitary loneliness of the valley, in the sacred atmosphere of their beloved Mission and in the deepening dusk of an ending day, one of their small group was laid away. May her simple soul rest in peace in the company of her forebears.

In a way, it is sad to relate that as one by one the older generation of the Zanja de Cota Indians was brought to the Mission's Campo Santo and to their last resting place, the custom of wailing at the grave ceased altogether.

TREASURES IN GOLD, SILVER, PEWTER AND COPPER

On our arrival we found three chalices at the Mission. One was of gold of modern make, another of hand hammered silver, the cup of which had several breaks and was otherwise battered and bent, rendering it useless. My memory eludes me about the third. In 1905, when the Santa Maria church was built, Padre's outposts of Sisquoc and Los Alamos were placed in charge of the new Pastor, the Rev. Mathias Ternes, and the chalice was left at one of these outposts. As nearly as I can remember, it too was of hammered silver.

There was also a ciborium, a thurible, an incense boat and spoon, a combination baptismal service set, a baptismal shell and a processional set of cross and two candlesticks. All these were of hand hammered silver and like the silver chalices, bear the hall-marks and other markings found on the gold and silver pieces brought to California for the Missions. The holy water vessel and aspersoria were in pewter and of modern make.

The thurible, in design, bears the inscription "San Miguel" on the rim near the top. Evidently it belonged to the Mission by that name. How it found its way to Santa Ines we don't know. The incense boat also bears an inscription. It has "La Purisima" on the inside of its cover. This piece is very ornate with elaborate chasings on bowl and cover. It was always my favorite. The explanation of its presence at Santa Ines is obvious since many of the vestments and other things were taken there when the Purisima Mission was abandoned.

The processional candlesticks and cross were about seven and eight feet high respectively. Their standards, resembling a bamboo stock, unscrewed at the joints, thereby making them quite compact for putting away. The cross bears the figure of Christ on one side and the Blessed Mother Mary on the other.

Padre was a little surprised to find there was no ostensorium, since all the other altar pieces were there. After much scouting and inquiring of representative families in his outposts, he discovered it in a ranch house in Sisquoc, together with a chalice, and, as I recall, two sets of vestments. These things, presumably taken to the little church at Sisquoc for some special occasion, were left in the keeping of this early day Spanish family. It took months of gentle persuasion and patient waiting before Padre could prevail upon them to part with the treasures, but eventually they were returned to their rightful place at the Mission. Other than being tarnished from lack of use, the ostensorium was in good condition· The chalice had a long break in its cup which made it unfit for use. Both were quite ornate and beautiful in design. There was a leather covered wood case for the ostensorium that was quite interesting. Made in two parts, it conformed to the shape of the ostensorium and opened like a shell, which, when closed, protected its treasure.

For many years it had been Padre's ambition and hope to have both the gold and silver chalices repaired. This was not granted him until 1916 when the Altar Society was organized, and they had acquired enough funds in their treasury to finance the cost. After some lengthy correspondence with the firm of Wiltzius in Milwaukee, Padre sent the chalices to be restored and once more they became useful in the ceremony of the Mass.

It may be of interest to state that on receiving the chalices the firm wrote Padre a letter, which in substance reads—"We wonder if you realize the treasures you have in the two chalices? One is pure gold and the other pure silver, without the usual steel rod in their stems. Both are not alone a century old, but many centuries old. As a rule, each chalice was made by one person alone, not with the division of labor practiced today. I would say they are priceless." The firm restored the chalices for the very modest sum of $30.00.

The altar bread irons and a set of large and small host cutters were among the sacristy equipment. They were rusty with age and disuse and so were relegated to the museum shelves. The altar bread box was of pewter and modern manufacture and no particular interest.

In our early exploring days we found a pewter container which, quite accidentally, I later discovered was one of a set that belonged in a quaint leather covered box. It was unearthed when we were doing some digging in the courtyard. One day when rearranging things in the sacristy, where we kept all such objects, I thought of putting the containers in the box to save shelf space, and to my surprise they fit perfectly. When I called Padre's attention to my discovery he at once identified it as the Holy Oil stocks and box. The containers are round, about seven inches in height and three inches in diameter, perfectly smooth and without any ornamentation of any kind. They have a screw top like the bottles. The box is covered with heavy black leather put on with large headed nails tacked closely together. Little grooves in the side boards show where two partitions had once separated the containers and held them in place.

According to the historian, Father Engelhardt, this is the same box which brought the Holy Oil from Mexico for Padre Junipero Serra and traveled back each year for a fresh supply. From it all the Missions were given their portions of the oils. We were delighted with the discovery of so rare a treasure.

The baptismal font and basin are of hand hammered copper. The font is ornate in design having two wavy lines encircling its bowl, and an eight point star-shaped design on the lid. The lid, with a six inch cross set upright in its center, is in two parts, held together with hand hammered hinges. This makes it possible to uncover only half of the bowl at a time. The basin is plainly encircled, with a straight protruding line three inches from the rim as its only ornamentation. We were told that it was made at the Mission.

An interesting utensil for dipping the water from the font was a beautifully fluted shell, perfect in design, about five inches across and of solid hand hammered silver. In taking tourists and visitors through the Mission we discovered that this was one of the many treasured pieces that required a sharp eagle eye to protect it from curio-seeking vandals.

Another piece in hand hammered copper was a large water pot, beautifully shaped, with two ear handles and a protruding line encircling the pot midway between the top and bottom, forming its only ornamentation. It was used for domestic purposes.

Other treasures unearthed were three altar stones, buried in the cemetery so long ago that no one knew or remembered where. It seemed they were buried for safe keeping during the dark days of the Mission. James Donahue, having heard about the altar stones, tried to locate them but failed. However, with Padre's persistence and an occasional tramp to do the digging, they were finally brought to light. Two of the stones were of white marble and the third was of a deep cream marble with soft rose veins and scrolls all through it. All three stones were broken, their relics still imbedded in them. Padre removed the relics and put the pieces of stone in the Mission's museum. In going through Padre's effects after his death, I came across the relics and returned them to the Museum.

We also found, buried here and there about the premises, stone bowls, metatas, pestles and two mill wheels. One mill wheel was found near the Mission, the other was hauled in from somewhere in the field on the little sled built to haul water from the river. Looking back through the cobweb of the years, I can see Padre puffing and mopping his brow as he and the chore man, John Mullinary, tugged and pulled at the huge stone wheels until they had them installed in the sacristy museum. The one found in the field was of good shape, about thirty-two inches across with an iron rod through its center. Padre was delighted with his find.

Other things gathered for the museum were hand-made locks, keys, door latches, hinges and nails of all descriptions and sizes. Most of the locks were too rusty for use, but we did manage to scrape and clean some keys sufficiently to be used. Padre then bought large locks for the front and side doors of the chapel and outside door of the sacristy and had the largest and best of the old keys adjusted to them and put to use. They were a source of pride to us and became polished almost to a shining silver from constant use.

There were three branding irons, some broad-axes, an old scale, and various other items in wrought iron. One day, when doing some digging and leveling of the ground back of the storehouses, Padre slashed his spade with the end of a large cross-cut saw. It was buried upright under a heap of melted adobes and it took him the greater part of two afternoons to retrieve it. The saw is about five feet in length with its teeth all running one way, indicating it is a one-man saw.

We found three branding irons on the premises. Later Mr. Shaw found another on his land a short distance from the Mission.

A ship's cannon, which inspires the weaving of stories by writers, novelists and would-be historians, lay silent and inoffensive among the museum's treasures. During our long stay at the Mission we never came across anyone who could tell us anything authentic about its history. Whence it came, or for what purpose it was brought to Santa Ines, no one knew. Mrs. Donahue told us that during their occupancy of the Mission, her sons, one New Year's eve, filled the cannon with gunpowder and set it off at midnight to enhance the dying of the old year and the birth of the new. The blast shattered several window panes, both of the chapel and the convento, which faced the court where the cannon had been installed.

Another implement, emphasizing the primitive war weapon of an earlier day was a fascinating heart-shaped bullet mold and quaint old pistol which attracted the attention of the tourist and evoked much speculation.

At one time Padre had markers made and placed over the graves of the Padres buried in the chapel. These were made of lumber three by four feet in size, about ten inches high at the head and sloping to about four inches at the foot. They were made by a tramp carpenter. A little later, as Padre put it, in answer to his prayers a tramp painter came along. He was a Dane with some ingenuity and knowledge of painting. The markers were painted white with black borders. Then in the enclosure in square black letters the names of the Padres were inscribed with dates of their birth and death. These markers served their purpose until the year 1912, when Mr. Nathaniel Bachelder of San Francisco, Calif., presented the Mission with two bronze plaques to take the place of the wood markers.

These were placed on the walls just above the graves and below the communion railing. The plaque on the epistle side commemorates the burial of three Fathers and the plaque on the gospel side the burial of two Fathers. The inscriptions on the plaques read as follows:

Sacred to the memory of
Fr. Marcos Antonio Saizar de
Vitoria y Odriozola
Born Cantabria, Spain, 1760
Died July 25, 1836

Sacred to the memory of
Fr. José Antonio Calzada
Born in Cuba Nov. 1760
Died Dec. 24, 1814

Fr. Ramón Arbella
Born Monforte, Spain
May 29, 1764
Died May 24, 1842

Fr. Felipe Arroyo de la Cuesta
Native of Cubo, Spain
Born April 30, 1780
Died Sep. 20, 1840

Fr. Juan Moreno
Born Montenegro, Spain
Jan. 27, 1799
Died Dec. 27, 1845

R. I. P.

A CASCARONES BALL AND A TRIP TO SANTA BARBARA

By this time we fully realized that we could not continue at the Mission under existing conditions. Something had to be done. Mrs. Donahue with four grown up daughters paid us a call, and during their visit suggested that the ladies of the parish give a benefit party to help in procuring a few necessities for our comfort. Padre readily agreed to this suggestion and commented: "Women are always resourceful and usually accomplish what they undertake."

Before many days the news that there was to be a Grand Cascarones Ball and supper in the village hall in Santa Ynez was spread through the valley. The Santa Ynez Argus, a weekly newspaper, had printed the announcement.

In due time the ladies were busy preparing good things for the supper. They boiled hams, baked bread and raised biscuits, cooked Spanish beans, made salads, cakes, and pies, to say nothing of preparing the cascarones.

Cascarones! That was an intriguing word to me. I pondered over it and could not decide whether it was something to eat or wear, feeling that it must be one or the other.

It was to be my first social function. How exciting! I knew absolutely nothing of what this ball would be like, what sort of people would attend, or what they would wear. It was with some anticipation that I unpacked my trunk, spread all of my pretty gowns on the bed and tried to decide which one would be most appropriate. Of course I really wanted to wear my prettiest, a champagne colored crepe dress trimmed in blue satin and lace. But Padre had cautioned me to dress modestly, explaining that those attending would be mostly from ranches and they would be simply dressed. I felt a bit downcast as I surveyed the wardrobe on which I had spent so many precious days in creating, only to find that it was too elaborate

53

for my environment. Finally, I chose the black silk taffety trimmed in corn-yellow chiffon, with its long skirt elaborately fagoted and ruffled. The accompanying petticoat, also of taffety, had three narrow ruffles on its full hem. Really my best dress but less conspicuous, I thought, as I fondled and folded the others and put them back into the trunk and closed the lid.

Mrs. Donahue as chaperon and her daughters in their horse drawn surrey stopped at the Mission for me and gaily we rode the four miles to the village ball. The place was a long narrow building with low ceiling. Evidently two additions had been added to the original, as the floor and ceiling showed piecing in two places. It was dimly lighted with coaloil lamps set in brackets on the walls on either side. Next to the entrance was a crudely constructed booth where men checked their hats for a small sum. Across the room was another booth, with counter, displaying two large Indian baskets filled with the intriguing cascarones. Along one side of the building was a lean-to which provided room for the women to make coffee and serve the supper.

I was feeling more and more self-conscious and uncomfortable as the guests arrived. Whole families came; mothers with babes in arms and fathers carrying blankets which they spread in corners on the floor for their children when sleep overtook them. Some young men, perhaps from remote canyons or hill tops, came in khaki riding clothes with yellow, blue, or red neckerchiefs, others appeared very much dressed up in white stiff collars and cuffs and colorful ties, their hair shining and their shoes highly polished. Most of the women and girls were in wash dresses, all ruffled and starched, a few in black sateen with colored trimming. The Donahue girls, being in mourning for their father, wore black sateen and did not join in the dancing. I felt like a clown on parade as the taffety ruffles of my skirts swished and rustled at my every turn and move. In passing, I wish to say that at this writing the same black taffety dress, neatly folded, rests on a shelf of my clothes closet.

Cascarones I discovered were egg shells filled with finely cut gold and silver tinsel on which the women spent hours in preparing. The broken open ends by which the eggs were filled were pasted over with varied colored tissue paper which gave them an attractive appearance. All cascarones, selling at from three for a nickel to ten cents apiece, were popped, cracked and broken on heads that evening, enough of their contents remaining in the hair to sparkle as the dancers whirled around the hall.

The proceeds from this interesting affair netted $50.00 for the benefit of the Mission—quite a sum of money at that time, but our needs being so great reduced the amount almost to insignificance. Nevertheless, we appreciated the efforts of the ladies and were very grateful.

I made out a list of things we needed most, revising it several times to fit into the allotted sum. Then, with Padre's approval, I made plans to go to Santa Barbara for the shopping. Miss Nellie Donahue, glad of some pretext, persuaded her brother Thomas to take us, by carriage, into Santa Barbara by way of San Marcos Pass.

The San Marcos Pass! The route Benjamin Foxen chose to lead General Fremont's army into Santa Barbara on that memorable day when the United States added California to its union. I was all agog with anticipation.

At seven in the morning in their two seated, fringed top surrey drawn by two black ponies, Nellie and Thomas stopped at the Mission for me. The weather was biting cold, the ground covered with white frost. We had to wear heavy clothing to keep warm in the open carriage. In addition to my heavy coat I wore a collarette and muff of otter fur. As I look back, I think it was the first and last time that I used the muff in California but it served me well on that trip. All the forenoon we crept on, ever upwards on the shady side of the range of mountains, most of which was damp and cold, but, oh, so beautiful. We were close to nature as we drove under the green, dense, spreading branches of the live-oak, the lacy limbs of the laurel which gave out such a sweet pungent aroma as our carriage brushed past them, and the picturesque sycamore in their weird, magical forms. The road for the most part was wide enough to allow for meeting vehicles comfortably. In very steep, narrow and rocky places, pockets were cut out of the sides of the mountain wall where one vehicle could turn out and await the passing of another. Not being familiar with mountain roads, those pockets were a source of great interest to me. I remember joking a lot about the "empty pockets" and on the whole trip we always found them empty. In fact, I cannot remember meeting a vehicle once we started to climb the mountain until we reached the bottom of it on the opposite side. At noon we arrived at a very picturesque spot, a sort of wooded alcove with large ferns everywhere under the trees. To one side, coming right out of the mountain was a spring of ice cold water. We stopped to eat the lunch we had taken with us, hard boiled eggs, bread and butter sandwiches and a piece of cake. The thermos bottle, an unknown commodity to us at that time, was not a part of our equipment. We satisfied our thirst with a cold drink from the spring, taking it from a rusty tin cup which we found on a flat rock close by, evidently put there by some thoughtful person for the convenience of the traveler. Our ponies, too, were enjoying their lunch. They had been unhitched from the carriage, their harnesses slipped off, nose bags filled with grain and fastened on their heads. Their meal over, they too were refreshed with the sparkling cold water of the spring. After an hour's rest we were glad to be off again. The place was beautiful, but very cold as we sat there on convenient rocks close to the mountain wall.

We were now nearing the summit and many panoramic views, like moving pictures, presented themselves as we rounded the sides of the mountain on our high shelf. Mere words cannot describe the scenes. The coloring and sublimity of changing views all defied description. It was so still that it almost hurt our ears, and how very small we felt in the prodigious whole. The final climbing was steep and we had to stop often to let the ponies rest and get their wind. In the meanwhile we were taking in the marvelous beauty. Through the trees now and then we spied either a coyote or a wildcat that fled for shelter at sight or sound of our surrey. Also the graceful, lithesome deer, not so wary, which stood at attention and looked at us in wonderment. But only Thomas' trained keen eye detected a mountain lion across the canyon in the distance. When we reached the summit and were riding on top of the world, as it were, we suddenly found ourselves looking out onto the vast ocean. What a great expanse of sapphire blue, reaching out to the far horizon! The day was clear and we could see the four islands, like sentinels guarding the shore, and the town of Santa Barbara nestled snugly between the range of mountains and the sea. All was so peaceful looking.

While jogging along in a deep canyon where trees were dense we heard dogs barking. Soon we were in view of the Kinniven home, a prominent pioneer family. As we approached the house one of the boys and his sister came out to greet us and to invite us to stay a while. They seemed disappointed when told we were on our way to Santa Barbara and could not tarry. The spot was so cold and shady and cheerless, with its old and dejected-looking buildings, that I was glad when Thomas applied the whip to the ponies and we were on our way.

As we descended the mountain the sun beat warmly upon us and before long we were shedding our outer wraps and kicking away the robes that were so carefully wrapped around our feet and knees during the forenoon. The grade was much shorter on this side of the mountain and going down so much easier on the ponies that we made very good time, arriving at

Santa Babara at four o'clock that afternoon. What wouldn't
I give today to live over again the thrill of that exhilarating,
alluring first trip over this pass!

We spent two nights in Santa Barbara, staying with a family
by the name of Orella, friends of the Donahues. Mrs. Orella,
a widow, and daughters Nellie and Mercedes, lived in an interesting adobe house on what was at that time "upper" State
Street, the main thoroughfare of the village. They received us
kindly and after the evening meal Thomas took us to the theatre,
the Lobero Theatre, of which the village was proud. Jose
Lobero, a musical genius and native of sunny Italy, with the
financial backing of an affluent citizen, purchased an old adobe
schoolhouse and, with some alterations and additions, created
this first community center in Santa Barbara.

The play that evening was entitled "Wedded and Parted."
It was a poor reproduction of a play I had seen in a large
theatre in St. Paul, Minnesota. The fact that the play was
uninteresting was distressing, but to be eaten up with fleas was
far more distressing, and very embarrassing. I am afraid I
was not altogether appreciative of the community's endeavor.

The quaint Orella house, still in existence, has gone through
many changes since my first visit in it. As I write this, many
years later, it is being used as a restaurant known as the "Copper
Coffee Pot," a charming place. Its deep frontage makes an
ideal court in which to arrange tables for serving meals out of
doors. With the rapid growth of Santa Barbara the building
now finds itself in the heart of the city. I like to wander there
occasionally for a quiet meal and to lose myself in reminiscence
of my first visit.

Mrs. Orella, true to the early Spanish Californians, was
very hospitable. An incident of our stay, which still shines in
the pocket of my memories, was that we were served frijoles
for breakfast. This was my first introduction to the California
pink bean. However, I cannot say that I relished them at
that time of the day.

What fun to go shopping with $50.00 to spend! Considering my youth and inexperience Padre must have had great confidence in my good judgment to give me "carte blanche" to do the shopping. I did considerable tramping from shop to shop looking over materials and getting prices so that I might fill my list at the least possible cost. Finding everything so much higher in price than I had anticipated, I began to have a sinking feeling that the $50.00 would be inadequate. Finally, at the "City of Paris," a mid-western firm that had just opened up a store in Santa Barbara, I asked to see the proprietor. Frankly I told him of the things I wished to purchase, the amount I had to spend and asked if he could make any concessions in view of the fact that the amount was considerable.

The man laughed graciously, said he wanted me to be pleased, and personally waited on me, doing all that he could in the way of concessions. We had many a hearty laugh as we dickered and figured while he measured out yards and yards of sheeting, pillow casing, toweling, linen for table-cloths and napkins, silkolene for comforters and netting for curtains. The selection of cotton batting, threads and needles and two blankets completed the list, which when added amounted to $53.00. I accepted the bill and paid the difference from private funds, feeling pleased with myself and my purchase.

With all this material in yardage, I just had to have a sewing machine to make it up. Padre had mentioned getting one, provided the firm would be willing to wait a little for payment. Sewing machines were high in price and secretly I had given the matter much thought, fully making up my mind as to what I would do about it.

As I walked into the Singer sewing machine shop I asked the clerk if he had any used machines on hand. He hesitated a moment and then said that he did have one and motioned me to follow him to the farther end of the store. There I found a Singer sewing machine, almost new, which the clerk assured me was in first-class working condition. After a little bartering I agreed to take the machine for $20.00 provided he would crate it and send it to the Santa Ines Mission. All this he agreed to do.

Dusk was laying its mantle of gray over the village as I stepped out of the shop, and I quickened my step as I suddenly remembered that Father Ealing of Our Lady of Sorrows parish had invited Nellie and me to have dinner with him at the parsonage. To be entertained for the evening was a welcome relaxation after the day's shopping.

It was a subdued trio that boarded the surrey in the early morning of the third day. With bundles of all sorts and descriptions around us, under us and over us we were off for the homeward trip, leaving Santa Barbara behind us.

Santa Barbara! A name so sweet and full of music. This visit left an indelible picture of its beauty and mildness of climate and has ever been as a bright flower in my bouquet of memories.

As the morning wore on, however, and new scenes greeted us we regained our alertness and enthusiasm. We returned via the Señora del Refugio (Our Lady of Refuge) Pass. The road, very narrow and for the most part very steep, was nothing more than a wagon trail. The scenery was superb, but the narrowness, steepness and roughness of the road kept us in such an anxious state of mind that most of the time we were kept busy hanging on to our seats and could not fully enjoy it. We arrived at the Mission at dusk, weary but pleased with our trip.

CHRISTMAS DAY

On Sunday preceding the feast of the Nativity Padre announced that there would be two Masses on Christmas day, one at five and another at ten o'clock in the morning.

Miss Flora Fabing came all the way from Lompoc the previous day to play the organ and, with her brother William and the four Donahue girls, sing a few hymns during the service. Also on the previous day Padre and I had gone to the sacristy to look over the once beautiful but now very dilapidated vestments to select one for use on Christmas day. Padre having made his selection I, at once, took the garment home to make the necessary emergency repairs.

Then there was the matter of altar decorations. There were no flowers in the Mission's garden and the best that could be done was to add a few green pepper boughs, which were laden with red berries, to the few silk and velvet artificial flowers that already were on the altars. These flowers, battered and faded by time, were in quaint and beautiful vases. After perking them up by straightening out the wires which held the leaves and petals, and adding the fresh green boughs, they took on a new appearance. Linens, freshly washed and ironed, added to the decorations as a whole and did much to give the chapel an air of festivity.

A little creche arranged on St. Joseph's altar consisted of small but beautifully hand carved wooden figures of Mary, Joseph and the Infant. These were arranged under a ramada of pepper boughs.

We were up and about very early on Christmas morning. Padre lit the many candles on the three altars and saw that everything was in readiness for the service. At the appointed time, I rang two of the five bells hanging in the tower by pulling the long ropes tied to and hanging from their clappers.

61

In the darkness and eeriness of early morning Mrs. Donahue and daughters Kate, Anna, Nellie and Lizzie, Mr. and Mrs. Peter Hanly and daughter Eva walked to the Mission. They carried lanterns to light them on their way. Miss Fabing, her brother William and myself made up the congregation. Faith alone could bring us together at this hour, I reasoned, as we sat in our pews in the cold, heatless, and semi-dark church, all bundled up in heavy clothes, shivering, as we followed the Mass from our prayer books. In compensation the bright taper-lighted altars, glowing with red pepper berries, crisp white linens and the exquisite fabric in the chasuble Padre wore for the occasion, looked beautiful and warmed the heart.

After Mass, in the thin crisp air, in front of the chapel we exchanged our cheerful "Merry Christmas" greetings, then the congregation was invited to the house to greet Padre and to partake of a cup of coffee and bread and butter in front of a glowing fire.

For our Christmas dinner, instead of going out of doors to use the old cast-iron stove, I now managed the meat, vegetables and coffee very well in the fireplace. An apple pie baked the day before served as dessert. To give the meal a festive air I served it on a small table before the open fire. From outside came the pitter-patter of a welcome rain as soft music tumbling down from heaven to bless and restore to beauty the dry, parched landscape.

There were to be many more "Christmas Days" for us within the soft gray walls of the Mission but none painted so vivid a picture on the canvas of memories.

A WOMAN'S TOUCH IN A MISSION

The arrival of the sewing machine really marked the beginning of a "Woman's touch in a Mission." It was then that I began, seriously, to take my position as a helpmate and home maker for Padre, taking real interest in doing things both for our comfort and to make the place attractive as well as livable. Many were the times I lay awake nights thinking out some plan to improve our surroundings and to add to our comfort.

Busy days followed with the sewing machine buzzing and my young heart singing. I adored sewing and the making up of all the new materials was a source of great joy. I was proud of my hand sewing and wished that my mother could see the rolled hems on the napkins and the hemstitching on the table cloths. I thought of the joys there must be for young brides, when starting out in their housekeeping, to have everything crispy new and shining. But alas! I dare not dwell on the subject of brides. I had just missed that sweet gratification so dear to a young maiden's heart. Previous to my coming to California the young man to whom I had become engaged was fatally wounded in an accidental shooting while on a hunting expedition. Busy and interesting hours helped to dispel the grief of that tragic accident.

Besides making up the new materials I converted all sorts of odds and ends into doilies, bureau scarves and small table covers. Even the humble bleached out flour sacks were put into use. With a bit of embroidery, applique or crocheted edge, to give them an air of dignity and character, they made useful and decorative pieces to be used in an otherwise unattractive room. Soon Padre caught my spirit of decorating and brought out many personal knick-knacks and acquisitions and distributed them here and there to make the place more homelike and good to remember.

Sandwiched between my sewing, Padre and I were busy mending doors, locks, window frames, replacing broken panes and patching up holes and broken places in the adobe walls in all the rooms that were used. We made small tables to be used here and there in the various rooms. Then there was the shelving for china, pantry things, books and what-nots. In the bed rooms we put up large shelves, with curtains suspended from them, to be used for wardrobes. All these were quite crude, to be sure, but with a woman's touch, a piece of oil cloth neatly covering a small table, a piece of chintz made into a curtain, artistically shirred or pleated, and tacked on the shelves used as wardrobes, did much to obliterate the crudeness. Netting neatly made into sash curtains for the windows and a little glue, putty and paint on a few pieces of furniture that fairly screamed for attention, did much to transform appearances.

Besides making the house tolerably livable there was much in and about the Chapel that needed attention. First of all the openings left by broken window panes had to be covered up, at least temporarily, to keep out the owls and bats that made the chapel their home, the statues and frames of the large oil paintings their roosting places. Not an easy task you'll grant, if you have ever visited the Mission and noticed how high the windows, set in their deep recesses of the adobe walls, really are. For this purpose, by piecing some old boards together,

Padre and I constructed a step ladder long enough to reach the recesses. True, this ladder was a bit shaky and much too fragile to carry Padre's weight of some hundred and seventy pounds so it fell to my lot to scale it and repair the windows.

Will I ever forget that day! Never! We started on the south side facing the court. With hammer, nails and some thin boards I reached the recess, crouched, and with fear and trembling tried to adjust the boards to fully cover the openings. Padre, standing at the foot of the ladder, was shouting directions as to how the work should be done. We argued back and forth but came to no agreement. Finally, to gain his point, Padre removed the ladder some two or three feet from the recess, saying as he did so, "You can stay there all night," and indignantly walked back to the house and disappeared. The strain of our being unqualified and unaccustomed to doing these many strange tasks had reached the point where we were sandpapering each other's temperaments with words.

I regained my self-composure, nailed the boards as well as I could, then with my arms folded, sat in the deep recess awaiting Padre's pleasure, for well I knew that when the inner man asserted itself in the requirement of food the ladder would come back into place. I did not have to wait long, for soon I saw Padre, his face wreathed in smiles, ready to replace the ladder.

"Are you ready to come down?" he asked.

I was.

With the openings closed, the owls and bats were forced to find new homes and roosting places and we could now give attention to doing some cleaning in the chapel. What a herculean task I thought, as I stood contemplatively near the front entrance taking in the condition of things. The cleaning of the statues and oil paintings would require some skill as well as patience. To remove the dried up owl droppings without marring the soft colored paint and gold leaf of the statues, without defacing the oil paintings, was a difficult procedure.

It would be a long, tedious performance. The statues were carved in wood, and painted in lovely soft colors trimmed in gold leaf.

With Padre's help I took down the statues of Blessed Virgin Mary, St. Anthony, Mother of Sorrows and a small madonna. Santa Ines, which was in a niche high above the main altar, required a ladder to reach it and we considered the one we made too wobbly and insecure to undertake such a feat. I spent hours on each statue in removing the offensive filth. Then, with the application of linseed oil and a soft polishing cloth, I was able to bring back, somewhat, the life and soft colors of the paints.

Poor Santa Ines had to wait a year, or maybe two (memory fails me here), before being cleaned and classed among the respectables. It happened when a tramp, a young man, came to seek food and shelter. The weather being cold and rainy he was forced to remain several days, during which time he offered to do odd jobs for his keep. Padre asked him to clean the statue. The man, young and agile, did not mind going up the wobbly ladder. It was then that Santa Ines too became respectable looking and worthy of her place of honor above the main altar.

Before leaving for his regular two days trip to Lompoc, early one Saturday morning, Padre assisted me in taking down some ten or twelve of the largest oil paintings from the chapel walls. There were at that time twenty-five oil paintings besides the stations of the cross and a small painting of the Good Shepherd adorning the door of the tabernacle. We carried the pictures out on the veranda, under the arches, and leaned them against the wall of the convento where they remained until they were cleaned. There were no visitors, much less vandals, coming to the Mission during those primitive days and we had no fears for their safety. In some respects the paintings were easier to handle than the statues but their cleaning was just as difficult and laborious. When ready for the task, I filled a washtub with water and, with a soft brush and soft cloths, proceeded to scrub and wash the paintings and their huge frames.

When Padre returned from his trip he was horrified to find me scrubbing and splashing water with, apparently, no regard for the preservation of the paintings. I can still see him, through my mind's eye, throwing up his hands and saying, "My Heavens, Mamie, you are spoiling the paintings."

"I know of no other way of getting this dirt off," I replied.

True, I was, at that time, too inexperienced in the knowledge of the high merits of old oil paintings fully to appreciate them. I regarded most of these, in their present dilapidated and soiled condition, as unfit for use. Others I thought positively ugly. Padre, on the other hand, studied them minutely, was appreciative and, pointing out their beauty and worth, tried to make me realize their true value.

When all were cleaned and dried they presented a dull and rather sad appearance just as the statues had before the application of the linseed oil. Padre did not approve of the use of linseed oil on the paintings but I argued that I didn't see how we could possibly do anything to make them look any worse than they were. Finally, we compromised by trying it out on "San Rafael," a very crude painting done by an early Mission Indian. It portrayed the saint as having wings, wearing a helmet, cheeks painted, carrying a staff in his right hand and a fish under his left arm. He looked knock-kneed and wore high boots. The oil wrought wonders in bringing out the colors of the paints and giving life to the painting. As a result the paintings received a liberal application of the linseed oil. Some years later Mr. John Gamble, the artist, recommended the use of banana oil for paintings.

At about this time we found the beautiful old oil painting of Saint Francis in the floorless room under the water tank, a dark and damp place full of debris. It was without frame, crumpled up, and partly buried in the soil and so decayed that it simply crumpled and had to be cut off, thus cutting off the feet of the saint. You can see the painting at the Mission today, in a plain frame just as it was mounted at that time.

After Padre's death, in going over some of his papers, I found a list of the paintings which were cleaned and rehung at that time. The list follows:

1 B.M.V. cum infanta	10 S. Theresa c. Jesu	19 S. John Baptist
2 S. John of God	11 S. Franciscus	20 S. Joseph
3 S. John of God	12 S. John Baptist	21 B. M. Guadalupe
4 S. Ignatius	13 S. Catherine	22 S. Franciscus
5 S. Familia	14 S. Theresa	23 S. Rafael
6 S. Agatha	15 S. Aloysius	24 Death of S. Ines
7 S. Antonius	16 S. Vibiana	25 Presentatio Templo
8 S. Ines	17 S. Maria inter agnos	
9 S. Gregory	18 S. M. cum infanta	

In the early part of February the Yankee couple left the Mission. Shortly after taking charge, Padre asked the couple to vacate the rooms they now occupied and seek other quarters. But they were loath to relinquish what they considered an ideal place for their chicken raising. They remained on and on, challenging Padre's right in asking them to leave. Padre was at his wit's end. He did not wish to be harsh or unkind but his sensibilities revolted against the cackling of hens and crowing of young roosters within the Mission building. Ultimately, after much urgent persuasion, they realized that although the old Mission was an ideal place for their chickens, the atmosphere of it was not in sympathy with their venture and occupation.

At ten o'clock one night, as Padre and I were returning from a neighboring farmhouse where we had spent the evening, we met the couple driving down the lane to the main highway. In the dim starlight we could see that their canvas covered wagon, which was bulging out on all sides, was loaded with their household possessions and their chickens. A water bucket, lantern, some pots and pans and such things as were hung to the end and sides of the wagon tossed and rattled as they sped on their way.

"Praise be to God," I heard Padre say as soon as we were beyond hearing distance of the couple. His elation over finding himself sole occupant of the Mission was such that he could not refrain from giving expression to it.

"What a sight!" "What a sight!" both Padre and I exclaimed as we waded through the foul, repugnant filth and dirt of the vacated rooms. The cleaning of our own rooms had been discouraging enough but this part of the building was revolting. Having previously been used as a blacksmith shop during the Donahue occupation, it had suffered much from neglect in every way. One of the rooms we found had been used, apparently for years, as a dumping place for all rubbish.

For more than three months I had scrubbed, scraped, washed and cleaned everything with which I had come in contact and, now, to face this veritable nightmare condition brought on a feeling akin to despair. What an arduous, disagreeable and seemingly impossible task it would be to clean the place, I thought, but Padre, on the other hand, laid plans for our undertaking the huge task.

"We will make a bonfire of most of this stuff," he said, waving his arm in a general direction indicating the debris in all the rooms.

"Ye-es," I managed to say as I turned away to conceal a flow of tears and walked back to our livable rooms for solace. Never before had I felt so discouraged or incapable of coping with a situation. To me the very thought of digging out the filth and dirt seemed inconceivable.

At six o'clock one bright morning, with an old wheelbarrow which we found on the premises, we started our cleaning. All day long we kept that wooden wheelbarrow creaking its way from the "dump" room to a bonfire in the middle of the road in front of the building and back again. What a conglomeration of paper, cartons, pieces of harnesses, parts of saddles, old shoes, boots, rusty tools, bottles, burlap and what-not was found in that room. In fact, as Padre kept saying, "everything but money." The whole mass, moldy, with offensive odor, was rotted and matted together by time. Sprinkled over all this was the filth left by the chickens that had made the dump a roosting place. Of all the tasks performed at the Mission the cleaning up of those rooms was by far the most arduous and repulsive.

A STORM AND AN EARLY DAY EASTER SUNDAY

Just as we were getting ourselves tolerably comfortable and settled along came a violent and terrifying rain storm, the most severe of that winter's storms, descending on us March 4, 1905. The wind had a velocity of a tornado. Huge portions of the roof were torn off from the convento and landed in an adjoining field yards away. Shakes loosened from the remaining portion were flying through the air in all directions. Garden tools, garbage cans and board ends, in fact everything that was loose or could be loosened, was being carried away by the strong wind. So terrifying it was that we did not dare open an outside door, much less venture out during the storm.

The water was coming down in torrents in nearly all the rooms and we were kept busy running hither and yon, shifting beds and other pieces of furniture, diverting the water into tubs, buckets, pots and pans and anything that would hold water. All around us were little puddles of soft mud that had oozed out of the water-soaked adobe walls.

"The windmill is going." Padre looked out of the window and saw the wheel and fan-tail of the mill being torn from its derrick. It fell in a crumpled heap on the ground. A little later we saw the derrick, looking very dejected, lying flat on

71

its side. A board fence seven feet high running about a hundred feet from the buggy shed to the north end of the chapel, forming the court back of the convento, was also flat on the ground.

It was terrifying and disheartening to listen to the wind and rain, not knowing what would happen next. I have often wondered at our courage at remaining in the building, but we did not realize the danger of an adobe building in such a storm and the possibility of our being buried alive should the walls crumble.

The loss of parts of the roof caused us considerable inconvenience during the remainder of the rainy season but the destruction of the windmill was a greater loss. As a result we were forced to haul water from the river for all household purposes. We were fortunate in that a few days later, a man appeared in search of employment and a place to stay. He did not long for work but his appetite was normal. He was an elderly man, apparently strong, and his name was John. Padre decided that John could at least haul water, and welcomed his coming. A day or two later he borrowed a horse from the Donahue boys. Under his supervision a sled was built on which a barrel could be placed. Thereafter each morning John would hitch the horse to this primitive conveyance and go whistling down to the river for water. Poor John, after driving over a rough road with most of the morning gone, would arrive with the barrel about one-third full. It was weeks before a new windmill was installed.

Our first Easter at the Mission has always remained a very vivid picture in my gallery of remembrances. All nature seemed to have been attuned for the occasion. The sun beamed its approval. The linnets were early in singing their "matins." Spring had spread her mantle of green over the hills and valley. Altogether it was one of those rare days when one's soul is filled with the thrill of being alive.

With the small attendance on Christmas and New Year's day fresh in his mind Padre had made no preparation for special services during Holy Week or Easter Sunday. He simply announced that the usual week-day and Sunday masses would take place.

It is high time that I should introduce the most unique and interesting character it was our good fortune to know in our long stay at the Mission—none other than Fernando Cardenas. Fernandito he was affectionately called, as an endearing term and for his small stature. Fernandito was not at all pleased at hearing Padre's announcements for Holy Week and Easter Sunday. He came to the Mission to protest in no uncertain terms, saying that there had always been the usual Holy Week ceremonies, that the people expected it, and that he would serve at the altar as an acolyte.

Padre explained to him that he did not have the proper facilities to perform elaborate ceremonies, but hoped by another Easter week he would be able to give it all the solemnity it deserved. Meanwhile if he wished to take part as an acolyte he would be glad to have his assistance.

On Holy Thursday, Good Friday, Holy Saturday and Easter Sunday morning Fernandito came to act as acolyte. A man four feet five inches in height, in his sixty-seventh year, wearing immaculately clean jumper and trousers of blue denim, he gave an impressive touch to the simple ceremony as he lit the candles and recited the Latin responses of the Mass.

Padre was pleasantly surprised to see a large attendance at the week-day ceremonies, especially to see so many of the Indians and Mexican-Indians. There was, and still is, an Indian reservation near the village of Santa Ynez but up to this time it was more or less unknown to Padre.

After the service, on Friday morning, I noticed that people did not gather in little groups for a chat as was usual, but all seemed in great hurry to get away. As I sauntered down from the church through the corridor towards the front door I caught sight of something dangling from a limb of the lone pepper tree in front of the farthest end of the corridor. I knit my brow and looked hard to make sure of what I saw. There was a man dressed in a blue shirt, black trousers and a black hat, hung by the neck and swinging from a limb of the tree. I turned to call some one. No one was there, everybody had disappeared. What did it mean? Trembling, I walked to the end of the corridor to take a closer look and if possible identify the victim. Fancy my relief and my indignation when I saw it was only an effigy of a man. By now Padre made his appearance and at sight of it burst into a hearty laugh. "An effigy of Judas hanging to a tree," he exclaimed. "The Indians must have hung it there." Then he wondered if that explained, at least in part, Fernandito's anxieties about observing Holy Week ceremonies.

On Saturday afternoon John and Ned Murphy from Santa Ynez brought a clothes basket full of flowers to decorate the altars. A feast for the eyes was this array of Cecil Brunner roses, bridal wreath, syringa and fleur-de-lis—really the first and only flowers I had seen in that dry and sun-parched valley. The men offered to help in arranging them, saying they had often decorated the altars. I accepted their assistance and was grateful, for I knew it was a long task.

Imagine our surprise Easter Sunday morning when, at six o'clock people began to arrive and continued to do so until time for service at ten o'clock. They came from all the surrounding country, Lompoc, Sisquoc, Los Alamos, Las Cruces and the nearby villages of Los Olivos and Santa Ynez; also from the almost inaccessible mountain tops and deep canyons. They appeared in all sorts of conveyances, stage coaches, tallyhos, lumber wagons, surreys, carts, and a number came on horseback, boys and girls riding alike, astride. Many came who were not of the Catholic faith, but all were welcome at the Mission on Easter Sunday and every Sunday.

Everyone was dressed in his best clothes and finery. Most of the small children wore sunbonnets, all ruffled and starched, to shield them from the hot sun. The young girls in stiffly starched wash dresses wore picture hats gay with inexpensive colorful flowers. Black predominated in the dress of the older women, while lace mantillas or bright little shawls made up their head dress. A number of the young men were colorful in boleros and decorated trousers, while those who rode on horseback wore elaborate chaps in all sorts of beautifully stamped leather, sheep skins or ornate bead work. Some of the sombreros were trimmed with red, yellow, green or purple hat bands, others with more sombre braided horsehair in black and white and maroon and white.

The horses, too, were groomed for the occasion with manes and tails all carefully waved, showing the care and artistic temperament of their owners. Their saddles and bridles were decorated either in ornate stamped leather or with mountings of shining silver. Gay colored tassels hung from their bridles just below the ears and amusing little peaked straw hats were set on the horses' heads to shield them from the sun's heat.

Many of these people made their long journey fasting in order to avail themselves of the opportunity of receiving their Easter Holy Communion. Padre was indeed a busy man, hearing confessions and giving communion hourly from seven till ten o'clock that morning.

I, too, found myself wholly unprepared; but busily occupied brewing coffee on the little cracked iron stove, and with bread and butter managed to serve many who came fasting. By now I had become accustomed to the cracked and chipped china and in the midst of the good cheer that prevailed they lost much of their offensiveness.

The church service was simple but impressive. Fernandito as acolyte made the Latin responses in his clear, soft voice while a choir composed of volunteer singers added to the glorification of the day. Among the singers were two old Indian women who, with their sweet, low musical voices and with great feeling, sang their favorite Spanish hymn, "Santa Ines Hermosa."

After the church services the large space in front of the Mission, green as if in preparation for the feast, was dotted with groups here and there, spreading their sumptuous food from baskets and boxes which they had brought with them. Little cook stoves were hastily made of a few rocks or broken tile to cook their coffee, and, in a short time the inviting aroma was beyond resistance.

It was a happy carefree day! A truly joyful Easter! All met their friends, chatted and were gay.

Not until the sun was setting beyond the purple hills did the last of the picnickers wave their "Adios" with many a "Ven otra vez."

RESTORATION BEGINS

As time wore on and as each day we walked about the Mission viewing the destruction and ruin on every side, it became more and more apparent that something would have to be done to the building if we were to remain in it. Up to this time, in spite of all we had done, things in general were most discouraging. At times Padre was tempted to write his Bishop that it was impossible for him to remain. I too was disheartened and just about as low in spirit as one could be. Only the realization of Padre's helplessness without me prevented my taking the next train home to Mother.

Much had been done to make ourselves tolerably comfortable inside the house, but nothing had been done to the building itself. Since the big storm of March the Mission was practically roofless, and the cracks and holes made by the rain in the adobe walls were growing larger and larger. As the water-soaked places dried out a fine dust was created which slid down in little mounds here and there on the floors.

Then there was the problem of getting water again. But most necessary and most difficult was the solution of procuring funds. We were willing and ready to do all that hands and brains could accomplish, but the purchasing of materials required money.

As spring burgeoned in its beauty of scenery and sweetness of climate one could not help but be thrilled at being alive. Padre was filled with new zeal and ambition and had many plans for his Mission. Early one morning he asked me to join him on the front veranda, where he could look out at the sweeping view of the valley and mountains. We usually held counsel on the veranda and, it was a long, long talk that we had that morning. There were so many things and problems to face and solve.

After a full, round morning of pros and cons Padre decided to put his difficult problem before his superior, the late Bishop Thomas Conaty of blessed memory. Ere the afternoon had faded into the purple shade of evening he had poured out his soul's longing and ambitions for the Mission and was tripping down the lane carrying his letter to the mail box where Uncle Sam's mail coach would pick it up and take it on its way. From the sprightliness of his step I knew that he was confident of an early and favorable reply.

Tense days followed the mailing of Padre's letter. We worried along almost breathless awaiting the answer.

"A letter from the Bishop," Padre solemnly announced, late one afternoon, as he opened his mail sack and proceeded to his sanctum sanc-torum to read it.

His face beamed with satisfaction as he emerged, the letter still in his hand. He re-read it to me. The good Bishop gave instructions to have the shakes on the roof replaced with shingles, the well and windmill repaired, and to send the bills to the Diocesan Chancery.

The repairing of the well for procuring water was our most urgent need. The old well, hand dug, was four feet square and ninety feet deep, lined with boards all the way down. During the course of time these boards decayed. Then a circular curbing of wood was placed inside the old square one and a windmill erected. This was done during the Donahue occupancy of the Mission.

From the firm of "McAdam and Smith" of Lompoc, Padre secured mechanics and materials to repair the well. At this time an eight inch terracotta pipe was placed inside the old circular casing and a new windmill put in place. Once more with the first strong wind the well gave forth its life-giving water.

The next task at hand was the placing of a roof over our heads before the rainy season set in again. In our isolation the securing of skilled workmen was quite a problem. Carpenters were needed. The few skilled men among the ranch people were busy with their own work. However, after some little time Padre learned of a man living in Santa Ynez, a Frenchman by the name of La Fontaine, who claimed to be a carpenter. Padre hired him, and with two Spanish Mexicans he went to work putting on the new roof.

What a slow, long drawn out affair the removing of the shakes and putting on the new roof really was. The men came from Santa Ynez each morning in the most "mañana" fashion, usually from fifteen to thirty minutes late. They donned their carpenter's aprons and worked until noon, when a hearty meal was ready for them. They then smoked their cigarettos until one and leisurely went back to work. When the hour for quitting arrived they promptly put their tools away, hitched their horses and were out of sight in a cloud of dust before we could say "Jack Robinson." All of this got under Padre's skin, as the saying goes, but what was he to do? Nothing.

The materials, namely sheeting, shingles and nails for the roof, came from San Luis Obispo and were transported on the narrow gauge railway as far as Los Olivos, the end of the railway, thence over the six miles to the Mission by wagon. They were unloaded in front of the convento.

Many times after the workmen left Padre and I carried sheeting through the house, or with the wheelbarrow transported bundles of shingles to the opposite side of the building, that they might be there and at hand when the workmen returned the following morning. In doing so we saved time and expense.

The preparing of the noonday meal on the old cracked stove, for three husky men, was anything but a joy. Furthermore, I was not accustomed to preparing meals for husky men and, with all the other tasks at hand, I found it very trying. One day when I was in front of the building helping Padre move some lumber one of the men came all the way around the convento with the sugar bowl in his hand. This he did to remind me that I had forgotten to replenish it for that meal. It struck Padre as being funny and he broke out in a hearty laughter. Then the man joined him, and the incident was treated as a joke.

O tiempo pasado! Only the memory of it remains.

This new roof, when completed, extended over the livable rooms which was half of the convento in its present state.

The cost of the well, windmill and roofing amounted to $2,606.27. This was paid for by the Bishop. At his own expense Padre retained the French carpenter to put partitions in four of the largest rooms so as to make them more comfortable and homelike. It was here that we discovered how very little the man knew about the trade he professed. One instance stands out distinctly when, at the end of a whole day's fussing and puffing he had accomplished the task of hanging a door and putting in its lock, only to discover that it was hung upside down. "It looks very funny," he jestingly remarked, as he put on his coat to depart. This took place on the eve of a holiday and I recall that Padre and I celebrated the holiday by re-hanging the door and adjusting the lock in its proper place. In view of the man's shortcoming Padre was most patient and assisted him wherever he could.

When all of the two-by-four timbers for the partitions were up and the one door hung the carpenter announced that he did not know how to do lathing and left the job.

For months we walked around the two-by-four timbers in the middle of these rooms, until one Saturday morning, when Padre was leaving for Lompoc to be away until the following Monday, I got the bright idea that I might do some lathing myself. As soon as Padre disappeared I got busy with hammer, nails and a stepladder and lathed a whole side of a wall eighteen feet wide and fourteen feet high.

When Padre returned he questioned my knowledge of lathing by affecting displeasure, but secretly, I knew that he was pleased. From that time on all of my precious spare moments were spent going up and down the step-ladder to nail on more laths, until all of the four walls were finished on both of their eighteen-by-fourteen feet sides. Many months later Thomas Donahue took compassion on us and offered to do some plastering. He was not exactly a first class plasterer, but all the better, for his work was rough and rather resembled the adobe walls.

Not until after the storm in 1912, when there was more extensive restoration, did these walls get finished, that is to say, the door frames put in, the doors hung and the mop boards put in place.

The fence across the west side of the courtyard still had to be replaced. The wind which swept in from that direction, almost every afternoon, was terrific and very annoying. Every thing that was loose in the yard would be blown about or out of position. To prevent a repetition of the previous catastrophe, Padre decided on building a row of storerooms, work shop, chicken houses and granary. These were built on a concrete foundation with but one slope to the roof, which faced the courtyard. This structure extended the whole length of the west side of the courtyard, which is to say, as long as the convento part of the Mission. For the most part all this was built from lumber salvaged from the old fence and that of the greenhouse. The windows used were also taken from the greenhouse, all of which was a great saving in expense.

This work was done by William Miller, a carpenter from Santa Ynez. With the help of the occasional tramp Padre undertook to put in the partitions and to do the shingling.

It developed that I, too, had to give a helping hand. Vividly do I remember that, when the rainy season was approaching and the "occasional tramp" did not appear, for three days I climbed on the roof and nailed shingles. Slipping down each evening I was so stiff and crippled from the cramped position that I could scarcely walk home; but the roof got shingled and that is what Padre wanted.

When Fall was again painting its gold, yellow and brown over all the landscape, we had been at the Mission over a year, working harder than we had ever worked in our lives and we had just made a small dent in the accomplishment of what was to be done if the Mission was to be restored.

The memories retained of this our first year at the Mission are many. Memories of loneliness, sadness and despair, with only the beauty of nature surrounding us to give comfort, hope and a little joy. Happily, the approaching winter had lost some of its terror, however, since we had a good roof over our heads.

Sometime during this late summer Bishop Conaty appointed Father Mathias Ternes, S. T. L., to build a church in Santa Maria, a small town forty miles north of the Mission. In making this appointment the Bishop assigned the churches at Sisquoc and Los Alamos as outposts of Santa Maria. This relieved Padre of considerable work. He now gave Lompoc and Santa Inez two Sundays each month instead of one as heretofore.

Of considerable importance in the history of the Mission was the Centennial of its founding on September 4th, 1904. To hold any kind of celebration on that date was wholly out of the question. Padre did not belittle its importance, however, and made plans to celebrate the following year.

We were still living under perplexing conditions when the date arrived, but managed quite a nice celebration. Rev. Joseph O'Keefe, O.F.M. of Mission San Luis Rey, Rev. Ludger Glauber, O.F.M. of Santa Barbara, Rev. Frederick Lack of Arroyo Grande and Rev. Mathias Ternes of Santa Maria were invited to participate.

At ten thirty o'clock a High Mass was celebrated; Father Glauber was celebrant with Father Lack and Father Ternes taking the parts of deacon and sub-deacon respectively. During the Mass Father O'Keefe gave a sermon in English and after the Mass another in Spanish. Padre made up the choir by playing the organ and singing the Mass. His strong melodious tenor voice harmonized with the music of the little melodian organ and filled the chapel. Padre was a talented musician. When the service was over the visiting clergy were loud in their praise of his voice and his performance on the organ. The inhabitants of the valley were not very enthusiastic about the celebration of the Centennial and only a few people were in attendance.

With the celebration over and mindful that the restoration must continue, Padre lost no time in furthering his plans. He immediately hired an Indian, José Solares, who understood working with adobe. The room we chose to use as a kitchen had no outside door. Capitán José, as he was known among the Indians, with pick, ax and shovel cut an opening in the thick wall. This took several days to accomplish. What a mess it created! The fine powder like dust of the dry adobe settled over everything. Even Capitán nearly disappeared from view as he stood in the big cavity to pick and chop out the opening.

The creaking old wheelbarrow was again brought into play as the huge pile of debris was hauled out through the new doorway and used to fill depressions in the courtyard.

Capitán then built a low ledge between the arches. These were made the same thickness as the buttresses, from broken adobe and tile picked out of the ruins. Three arches were left clear, two leading to the front doors and the other to the back entrance of the house. Several years later they received a coat of concrete to protect them from the rains and make them more lasting. They proved a great protection against the sand and dust that blew in through the arches and later, as we acquired all sorts of potted plants to set on them, they added to the appearance of the veranda.

Another task for Capitán was the building of an abutment to support the last arch of the corridor and keep it from crumbling. This he did with rocks and adobe and it required several days labor. When all this was accomplished funds for repairs were exhausted. It was then up to Padre and myself to patch the crumbling inside walls of the rooms we were using. This proved to be an endless task. During our long residence at the Mission there never was a time when there were no defects in the walls to be mended. The rains had so saturated the almost roofless, thick adobe walls that it was a long time before they thoroughly dried out. As they did so they crumbled into fine dust, leaving cavities of every dimension and shape to be filled in and patched. We would mix mortar and patch the holes, then in a few weeks the adobe around these patches would dry out and crumble, making it necessary to do more patching.

The floors, too, were a problem in our efforts to make the place cozy. The unattractive black asphalt floors of the dining room, kitchen and my bedroom and large room next to the living room were uneven, unsightly and hard to keep clean. Those of the living room, Padre's bedroom and guest room were of pine boards, worn down to slivers that caught on to the floor mop when I tried to clean them.

It must be borne in mind that these rooms were built not as a dwelling but as shops, and the asphalt floors served that purpose very well. Now that it was to be used as a dwelling I particularly wanted something different. I gave the problem considerable thought, always keeping in mind the fact that funds for anything outside of bare necessities did not exist.

From the start we decided on paint for the wood floors. The next time Padre made the trip to Lompoc he brought home some terracotta colored paint and a paint brush. I loved painting and was delighted. When Padre again left home to be away for a few days I spent all my time painting, scarcely taking time to prepare meals—and most of them were eaten standing over the cook stove or work table.

Just as I was having a beautiful time painting the big front room floor, singing and keeping rhythm with the strokes of the brush, who should appear in the front door but Mrs. Donahue and daughter Lizzie.

"Oh my; you are painting the floor," Mrs. Donahue commented, and looking not at all pleased.

"Oh yes," I said, "They are so rough that I thought a little paint would freshen and make them easier to keep clean."

"During our long stay at the Mission we never used water on the floors," she said with some pride.

"But how did you keep them clean?" I asked.

She then related how she sent the children down to the river to get fine sand. This she sprinkled over the floors and, after a day or two when the sand had scratched the dirt from the boards she would sweep it up. "It left the floor much cleaner than if I had scrubbed it."

Perhaps that was all very true, the sand may have had its good merits, but in my own young mind I still wanted the floors painted and the slivers eliminated. The floors of the living room, Padre's bedroom and guest room were all given two coats of paint.

Covering the asphalt floors proved to be more of a problem. Padre suggested matting, which was so much in vogue at that time and not too expensive. Unfortunately matting could not be tacked to the asphalt floor. I pondered over the idea. It then occurred to me that it could be sewed together like carpeting. At first opportunity Padre went to Santa Maria and from the Jones Furniture Co. bought enough matting to cover the floor in the dining room and the large room next to the living room. It was a long, slow procedure this sewing of the matter. It was stiff, cumbersone and difficult to handle. It had to be done by hand with heavy thread. After sewing the strips together the ends were tacked to a wood quarter-round and these in turn were nailed to the mop boards. This stretched the matting in place. When the room next to the living room was finished it looked so attractive that I decided to move into it and use it as a combination sitting and bedroom. I occupied it until 1912 when more extensive work was done on the building.

In covering the kitchen floor we used linoleum. Then Padre had a workman put up a terra cotta pipe to be used as a chimney for a cook stove. Shortly afterwards he bought a wood range. The old cracked stove which had served its purpose for so long now landed in the "junk limbo", a gulch cut into the hillside by the earthquake of 1812, a little southeast of the Mission.

So depressing and disheartening were the aspects at times that nothing but sheer force of will gave us strength to stay at the Mission and carry on. But now much had been accomplished, we felt more encouraged, and life took on a more cheerful aspect. From time to time we acquired a few pieces of furniture and smaller and lesser objects that contributed to the appearance and comfort of the house. The rooms were so large with such high ceilings that it took a great deal to make them look homey and give them a feeling of warmth and friendliness. However, in due time all this was accomplished. There was nothing elaborate or expensive in all the furnishings but they had that atmosphere of being usable and inviting. Housekeeping was beginning to lose some of its drudgery. There was a sense of great satisfaction as we looked about and realized all that we had accomplished by the work of our own hands. Some of our dreams had become an actuality.

The winter of 1906 had been very mild, with a good rainfall of 22.89 inches. When spring arrived the landscape, in its harmony of coloring, stretched soft and undulating. The tang of the earthly smells was sweet to inhale. As time wore on and days lengthened Padre seemed to think, or perhaps realized, that I should have a vacation. He suggested my going home for three months. At first mention of it I demurred saying, "I cannot possibly leave you here alone," but he insisted and on May 31st I found myself aboard the Santa Fe transcontinental train on my way to the big metropolis of the twin-cities of the middle west. "Going Home!" What a mixture of feelings the words had for me. With a longing half pain and half rapture,

I was torn between leaving Padre to the loneliness of the Mission and the anticipated joy of being reunited with my family.

Life had been so full that I had not realized how very tired I was or how pale and pinched my features were until I had reached home and the family displayed concern about me. However, youth was in my favor and after a few weeks of complete relaxation and rest, health and vigor was restored. There was nevertheless a secret tugging at the heart when, in the solitude of the sleepless wee small hours of the night, I thought of again bidding farewell to loved ones to return to isolation, hardships and self sacrifice.

Happily the vacation, besides relaxing my taut and jagged nerves, seemed to have given me a broader perspective on things in general. The drabness and solitude of the place seemed to take on a rose colored hue and I began to adapt myself to conditions and to the new and strange ways of unfamiliar people. Song and laughter were coming back to a sore and troubled heart and more and more I found myself giving in to a sort of contentment with renunciation, the memory of which grows sweeter with the passing of years.

Padre seemed to have fared quite well during my absence; at least he did not complain. Preparing his own meals besides attending to his priestly duties left him little time for loneliness.

It was shortly after this vacation that I undertook the very extensive and intricate work of restoring the church's vestments and linens.

A VENTURE AND A FAREWELL TO ADOBES

On October 22, 1905, Mr. and Mrs. Joseph Fratis came to live at the Mission. For a whole year with the occasional help of John Mullinary and a few tramps, who were anything but dependable, we had worked like Trojans trying to make the place habitable. Then we realized that the burden of carrying on at such a pace would be humanly impossible without help.

There were no funds with which to hire help; but there were some thirty acres of land surrounding the Mission building, fourteen of which was good tillable land and the rest could be used for pasture. This acreage, Padre reasoned, might be leased out in exchange for labor.

Mr. Fratis, a Portuguese, from Arroyo Grande, came to look over the land. An agreement was reached whereby Mr. Fratis was to have use of the tillable land and all profits from it, as well as a place in the Mission for housing. In return he was to do all small chores about the place and with his team of horses drive Padre to Lompoc twice a month for Sunday services.

Mr. and Mrs. Fratis loaded their belongings, including a few chickens, into a big lumber wagon and came down to establish themselves at the Mission. Three rooms, partly furnished, were assigned to them. On arriving they unloaded and arranged their few pieces of furniture, bedding, dishes, etc., made themselves comfortable and seemingly were content. Born on one of the

Azores they had migrated to America and to a colony of Portuguese small land owners near the town of Arroyo Grande. They were a charming couple, quiet of manner and speech and ever anxious to be helpful and to please.

On March 6th of that year Padre bought a cow, a black Holstein with a white face. I recall that the purchase was made from John Loynihan, a rancher near Lompoc and that the price was $30.00. In addition he paid Mark Mullinary $5.00 for bringing the cow down to the Mission, a distance of twenty three miles, in a horse drawn truck. Also he purchased two baby pigs. We had by this time quite a flock of chickens besides those of Mr. Fratis'. The care of all these animals was turned over to him. In the spring he planted beans in the tillable fourteen acres of low land and reaped a fairly good harvest. The upper land surrounding the Mission was used for pasture.

To the disappointment of Mr. and Mrs. Fratis, and of Padre, the arrangement was short lived. Mr. Fratis in his seventy-fifth year soon became too feeble for the hardships of six day's toil in the field and the long tiresome drives to Lompoc every other Sunday. His wife, considerably younger in years, was not altogether happy. The drab rainy days of a long winter in poorly lighted rooms was not conducive to good cheer. Although their little house in Arroyo Grande would have fitted into their living room at the Mission, she had been happier there. She missed her friends, the friendly little visits of her neighbors and some of the conveniences of her own home which the rooms at the Mission did not have. Too, she was concerned about her "Ole Man" as she affectionately referred to her husband, realizing perhaps better than we did that the work was too strenuous for him.

Consequently, after the hardships of over a year Mr. Fratis' health began to fail quite noticeably and in June he became very ill and finally was confined to his bed. After three weeks confinement he wrote to his daughter, by a former marriage, asking her to come and see him. The daughter, now married and living in Santa Maria, came with her husband, making the trip in a small buggy. They stayed a week during which they sent for a doctor and did all they could to make the sick man comfortable and to console the worried and anxious wife.

Mr. Fratis' condition did not improve and with the doctor's permission, they took him and his wife back to Arroyo Grande and their little house. Three days later the sick man passed away. No doubt it was some comfort and consolation for Mrs. Fratis to have her husband end his days in their own home close to friends and neighbors of long standing. Thus ended what Padre had hoped would be an ideal arrangement, and again we had to take over doing chores. This time, with the acquisition of more animals, it was a bigger assignment.

During the weeks that Mr. Fratis was confined to his bed Mrs. Fratis took over the milking of the cow; but with their departure we were left with a problem of what to do about Bossy. As was her wont, she came to the pasture gate near the house that evening, industriously chewing her cud. She stood there awaiting our coming to milk her. It was all very wonderful to have our own cow; our menus were dotted with fresh, unsalted butter, whipped cream and rich, smooth cottage cheese, to say nothing of butter used in frying and baking food. But who would milk her now?

It was a bewildered Holstein that witnessed Padre and myself taking turns sitting on the milk stool, tugging, pulling and otherwise torturing her, while the other stroked, petted and coaxed Bossy into giving her milk. Whether it was my gentle touch or greater persistence the patient cow finally yielded and, at least, gave us a portion of her usual amount of milk. After a few days I had acquired a new art, and, incidentally, an added item to the already crowded curriculum of daily duties.

The pig gave us very little trouble. With plenty of milk and some grain mash it responded very well and in a short time required more food than we had to give.

In August of 1906 John Mullinary came back to the Mission. A bachelor past middle age, John went back and forth between

Lompoc, where he made his home with a sister, and the Mission. He would come for a week or two, or for a month or more, as the mood moved him· Tall, wiry and strong, he was always enthusiastic for new adventure and would work like a Trojan while interest lasted. With a little guidance and approbation John did a lot of work about the Mission. Whenever it was possible Padre worked with him. Together they rebuilt the fence surrounding the Mission property; built a fence dividing the tillable from the pasture land, and also did endless odd jobs to improve the place. During this time John milked the cow and looked after the pig.

In taking over the care of the pig John did not do so well. On a very hot day after churning the cream into butter he took the buttermilk out to the pig. He had already fed it its portion of sweet milk and the buttermilk was just too much; the pig foundered. Discovering that something was wrong John came to tell me that the pig was sick. Going out to the pen I found the pig lying on its side and bloated like a blown up balloon.

Padre was in retreat in Los Angeles and I did not know what to do. In my frenzy to do something to save the pig I ran practically all the way to the Donahues, a quarter of a mile away, to solicit advice. Mrs. Donahue and daughter Lizzie were in the dining room as, exhausted and breathless, I ran through the open door and said, "Mrs. Donahue our pig is dying; what shall we do?" Lizzie, who could always see the humorous side in everything, broke out in hearty laughter and said, "Bury it!"

Realizing how ridiculous I must have appeared I simply told Mrs. Donahue that I thought she might know of some remedy to administer to the ailing pig, then went home to find the pig had died. It must have weighed well over three hundred pounds and was a great loss. I felt dreadfully about it. Padre had experienced such a thrill in raising a pig. To have to tell him what had happened to the pig was a hard piece of news to break to him.

Along about this time Padre bought a small black horse so that John could take him on his trips to Lompoc. Since the departure of Mr. Fratis Padre had to depend on the good will of the neighbors, which at best was not very satisfactory. In his whole life Padre had never had occasion to handle horses and was more or less timid about driving.

One of the really big things John did was to tear down the adobe house north of, and adjoining the cemetery. It was a long, low building divided into two rooms, one 13 feet and the other about 30 feet long and 17 feet nine inches wide. The flooring was of wide pine boards which covered the small room and 25 feet of the large room; the rest was dirt. There was no ceiling, canvas having been nailed onto the rafters as a substitute. This building, we were told, was built during the reign of Bishop Thaddeus Amat and had no particular historical value. A nephew of Bishop Amat occupied it for a time and kept a general merchandise and grocery store in one of the rooms. Tracings of shelves left on the walls confirmed that. Evidently the store changed hands several times. José Dolores Solares, Gerardo de la Cuesta, and more recently, Thomas Donahue occupied the building. Judging from an account book kept at the store, and treasured by its present possessor, the sale of wines and liquors were included in the general merchandise and groceries.

It was with some hesitancy that Padre had the building demolished. The task of restoring it to use again seemed too costly. The building was roofless, the doors and windows battered, and their frames were at all angles owing to the large cracks in the adobe walls. Too, it was an eyesore, as driving up from the highway one came upon it before reaching the Mission.

John adjusted the ladder against the building, climbed to the roof and worked with a vengeance, tearing out shingles. At the end of his day's work he tried a shortcut by letting himself down the side of the building instead of using the ladder. In doing so he came down with such a thud that he bit the end of his tongue almost clean off. It bled profusely and became very swollen as he ran to the house to tell us of his mishap. He was quite frightened too, and so were we.

Padre suggested my going to Mrs. Donahue's for some remedy and advice in treating the bleeding tongue. Recalling my previous experience in going to Mrs. Donahue's for advice I felt anything but happy about the suggestion. However, the bleeding tongue had become so swollen that something had to be done.

John's plight, as I related it, evoked a hearty laugh from Mrs. Donahue and her daughters, particularly Lizzie who was quick to see humor in the incident and could not refrain from remarking, "We always told John that his tongue was too loose and too long." They had known John and his family for many years and really were sympathetic. Mrs. Donahue advised a strong solution of arnica and water be kept in the mouth as a disinfectant and curative, and gave me a small vial of the arnica.

Arnica, I discovered, was an indispensable remedy for the ranch housewife. Its uses were almost endless. They applied it internally or externally for either man or beast as the case might be, only varying its strength by diluting it to fit the need.

For several days special foods had to be prepared for John but he was faithful in applying the arnica and soon was able to resume his normal speech and the work of tearing down the adobe building.

There was something mysterious and eerie about the "Amat House" as it was called. Its battered windows, gaping open doorways and cracked gray walls presented a weird and gloomy appearance which stirred the imagination. Some of the valley people claimed it was haunted and were timid about passing it after dark. In tracing down clues for the basis of that claim and what could have stimulated the story, we found that at one time the body of an infant had been found in the building. In piecing the story together it appears that the body had been brought to the Mission for burial in the adjoining cemetery.

The party did not find the resident priest at home and, instead of burying the remains without the priest, left it in one of the rooms of the abandoned house. In all probability they left it with the intention of returning later. Perhaps they came from a great distance and never did come back. Since the house was not used, the remains were not discovered for weeks, or perhaps months later. When the news of finding the remains got into circulation the story probably grew to such proportions that the house became an object of mystery with an atmosphere of eeriness. Indeed, situated as it was adjoining the cemetery, if one happened to pass it on a windy night when the loose shakes flapped, the broken windows played their rap-tap-tap and the gale shrieked and whistled through the thick, cracked walls, a stout heart and screwed up courage were certainly needed.

Another crumbling and almost roofless adobe structure to be demolished and cleared away was a room built back of the sacristy. As nearly as I can recall, this room was about 12 by 16 feet and its roof was tile. It had no windows or floor. An arched doorway and a heavy door led into the sacristy and an outside door opened out into the courtyard. Evidently it was built later than the chapel and sacristy as the adobe bricks did not tie in with those of the sacristy wall. Apparently its use was for storage. Like the "Amat House" this room was so dilapidated with its cracked wall, caved in roof and doorless opening that nothing remained but to tear it down. For this work Padre hired Capitán José Dolores Solares from the Indian Reservation, who, with another man, came on horseback daily to work.

When the building was about half demolished there appeared two men who demanded that José leave his task of demolishing the adobe room and immediately join them in an expedition to the San Rafael mountain. José was reluctant about going, saying he had to finish his work for the Padre. The men persisted in their demand for José, but Padre, knowing that there usually were plenty of mañanas for these men, pressed for more details about the expedition and their reason for being in such a hurry. After some hemming and hawing and evasive answers the men explained that they had always heard of a gold mine, discovered by the early Padres of the Mission, and that Capitán had on several occasions told them he could remember, when a small lad, having visited the mine with his father. They believed he knew approximately where the mine was located. Moreover it was late autumn and they wished to make the trip before the winter rains set in.

The two men (I have forgotten their names) had rigged up and equipped a wagon with bedding, cooking utensils and food and were ready to be on their way. Somehow Padre was not impressed with the urgency of the expedition and offered the men a compromise, telling them that if they stayed and helped José tear down the building he would release him until he could return to clear away the debris. It was early forenoon and the men agreed to help José. All the rest of that day and the next the four men worked diligently with picks, axes and shovels tearing away at the adobe-brick walls.

The men were on their adventurous trip before dawn of that third day. With their wagon creaking under the load of tools, provisions for their horses and for themselves, their hopes were high. The spot they set out to explore was high up in the mountains in the vicinity of big pine trees where the neophytes cut and hewed the heavy timber beams for the Mission building. They explained they would follow a long disused wagon trail as far as was favorable and then continue the journey on horseback.

What really happened on the expedition was not quite clear. The men had provided for three weeks' adventure but at the end of the second week José was back to clean up the mess created in tearing down the adobe room. He was reluctant to talk about the expedition and seemed willing to forget about the existence of a gold mine.

Another example of how individuals became obsessed with the get-rich-quick idea was evidenced when on a rainy day a tramp came to the Mission to ask for food and shelter. He told of how he had spent the greater part of a month in the vicinity of Chalk Rock on the bank of the Santa Ynez river, with pickaxe and shovel trying to locate a buried treasure. By following a clue some one had given him he was convinced of its whereabouts.

The heavy down pour of three day's rain and lack of sufficient food had shattered his dreams, dulled his ambition in his hunt for the proverbial "Pot-of-Gold" and forced him to seek food and shelter instead.

There was also the story of a buried box of gold in the ruins of one of the row of houses built close to the Mission. These houses were erected for the neophytes and were destroyed during the earthquake of 1812 along with the upper story of the convento. The treasure, supposedly hidden in a hollow of the thick adobe wall and buried in the debris when the building collapsed, was never found. At least so the story was told.

We had at one time a middle-aged couple spending a week's vacation at the Mission, and, upon hearing of the buried treasure, the man spent considerable time with pickaxe and a shovel digging and shoveling in the hope of being rewarded with finding the treasure. But alas! Only disappointment.

In the languorous days of many mañanas the air was redundant with fabulous stories about gold in the hills, buried gold and other buried treasures. Each story was replete with instructions for following marks of identification in locating the treasures, some marked by signs cut in the bark of a near by tree, or by special knots tied with branches in trees; others by rocks laid out in certain formation and leading to the secret hiding place of the treasure, etc., etc. In time these illusory and fantastic stories receded into oblivion and we heard no more about them.

UNDESIRABLE INTRUDERS

As we carried on our cleaning campaign we found ourselves facing another equally important problem: that of getting rid of all sorts of animals, bugs, insects and other intruders.

When up early in the morning, as we usually were, we often saw coyotes or wildcats prowling about the place· They came from the foothills across the river, attracted, no doubt, by the few chickens that we had by this time acquired. There was nothing we could do except to frighten them away. They were so wary that Padre never did manage to shoot one.

Padre had a shotgun and shortly after my arrival he presented me with a .22 rifle. With these firearms we shot ground squirrels and gophers. Up to this time I had never handled a gun. I became quite adept as, day after day, I walked about the place with never a lack of something to practice on.

We set all sorts of traps for skunks, weasels, rats, moles and mice. The skunks, though numerous, were not often seen. Nevertheless they always managed to make their presence known. My first sight of one was one evening after dark when its scent permeated the air of the courtyard. I was curious to see what it was like. With lantern in hand I started on a still hunt. All around the arches, the wood pile and under brush I flashed my lantern light and poked with a stick I carried. Then right between a rain-water barrel and the adobe wall near the kitchen door the dim light of the lantern revealed the black and white stripes of the skunk. Luckily, Padre appeared at the kitchen door just in time to prevent me from poking at the skunk with my stick, and perhaps remembering the skunk much longer than I desired to.

Besides leaving an offensive trail behind, the skunk was adept at robbing the hens' nests. On discovering the loss of eggs I fixed some especially for the robber. By breaking the shell on one end I inserted a few grains of strychnine, then pasted a bit of paper over the opening. Each night a special egg was placed where the skunk had easy access to it. In this way we soon exterminated the annoying quadruped intruders.

The sly weasel also caused us much grief in our little chicken coops. Since a weasel does not eat eggs our only resort was to shoot them. This often meant dozens of trips a day to the coops, and sometimes more trips before getting a shot. They were wily animals.

The reptiles, too, kept us on the alert. Continually we had an open eye for snakes such as the coral, the gopher, water, garter and the red racer. In addition we were forever bumping up against the horned toads, tarantulas, centipedes, lizards, wicos, matavenados, pinacartes and innumerable fleas.

On Father Zephyrin Engelhardt's arrival, on one of his many visits to the Mission, he found me near the front door in the act of killing a gopher snake some four feet in length. Having a strong aversion to snakes, he was very much impressed by what seemed to him my courage in killing the reptile instead of screaming and running away from it.

The incident was not forgotten and when the good Father was gathering material for his history of Santa Ines, he asked me to tell him something about the snakes we encountered.

In part, I wrote him as follows: "As to snakes in particular, I have never tried to put their story into print, although I have, on a number of occasions, put them into bottles and covered them with alcohol." I then related a few episodes of our coming in contact with them.

I have, in a previous chapter, related my encounter with a gopher snake sunning itself in the recess of the dining room window. Some time later, on opening the sink door one of the pesky things noiselessly crawled out. Thereafter for the small ones I had a broom and fruit jar handy. I placed the broom on them and the jar in such a position that as they tried to get away they found themselves in the fruit jar. Then it was easy to fill the jar with alcohol and later transfer them to smaller or more suitable containers. At one time we had about thirty specimens of snakes, centipedes, tarantulas and other repulsive reptiles.

On one occasion Padre, late at night before retiring, wanted a drink of water in the kitchen. As he came along in his bare feet, candle in hand, he just missed stepping on a coral snake. It was coiled in the middle of the asphalt floor in the hall leading to the kitchen. Never again would he go in his bare feet, or without bearing a light.

A gopher snake is not poisonous, but the coral is said to be so at certain periods of the year. Furthermore, the gopher snake is not always easy to see or discover, because it is the color of dry grass. The coral is easier to detect, for it is black and white, or black and yellow, the stripes alternating on its body.

Snakes, to me, became very interesting as numerous episodes brought me in close contact with them. I sometimes spent hours observing them. Of course I always tried to lay eyes on them before they saw me. But always I found they would go about their business perfectly harmlessly as long as they were not molested.

My first real interest was aroused one day as I walked about in the courtyard. Seeing our big yellow cat sitting very upright and rigid near the gate of the fence that formed the court, I walked over to see what held its attention. There on the other side of the gate, which was of wire netting, was a gopher snake about four feet in length, coiled, with its head raised so that its eye was exactly opposite that of the cat's. They were in such a position that each had a side view of his opponent. Here they were, the snake hissing and sizzing and the cat purring and gur-ring, but never taking their hypnotic eyes off each other.

They paid no attention to me as I came very near for closer observation, but continued their sizzing and gur-ring. The cat, every now and then, quick as lightning, would stick her paw through the wire netting and slap the snake on the back of the neck. In return, the snake hissed a bit louder, stuck out its fangs but held its hypnotic glance on the cat. Neither the snake or the cat moved one iota out of position during this procedure.

It was about noon when first I discovered them and my whole afternoon was spent in going to and from the gate to witness this unusual contest. It was with great reluctance that I left them long enough to prepare the evening meal. When I returned the big yellow cat, still on his side of the fence, was purring audibly over its victory and sumptuous meal of gopher snake meat. The snake's head, which had been cut off at the neck, was lying on the ground close by and a goodly portion of the snake was consumed. My regret was that I had missed the grand finale of the endurance test.

In the same courtyard at another time Padre, with the help of a tramp, was industriously engaged in cleaning and removing huge rock boulders that were piled a short distance from the kitchen door. With pick, shovel and crowbar as they tugged and lifted the rocks they uncovered a snake's nest, a huge mother snake and, at rough estimate, thirty baby snakes each about five inches in length.

"A snake! A snake! Bring my gun. Quick," Padre called to me as he dropped the crowbar and hastily stepped back several paces.

The tramp, also dropping his tool and stepping back, let the snake crawl to shelter in a thick bush of pampas grass.

I brought the gun. The tramp poked and stirred the pampas grass and soon a shot from Padre's gun sent the mother snake to her Eden, or wherever it is that snakes go when they depart from this universe. In the meantime the baby snakes made their get-away. Being so small, they easily lost themselves in the grass and bushes.

The mother snake was the largest and longest gopher snake we ever encountered. After killing it Padre stretched it out full length parallel with his measuring tape and found it to be five feet and three inches.

So repulsive was the sight of this mother snake coiled in a circle and the slimy babies, squirming and crawling over each other, filling the circle, that I could not dismiss the incident for days.

On another occasion, in the late afternoon, when feeding the chickens, I noticed a young rooster running around in circles, apparently in distress over something he was trying to swallow. I could not get close to him. After a while he became tired of running and just walked. There was something sticking out of his beak which I thought was the tail of a small lizard. I picked him up and held him in my left arm and with my right hand tried to relieve him of this distress. He soon wriggled out of my arm's clasp but I held fast to the tail and shook it back and forth, and up and down, the rooster dangling in mid air. Inch by inch he relinquished the obstructing morsel until I was holding, by the tail, a slim garter snake about a foot long. The relieved rooster, on falling to the ground, gave a couple of grateful "squawks" and proceeded to eat his meal of grain with the rest of the chickens.

The smaller snakes, such as the garter, water and racer, are not as easy to capture as are their larger and longer full grown kinsfolk. They usually manage to reach cover before one can find a weapon to kill them. On one occasion as I stood near the kitchen door I spied a water snake, striped in black and yellow, the stripes running from head to tail over its back. Its reverse side was yellow. With my weapon the hoe, I gave it a hard "whack" as it crawled over the few brick tiles near the door and the result was that the snake was cut clean through its middle. It was about twenty inches long. The tail-end half wriggled and remained on the tiling while the head-end crawled under some stove wood that was piled under the arches. The incident was forgotten until two weeks later when I was picking up the last few pieces of wood from that wood pile. The head-end came to light and crawled away! By the time I had disposed of the wood in my arms the snake was beyond finding. I never saw it again.

My choice experience with the slimy, noiseless occupants of the Mission premises was with a gopher snake and a grimy, crusty looking toad. One hot, still afternoon as I sat on the front veranda with my sewing, listening to the droning of insects, the music of which almost put me to sleep, I was suddenly brought to attention as a discordant note broke the harmony of the droning. The sound was not familiar. It had a tone of distress. I rose and walked out among the flower beds to locate it. Near a rose bush I discovered a gopher hole and peering into it, I saw the two hind feet of a toad. Again I heard the strange noise. It came from that gopher hole. For a moment I was puzzled as to what to do, then decided to reach down and take the toad by its tailless end and give it a quick jerk and throw it on the ground.

Reaching down I took hold of it all right, but its stub end was so short that it slipped through my fingers as if it had been greased. I tried again, this time more deliberately and, firmly as possible, I pulled and tugged but could not budge the toad out of the hole. I then took hold of its two feet and little by little it began to come out. To my great surprise I found that I was not only pulling a toad out of the hole but a large gopher snake as well. The snake was trying to swallow the toad. So far it had succeeded in getting the head and two front legs in its mouth and throat; the toad every now and then giving out the peculiar muffled croak that had attracted my attention. Knowing that the snake was harmless with its mouth full of toad, I hung on tenaciously as I slowly pulled the toad and the snake out of the hole. After tugging and pulling for some time I finally had about six or eight inches of the snake out of the hole when it opened its mouth, relinquished its morsel and slipped back into the depth of its hiding place. The sudden release almost threw me over on my back. Whilst trying to regain my balance I dropped the toad in mid air. As it struck the ground I again heard, but much louder, the same strange "croak." Then it hopped away among the flowers. Feeling that was its way of expressing gratitude for its release, secretly I answered, "No hay de que."

Have you ever chased a snake called a red racer? If you have not you will not understand the many weird contortions I exercised to capture one of the elusive species.

On one of those dry, parched, hot afternoons when all is painfully quiet which so characterize the Santa Ynez Valley, a little red snake found its way into the flower garden in front of the Mission. From the veranda I could see it as it lay very still, full length, in the walk near the picket fence. At first sight I could not make out what it was—a beautiful, rich rose-red streak like a twisted ribbon against the gray of the adobe soil and the weathered brown of the picket fence.

"Oh look, look, Padre." Almost in a whisper I spoke. "A little red snake. I must have it for my collection."

Very quietly and slowly I backed into the house for the broom and fruit jar. More slowly and stealthily I advanced with them towards the snake. Although I did not at the time know its propensities for racing, I did not wish to lose so beautiful a specimen. Alas, when near enough to pounce upon it with the broom, I only struck the tail end of it. It had been frightened. Like a streak of lightning it raced away, seemingly not even touching the ground. Then I realized that it was not an ordinary snake. More than ever I wanted it for my collection and the chase began. All over the garden walks, in the flower beds, along the concrete wall of the veranda and in and out among the flower pots, with broom in hand, I pursued it until I was almost exhausted.

Padre, who had been sitting on the veranda perusing his afternoon mail, now held his sides with laughter at my various contortions and grimly set features in the determination to capture my prize specimen.

"You'll never capture it. You may as well give up the chase," he kept saying to me. At last, plunk went my broom right over the snake's head and over hard ground which made it easier to hold it there. Padre handed me the fruit jar, which I had lost in the chase, and soon I had my precious prize safe and intact in the jar. It measured fifteen inches in length.

Only on one other occasion have I seen the red racer snake; that too was at the Mission. But on that occasion I failed to capture it, perhaps from lack of persistence or real interest in the specie.

On another afternoon, after sitting on the front veranda a long time, I wanted something from my bedroom. On opening the door I just missed stepping on a gopher snake about a yard long, lying on the braided mat. I confess I did not enter through that door. Instead, I closed it and ran for the broom and fruit jar; then entered the room through a door which led out on the veranda.

In the meanwhile, what happened to the snake remains a mystery to this very day. I never saw it again. Being under the impression by this time that the adobe walls and asphalt floors were sufficiently patched and mended to exclude all such intruders, I was truly puzzled. Search as I would, moving all furniture, lifting and turning over all the rugs and poking into all possible nooks and corners, I had at last to admit that the snake had made a complete but mysterious get away. The thought of it was not the most comforting, as I put out the dim light of the coal oil lamp on retiring that night.

Another gopher snake, or perhaps the same one grown older and longer, some time later I discovered must have practiced remarkable stunts and was not afraid to show off.

Working in the front garden one morning I was suddenly aware of a great fluttering and chattering among the many linnets that made the Mission garden their summer home. Back

and forth in circles around my head and through the arches
they flitted and winged excitedly, chattering and screeching
loudly. "I've never seen these birds acting so queerly; something must be wrong," I thought, and looking upwards, I saw
the head and about eighteen inches of the body of a snake
dangling from the tin gutter under the roof in the middle arch,
just over the front entrance. Not daring to chance the possibility of being pounced upon, I called Padre to bring his gun,
which he always had ready for such emergencies, and, from the
veranda, he shot it in the head. It wriggled a while and then
came tumbling down on the tiled walk.

We had at that time a baby rambler rose bush opposite each
pillar of the veranda, reaching to the roof and following the
contour of the arches. The snake must have found its way to
the gutter by means of one of these bushes. The serpent had
been enjoying the rare treat of linnet egg tid-bits, we discovered
as we scrutinized the ground and found the broken shells of the
tiny eggs. No wonder the birds made a big fuss, and our hearts
went out to them in their loss and grief.

The reptiles appeared as late as the year 1918 or thereabouts.
People told us not to kill them as they would eat the gophers.
They may have been all right in the fields, but not wishing to
have them share the Mission with us we disregarded such advice.

Fortunately we seldom saw a rattlesnake around the Mission
premises or in the valley. But we sometimes came upon them
on the road in the wooded hills. My first sight of one, outside
of captivity, was on the Nojoqui grade on the road to Gaviota.
I was enroute to Santa Barbara aboard the Los Olivos-Gaviota
stage-coach. Before sighting the snake the horses must have
heard its rattle, for they pricked up their ears, snorted and shied.
Suddenly they jerked backwards in their harnesses and stopped
dead still. A huge rattler was leisurely crossing the road directly
in front of them. The wise driver spoke gently to the frightened
horses, still snorting and pawing the dirt road. When the rattler
had completely disappeared in the underbrush of the hillside,

he let them take their own time in starting. With one big lurch forward, which nearly dislodged us from our seats, they galloped up the grade and continued on their way.

We also discovered that a horse fears a tarantula as much as he does a rattlesnake· One instance, which still lingers among the cobwebs of past experiences, took place one Saturday afternoon as I was taking Padre on one of his regular trips to Lompoc by horse and buggy.

We were traveling at a slow pace under a torrid sun untempered by clouds. The road was almost hub deep in fine dust. The reptiles seemed always to be out in greater numbers when the day was extraordinarily hot. We noticed the horse prick up his ears, give a disgruntled snort and stop traveling. Looking about for the cause of this procedure we saw a big black tarantula in the middle of the road in front of the horse. Remembering the stage driver's gentleness with his horses in the rattlesnake episode. I tried the same tactics on Mascot. But coax as I would, he would not go forward; just stood there pawing the dust in the road. Ultimately, when drastic measures had to be taken, I gave him a tap on the back with the whip, he lurched sideways and made a wide circle around the offensive looking tarantula. Luckily for us, the ground adjoining the road was level. Thus we avoided being upset or thrown from the buggy.

The tarantula was the largest I have ever seen. With its legs spread straight out it would have measured at least nine inches across.

Among our collection of bottled reptiles we had three tarantulas, one black and two chocolate colored. Padre caught and bottled the black one and one of the chocolate colored. The third one was my prize.

Early one Sunday morning a jaunty looking couple on their honeymoon, as they later revealed, came to the Mission and asked to be shown about.

"I will be glad to show you the things of interest," I replied, as I reached for the big key to the front door of the chapel. As we arrived at the door we saw a chocolate colored tarantula directly in our path close to the door.

Was the bride frightened? Or was she soliciting a little more attention from her enamored husband? Anyway she made a big fuss at sight of the tarantula. Truthfully, I thought the young man, without display, was the more frightened of the two. I ran to the house for my indispensable broom and fruit jar and, without further ado, took possession of the tarantula, to the amazement of the frightened couple.

The centipede, that small articulated animal, is something to be much more afraid of than snakes or tarantulas, according to the Indians. An Indian will pick up a snake by the tail, whip its head on the ground until he has killed it. But show him a centipede and watch him run.

In our collection of bottled species we had but one centipede. Capitán, an Indian whom Padre employed to do some weeding in the courtyard, came upon it as he was stooping and picking the weeds with his hands. "Centipeda! Centipeda!" he shouted as he got up and ran out of the way. Padre, who was ever on the look out for new specimens, searched the spot among the weeds until he had found and captured it. Capitán would not venture within a radius of three feet from where he had discovered it.

In the old days when dusk came the doleful, lugubrious and persistent "Whoo-Whoo" of the many owls blended with the atmosphere of the place, stirred the imagination and enhanced the charm.

Quite oblivious, though, to this bit of sentimentality was practical Padre, when, on opening the big front door each morning, he was confronted by a series of huge "visiting cards" deposited opposite each door and window on the board walk of the corridor.

The owls would sit on the deep recesses of the top moulding of the door and window frames, there to chant their plaintive "whoo-whoos" during the night and, inadvertently leave their visiting cards.

Each morning with a bucket of water and a broom Padre performed his first manual task of the day by obliterating the traces of his nightly visitors. But his practical mind soon found a means of keeping the intruding owls away. By nailing a board on the slant over each door and window frame the owls could no longer sit on the recesses and were forced to distribute their nightly evidence elsewhere.

On visiting the Mission nowadays I am amused to find that the slanted boards are still over the door and window frames and I feel sure that no other person knows the reason for their being placed there.

As the work of restoration progressed and the decayed and broken walls were repaired or replaced, the owls were driven to new abodes, presumably in the gnarled oak trees of the vicinity. Only a few chose to occupy the new bell tower where they found places for their daytime hide-out.

As for the bats! Hundreds of them, however, chose to remain about the place. They had no difficulty in finding places in which to hide. With their wings neatly folded they could get under the roof's tiling or hang themselves in dark nooks and crevices between the rafters under the eaves. By night they came out in great swarms and flitted through and around the arches. Like so many spirits of another world their noiseless, swift and almost invisible flight made their presence felt rather than seen.

Anyhow it was years before serpents and kindred inhabitants of the old haunts had been completely driven out of the Mission buildings and adjoining premises.

VESTMENTS AT THE MISSION

Hand Loomed Brocades and Linens

The Mission's vestments—oh, the beautiful, dilapidated, frayed and ragged vestments. They were my despair, but later my great pride and joy. Young as I was, and inexperienced too, I loved beautiful materials. It hurt me to see all those lovely old fabrics in such disrepair, as well as all those old linens in such a shameful condition. These priceless vestments were shoved into the big drawers of a fine old chest in the sacristy—no order or system whatever.

Many Sundays came and went before I got things straightened out in such a way that Padre could have a whole set of vestments in one color.

Some of them had parts missing, and others had parts so ragged that they could not be worn. Many a Sunday, too, before I could do more than cut the rags that hung from them, or put in a stitch or two, here and there, to hold them together till I had more time, as so many things were demanding my attention during those trying days.

As the work had to be done entirely by hand it was a long procedure. The sewing basket containing parts of vestments or linens was ever in evidence, and like my shadow was always found next to me.

Those beautiful brocades, centuries old, all hand loomed, were almost too sacred to touch. What a privilege to be able to repair and restore them to their former use in the service of Holy Mass.

The linens, too, exquisitely made by loving hands, were neglected, soiled and in urgent need of repair. It was a huge task and I had so little time with all my other duties. Five years elapsed before the last vestment was finished, suspended from its hanger and placed in the vestment case with its companions, the last piece of linen finally repaired, ironed out and laid away in the same huge drawer of the lovely chest where I had found them in confusion and disrepair.

The work of restoring the vestments became very interesting as I studied the cut, or style, of the various pieces, namely, the copes, chasubles and their accompanying stoles, maniples, burses and veils. The period and design of the materials, too, were interesting. Some were in rich, creamy white, others in a soft rose with intricate designs in pastel shades interwoven with pure gold and silver threads. The attractive cardinal reds in damask patterns, the reds with bold designs in yellow, blue and green, or the vivid royal purple with brilliant designs of gleaming silver, were all most fascinating.

Some of these precious materials were woven as early as the Fifteenth and Sixteenth Centuries. Because of the fine texture and intricate design a piece of material was often in the weaving for two or more generations. These rich brocades were made up into elegant and dazzling gowns for the "Grand Ladies" of Spain, Italy and France to be worn at elaborate Court functions. After they had served their purpose many were sent to some convent where the Nuns made them into church vestments to be sent to missionaries in foreign lands.

At the Pan-American International Exposition at San Francisco, in the year 1915, in the French building, I saw exhibited there the bed of Napoleon. It had been covered in French brocade. It was interesting to find, on close examination, that the brocade used was identical, both as to cloth and design, with the material of one of the copes I had so recently repaired at the Mission.

The interlinings of the vestments were of coarse homespun, hand woven linen. This gave the finished garment a great stiffness and preserved the brocade from becoming creased or worn from folding. Their outer linings were also of hand woven linen, but of a much finer texture and softness and in most instances had been reduced to shreds. Some of the linings were in natural linen, while others were colored with vegetable dyes in soft blues, old rose and brick reds.

The thread with which these garments were put together was also of homespun linen, of different sizes and very strong. It made ripping, when necessary, slow and difficult. I found that a discarded razor blade proved the best implement to use, especially in ripping off the braids.

Quite a study in themselves were the old braids. I found them marvelously bright and in excellent condition. In most instances they were of pure gold, flat thread, woven over a warp of yellow linen, or a silver flat thread woven over a white linen warp. On one of the chasubles of red damask a very elaborate braid was used. Instead of the usual straight braid with small scallops for borders, it was woven in a serpentine wave outlined with tiny scallops. It was then ornamented with a design in red and green glaze stamped into the gold braid. Ornate and very unusual.

Much of the work of repairing was done on the front veranda as I entertained a neighbor, or house guest, or, while sitting near the fireplace, on a winter's evening, listening to Padre read the daily newspaper, or as he outlined ambitious plans which he always had for his Mission.

Stitches, stitches, stitches; how endless they seemed and what dreams went into them as I fancied the day when all would be accomplished. As a stimulant to more effort, Padre would sometimes ask, "Will I have the white chasuble for Easter?" or, "Will the black chasuble be finished for All Soul's Day?" Somehow, when the special day arrived the chasuble was in readiness.

One of the chasuble sets I considered too sacred to desecrate with any changes. It was a white satin, yellowed and mellowed with age, having an intricate design of gold thread woven through it. Really what one would call a beautiful cloth of gold. We were told by Father Lack who traced its presence at the Santa Ines Mission, that it had been worn by Father Junipero

Serra, founder of the California Missions. Because of that fact and our reverence for the beloved founder we decided not to restore it. To leave it untouched would also serve as an example of the condition in which most of the vestments were before their restoration. This one, however, was in better condition than many of its companions.

Among the brocades were parts of three sets of candlestick covers, quaint, interesting and new to me. These were made like little aprons, about nine inches around the top and twenty-four at the bottom. The aprons had little ribbons fastened at the sides of the top and, when in use, were tied to the top of the candlestick. The wide flaring bottom of the apron gave them graceful folds as they covered the candlesticks. These aprons were of the same material as some of the vestments. They proved useful in restoring the garments.

In 1917, in the early part of the year, Padre began making preparations for a contemplated double church celebration, to take place on May 30th of that year. One was to commemorate memory of the five early Padres buried in the chapel, and the other to celebrate the thirtieth anniversary of his priesthood, which fell on that date.

It was at this time, too, that Padre conceived the idea of using the materials of a huge canopy for making a set of dalmatics, a cope and benediction veil for the solemn occasion. In view of the fact that by now I considered the vestment problem finished, it would be superfluous to say that I was not keen on the idea. But, as it seemed a part of the work I had undertaken, I acquiesed, and, after a little urging, went to work.

Padre, I think, felt a bit uneasy when he realized the huge task imposed upon me, and the shortness of time in which to accomplish it. "I'll help you do the ripping on the canopy," he offered, "and I'll do all I can to help you with other things too," he added.

This very large canopy, evidently used for out-of-doors processions, too big and cumbersome to be used in the narrow aisle of the church, was quite useless. How old it was we could not say. The silk used was different from the heavy brocades of the vestments. It was of a fine texture with satin finish, woven in alternating stripes of old rose and ivory white, separated by lines on green and yellow threads. The stripes had little scrolls of green and yellow flowers running through them, giving it the appearance of Chinese rather than French or Italian material, possibly brought to California on an early trading vessel from China and later made up at the Mission into a canopy.

Padre made good his offer to help with the ripping of the material from the canopy. If the meals were late and the biscuits burned he did not complain. Then the problem of cutting out the garments arose. I could cut patterns for the cope and veil from those at hand, but I had no pattern for the dalmatics. I pondered and worried over the situation considerably for several days. Since the dalmatics are worn only on very solemn occasions I knew that only the larger churches would have them. Furthermore, I did not wish to copy from modern garments if it was possible to do otherwise.

"I have it," I announced to Padre one morning at breakfast.

"What have you?" he asked.

"I recall, when on my visit to the San Miguel Mission seeing a set of quaint looking dalmatics. Why not ask for the use of one of them as a model?"

A letter to Father J. D. Nevin, pastor of San Miguel, brought the dalmatic to me. Padre was delighted over my resourcefulness and what he termed prudence, in adhering to the original design and style of the garments. Often he exerted himself to be helpful while they were in the progress of being made. To his great joy when the day of the celebration came the cope, veil and dalmatics were ready for use.

After I had finished making over and mending the vestments there remained a lot of pieces of various colors and odds and ends of braids apparently too small to be of any use. Padre, ever provident, asked if I could not patch the pieces together, dye them black, and make them up into a chasuble, stole and maniple in which he could be buried.

In my youth and inexperience, the very thought of such a thing was repellent. For a rash moment I wished I had burned the left over pieces instead of carefully preserving every scrap. But, as it was Padre's wish what nicer thing could I do for him, and to what better use could I put the precious pieces than to make them into a burial shroud for one who loved and wanted them.

So I gathered the brocade scraps, pieced them together as well as I could and after some manipulating, managed to get the garments out of them. These were dipped in black dye and then decorated with the odds and ends of gold braid. Years later when Padre retired from the Mission to move to Santa Barbara, he took the chasuble set with him. When he passed away I appreciated his prudence of having the burial shroud in readiness and his body was tenderly laid away in the garments of his choice.

When the work of restoring and mending these old brocades was completed, I was able to list: nine copes, three red, three white, one purple, one green and one black; seventeen chasuble sets, six white, three red, three black, two rose, two purple and one green, the burial chasuble not included; also, six anti-pendiums, or frontals, two white, one purple, one red, one black and one green, and the set of dalmatics and two white benediction veils.

Padre had a case built in the sacristy for the vestments, and some large hangers made by which they could be suspended without folding or wrinkling the garments. The placing of a finished garment on its hanger was always a reason for joy.

With great pride I would open the case doors to display the vestments to visitors or tourists. Their exquisite beauty was ever a marvel to me and I never tired of extolling them.

Visitors, especially the women, displayed much interest in the old brocades and soon the fame of the Santa Ines Mission vestments spread far and wide. Visitors from all over the country asked about them. Also they began to inquire at other Missions about old vestments, until the Fathers at such Missions as had any were impelled to put their vestments on display.

As an example, the late Father Saint-John O'Sullivan, of pleasant memory, on learning of my work with the vestments at Santa Ines asked me to come to San Juan Capistrano, there to go over the vestments with him and segregate the old ones from the modern. He, too, wished to put the old vestments on display with the many other treasures the Mission still possessed.

Some time later Father Tibureio Wand was trying to create interest at Mission San Miguel by exhibiting old vestments and other treasures. Having seen the vestments of that Mission on several occasions and, knowing their condition of disrepair, I offered to restore them sufficiently to be put on display.

Shortly thereafter Father Augustine Hobrecht of Santa Barbara had occasion to drive to San Miguel and Father Wand availed himself of the opportunity by sending a trunk full of old vestments to be repaired. Out of these sixteen pieces were mended. Two copes and a chasuble set were still in a condition to be restored for use, the rest were odds and ends and were mended sufficiently to be put on display in the Mission's museum.

Up to the time that I began to take an interest and repair the vestments at Santa Ines, little seemed to have been known about their being at the Missions or of their priceless worth. For the most part they were tucked away in musty sacristies and looked upon as old garments too worn and frayed to be used.

The altar linens, hand spun and woven, were in various textures, ranging from very coarse to extremely fine materials. There·was much bobbin lace, also done in hand spun linen thread, used in making up the linens. The albs, surplices, altar and communion rail cloths, and the smaller pieces, namely, the amice, corporal, purificator and finger towel all came in for their share of lace trimming.

The hand sewing that went into the making of the linens was most fascinating and a perfect marvel to me. Step by step as I took up the work on the various pieces I found it an interesting study.

The fine, decorative stitches spoke eloquently of the love and devotion that went into the making up of the linens. The back stitches used in the seams and the exquisite ones used in the felling were so fine it was impossible to detect them with the naked eye. Little herring-bone stitches, blanket stitches, and many other types with which I was not familiar, all finely, evenly and elaborately done, were used on cuffs, neck bands, around armholes and above hems of albs and surplices. The smaller pieces came in for fine rolled hems and intricate hem-stitching. Some of these were done in marvelously fine drawn work with elaborate patterns or designs worked into them. Others were in equally elaborate designs in satin embroidery, all representing infinite care, time and patience.

The work of restoring the vestments and linens would not have been so great had it not been for the hectic conditions under which it was done. But appreciation and compensation ultimately attend great efforts. Many nice letters received and prized by the author attest to this appreciation. Particularly was this true in a letter from our own beloved historian of the California Missions, the late Rev. Father Engelhardt.

An interesting episode occurred one day while taking a party of three gentlemen through the Mission. I was surprised at their keen response when I asked them if they would be interested in seeing the old vestments.

"We certainly would like to see them," one of the men replied with marked emphasis.

They kept up a chorus of admiration as I took out several of the garments for their closer examination. They marveled, not only at the exquisiteness of the fabrics, but also at the great number of pieces the Mission possessed.

It was when I brought out the old yellow umbrella that I discovered who the gentlemen were and the reason for their keen interest in the old silks. On opening the umbrella, in my usual little talk to tourists, I went on to say, "This is an old Spanish, pure silk umbrella, mounted on a frame of whalebone ribs and brought to California by the early Padres."

One of the men smiled a bit sarcastically and said, "If it is as old as that it should be entirely eaten up by moths."

"I never knew moths to eat pure silk," I said.

This brought on an interesting discussion of moths and their relation to various fabrics. Then one of the men asked if he might take the umbrella out in the open light for closer examination. I opened the sacristy door leading into the courtyard· The men walked out with the yellow umbrella and the examination took place.

"I am from Marshall Field's Silk House in Chicago," the man announced as he handed me the umbrella. "I profess to know something about silks and I want to compliment you on your knowledge of fabrics. The umbrella is of pure raw silk in the finest of weaves."

My statement that the umbrella was of pure silk was really a supposition on my part, and had I known that I was talking to a silk expert I should never have made such a rash statement. However, we had a nice visit. I learned many things about silks and silk brocades and the incident left a pleasant impression.

PEDDLER, HORSE TRADER AND PHOTOGRAPHER

Many strange and unusual, sometimes extraordinary things happened in our remote place of abode during these days of primitive living. I recall with amusement the visit of Mr. Phillip Kieran. It was late afternoon when he arrived driving a one-horse buggy the back of which contained two huge suit-cases.

Mr. Kieran was a small man with the map of his native Ireland stamped in every feature of his genial face. His brogue was captivating. To add to his picturesque appearance he wore a black derby hat perched rakishly on top of his heavy black hair.

Padre greeted him cordially and, knowing that he had driven all the way from Lompoc, invited him to put up his horse and stay for the night.

A man without any trade or occupation in particular, he was ever ready to try his hand at something new. His latest adventure was selling shoes. He explained to us that business in Lompoc shoe stores had taken a decided drop since Christmas and that he had undertaken the task of going out among the ranch people throughout the valley to peddle shoes. He proved a good salesman. After the evening meal when we had retired to the front room he brought in the two huge suit-cases and emptied their contents of shoes on the floor.

"There's a foin pair, Miss, no bether made," he persistently repeated as he handed me pair after pair of high, buttoned shoes with toes so pointed they curled upward when I tried them on.

"They're very stoylish, Miss. Look at the foine heels of thim. No bether made," he still persisted.

Padre's whispered admonition, "Buy something to help the poor man along," was still ringing in my ears as I picked up a pair of flat heeled, square soled shoes, with rubber inserts in their sides, known as "Mother's Comforts". I had an aversion to the name but thought they would be a source of comfort of an evening after a long day's tramping on the uneven asphalt floors. The deal closed, the suit-cases strapped, we settled ourselves comfortably about the fireplace to enjoy the evening.

"Is the Mission haunted?" Mr. Kieran suddenly asked as he looked about him. An eeriness accentuated by the dim lamp light seemed to pervade the large room.

"Sometimes I think it is," Padre replied, and related how, on several occasions, he had heard noises that resembled the dragging of chains across the floor in the unoccupied rooms above.

That started things! Both men seemed to have a flair for the gruesome, the setting was perfect and they spent the rest of the evening recounting all sorts of weird, fantastic and unbelievable stories about the departed. Not until the embers in the fireplace were dark and the room growing cold did Padre knock the ashes out of his pipe and announce that we had better retire before the ghosts took their nightly stroll.

Padre had escorted his guest to his bedroom and, after lighting a candle and placing it on the dresser near the bed, bade him good night. He had scarcely reached his own room when he heard screams and yells from the guest room. On returning he found Mr. Kieran in the middle of the room, disrobed, doing a cross between a highland fling and a toe dance, his arms waving and his feet beating time on the asphalt floor as he shouted, "They've got me, they've got me! Fa-ather, they've got me!"

"What is it that's got you?" Padre asked as he flashed the light of his candle full on his guest. They looked at each other for a brief second then, realizing the situation, both burst into hearty laugher.

When ready to retire, Mr. Kieran had put out his light and in turning to get into bed had stumbled against a mouse trap, which had been set under the dresser in such a way that it snapped and caught him by the big toe. In the darkness he was too frightened to think of anything but that the ghosts had caught him.

Poor Mr. Kieran, he never came to the Mission again, but for a long time the story of his strange episode was a valued asset of Padre's in the entertainment of his guests and often served as a spicy "pousse cafe" after an evening meal.

Time weaves romance around the most commonplace but often amusing events. The romantic, unusually thin, gaunt horse trader with his house-wagon and from two to six lean, half starved horses is now folded away in the mist of years. Time was when this tradesman frequented the countryside and surrounded himself in speculative mystery. He traveled leisurely; to him yesterday made today and both made tomorrow.

In choosing the Mission grounds for his short stay the colorful, crafty and persuasive horse trader was another of the Gypsy tribe to suffer the loss of his romanticism. This perfunctory roamer did not bother asking permission to establish his camp on the grounds. He preferred to move in by stealth under the canopy of the stars and darkness of the night. Squatting himself in a favored spot he would remain as long as he could muster some sort of business with rangers in the surrounding vicinity.

According to accounts from neighbors, the wily horse trader was not always overly scrupulous; the disappearance of bales of hay, sacks of grain or anything useful to man or beast gave rise to some speculations among the ranchers. Some housewives, too, complained of raids on their vegetable gardens. Moreover, as far as the Mission was concerned, what could possibly be more unsightly than a spot littered with the remains of several day's camping by a slovenly horse trader!

With the coming of the automobile and the farm tractor the sagacious and shrewd horse trader slowly but surely drifted into oblivion, thus closing another chapter in the history of Western frontiers. Only the memory remains.

The horse trader left a litter behind him which was unsightly and generally objectionable, but at least it was out of doors. Not so the havoc created by the amateur photographers.

Names of the photographers, kodak fiends, and in later years the moving picture cameramen often appear on the visitor's register.

Human nature being what it is there were times when the propensities of these geniuses proved quite a nuisance, if not a menace. Not only did they expect the guide to be ready at all times to pose smilingly but often they disturbed every movable piece of furniture within sight. In order to obtain the desired position for themselves and their cameras, benches and chairs from the veranda were stacked up, flower pots shifted, and all loose boards and garden tools brought into play in one way or another. All of which was perfectly legitimate if the cameraman's memory had not failed him at this point. Our having to return these things to their proper place after the geniuses had departed did not promote the best feeling towards the cameramen.

At all events let it be said that these thoughtless picture-taking individuals were in the minority. In a collection of greatly prized albums are pictures of all sorts and sizes taken of the Mission by visiting cameramen and camera-women. To be sure some of these were taken to show off their own party who posed conspicuously in the foreground. Or if, as in the early days of automobiling, they happened to be sporting their first "tin Lizzie" the Mission was a good back drop. Be that as it may, many pictures sent to us, as a kindly gesture by thoughtful and appreciative people, led to a warm and lasting acquaintance, as invariably they were accompanied by a friendly letter or short note.

Some of the photographers proved very skillful. A surprising number of these Mission pictures could, at least from one point of view, be classed as masterpieces. A few choice enlarged reproductions, some in the original color and others having the embellishment of tinting, adorn the walls of my home at the present time. Each photograph recalls a happy story of Santa Ines Hermosa.

AH GIDI

The lovable Ah Gidi, the Chinaman peddler who made his semiannual visits to the valley, traveled all the way from San Luis Obispo to Santa Barbara on foot. With a sort of yoke made of wood and fitted to the back of his neck and over his shoulders he carried two large round wicker baskets the size of wash tubs. These baskets were tied to and suspended from either end of the yoke and reached to the ground. Ah Gidi, with a kindly weather-beaten face from which dark eyes twinkled, was a short man. He wore an impressive moustache and a short chin beard. He was a picturesque figure as he plodded along in his high crowned straw hat and faded coat and trousers. When he first came to the Mission in 1905 he was seventy-seven years old.

Through his many visits to Father Lack in Arroyo Grande, Ah Gidi became a convert to the Catholic faith. Father Lack having spent many years in China spoke the Chinese language fluently. In speaking of Father Lack Ah Gidi would say, "Luie Gallanda (Arroyo Grande) him heap good man."

On coming to the Mission Ah Gidi would, as he approached the chapel, kneel on the ground facing the church door, take out his beads and recite his rosary before coming to the veranda. Here he would sit on one of the old benches, roll his cigarette, smoke and rest. Then squatting on the veranda floor beside his baskets he would invite me to come and inspect his wares. These baskets were filled with exquisite imported china and objects of choice lacquer, all wrapped in tissue and tightly packed in straw.

I would join Ah Gidi by squatting on the opposite side of the baskets and help him in taking out and unwrapping the precious pieces. What fun it was! If I particularly admired a piece of china or lacquer Ah Gidi's price would go up, if I laid it aside without showing interest the price would go down. When the baskets were empty and the china soup bowls, sauce dishes, nut and fruit bowls and figurines, the lacquered trays, boxes and other objects were all on display, Ah Gidi would straighten up and say, "You lik-ey? You tak-ey· You no lik-ey, no more talk-ey," and with that short speech he would immediately start to wrap and pack the precious china and lacquer. Today my china closet still displays many choice pieces from Ah's wicker baskets.

KNIGHTS OF THE ROAD

The wayfarer, tramp, hobo, Dick Turpin or bum as we called them, were always kindly received at the Mission. Padre was most generous, patient and tolerant with them. He had a way of making them feel at ease, and the first thing they knew they were telling him their life's history, their tales of woe, their reasons for being on the road, where they came from and where bound for. After this voluntary and sometimes elaborate introduction, Padre made his decision as to whether he wanted to engage the knight of the road for a few days' work, or whether he thought it best to fortify him with a plate of beans, bread and coffee and send him on his way.

They were always walking up and down the coast, coming from everywhere on the face of the globe and bound for somewhere which generally led nowhere in particular. Usually very optimistic, these "knights" had nary a care or responsibility other than to forage for food and shelter. Consequently, the majority of them were extremely humble, polite and respectful on arrival, depending on the impression they could make to secure a meal or lodging or both.

The rainbow's end was forever calling, and the "pot of gold" was still to be discovered. The search must continue. But if sore feet or inclement weather prevented traveling, the wayfarers were apt to show their true colors and take out their grievances against the hospitality of the Mission. Some of them became surly, grouchy and sometimes abusive, complaining of the food given them out of pure charity of heart from the Padre's larder.

Happily, the grateful and appreciative far out-numbered the disgruntled and dissatisfied. In the long run much work was done in the way of cleaning up around the premises and rehabilitating the Mission by these migrating "knights".

If a man asked for a meal, or a meal and night's lodging and was able-bodied, Padre in return asked him to do a little work such as chopping wood, weeding, hauling away decayed adobe, cleaning chicken houses or other light jobs. If he did his work willingly and well, Padre rewarded him with some chewing or smoking tobacco which he always kept on hand for that purpose. He soon learned that these men were happiest in their work if they had a good meal in their stomachs and a pipe or quid of tobacco in their mouth. With few exceptions, all used tobacco in one form or another.

After the big reconstruction work, the tramps helped in cleaning up and leveling the huge pile of debris left by the fall of the bell tower and huge buttresses.

Of course some were not anxious to work and did little or nothing. Also a few were so desperate looking that we just gave them a meal and sent them on their way.

When there was much work to be done and a man was willing to stay for a week or even a month or more, Padre would give him some money. The amount depended on how well the man worked, the nature of the work, or how rich he felt at the time. Some of these men were glad to work at odd jobs simply for their keep, especially during the winter's rainy season. Others were willing to stay for very little, perhaps a pair of shoes and some underwear and socks. Now and then men who claimed to be tradesmen of some sort or other demanded big money and felt highly insulted when asked to do a little work in return for food and lodging. Again there were others, carpenters, painters, plasterers and cabinet makers, well-trained in their respective trades who were willing to work for a dollar a day, five dollars a week, and sometimes for ten dollars a month during the inclemency of the winter when there were so many days that it was impossible to work. These proved to be a great help towards the restoration of the Mission.

In our early years at the Mission Padre always had open arms for a man who could wield the hammer and saw and pick and shovel. He, too, liked to deck himself in his khaki coat and "carpenter's"˙ apron to work with the men when time from his priestly duties permitted.

When a man appeared who was old, decrepit, crippled or otherwise incapacitated, he received food, shelter and the usual tobacco with no work asked of him. But when one of those big bombastic "See who I am; the world owes me a living" sort of fellows came along, Padre would, in his most tactful manner, very politely advise him to keep on traveling.

There were other types among our hoboes such as the habitual and periodical drunkards. Unfortunately for themselves, they were mostly among the men who were willing to work.

The habitual drunkard always asked for pay for his work and usually held a high esteem for his abilities and skill. He only worked long enough to get sufficient money to indulge in a couple of good "jags", and therefore found himself on the road, sleeping under some bridge or on a river bank most of the time.

His less depraved brother, the periodical drunkard, was less demanding and content to work a whole season in the bean field, fruit orchard, or at some construction work. He saved his earnings to the end and then went on a "grand" drunk. They often told Padre, "Had a helofa good time." In this way they would lose months of hard-earned cash in a couple of nights of brawling. Not infrequently these men, when arriving at the

Mission would tell Padre that they wished to sober up. After a day or two lounging in the Hobo Villa and eating proper food, they were ready to do a little work in compensation and then start in quest of another job and another "helofa good time."

These migrators were of all sorts as to nationality, creed and color. Each had his particular temperament and trait, ability and handicap, favorable or unfavorable general appearance and dexterity in pleading his case when faced with the pangs of hunger. Many of these were from good, respectable and oftimes affluent homes. One wondered by what decree of fate they were brought to their vagabonding. I dare say that none of these individuals started out with the idea of being a tramp in any sense of the word, but the call of the wild, the great open spaces and the carefree life of the out of doors always proved too great to be resisted and before they realized what was happening, they were full-fledged members of the "knights of the road" initiated in all the traits and language of the veterans. Seldom, if ever, did they express regret for being on the road, rather they considered themselves blessed with a certain amount of good fortune and gloried in their independence from the ties and demands of organized society.

The work done by the tramps at the Mission was slow and sometimes very aggravating. The virtue of patience had to be practiced and was often put to the test by both Padre and myself and perhaps by the tramps too, as they sought food without the exertion of having to work for it. Invariably, they had to be coaxed, humored and cajoled a lot in order to get much work out of them. But by keeping a good sized cemetery in our hearts in which to bury their faults, we did manage to get along quite peacefully. No persuasion was necessary, I am frank to say, when meals were announced! The weary, footsore, limping individuals became spirited soldiers at sound of the bell.

Padre had two drop-leaf tables built and attached to the wall, one under the front and the other under the back corridors. These he called the Poor Sinner's tables. A tray of food placed on one of them would fortify the tramp that stayed only long enough to partake of one or two meals. If a man remained a day or more to do some work, he ate his meals from the kitchen table.

Notwithstanding our isolation in those bygone days when work was being done at the Mission, the tramps learned of it and turned their steps in its direction; not many at first, but increasing in number as Padre acquired fame for his kindness to the wayfarer and won for himself the title of "The Padre of the Down and Out." Oftentimes they would tell us that they had changed their course of travel in order that they might come to the Mission and see the man who possessed a sympathetic heart for them.

Sometimes these migrators came at opportune times when there was urgent need for work and we were glad to have them. At other times they proved quite a nuisance, especially when work was dull and the larder almost as bare as the proverbial "Mother Hubbard's Cupboard." It required some brain cudgeling to prepare food for husky out of door men who tramped the road the greater part of the day and anticipated a meal cooked on a real stove with coffee made in something other than a tin can.

The food that we gave out consisted mostly of beans, bread and coffee and whatever vegetables or other things there happened to be on hand, perhaps cottage cheese, scrambled eggs and a glass of milk, as we had our own cow and chickens at that time. Frequently a short order meal of hot biscuits or hot cakes with coffee or a glass of milk was all the larder had to offer.

Muchos frijoles but little dulces was the usual fare, and always when the rainy season came on I would put the bean pot on the stove and keep it going till the warm days of spring when the gardens began to give out their fruits and the tramp could help himself along his way. He usually preferred to do his own cooking under a bridge or under the shade of an oak tree by the road side.

Some of these roamers still retained a certain amount of deference towards organized society and established camps along their roads of travel. These were of the higher type and found among those who worked in seasons and took their vacations and recreations in one of the camps. Billie Muller who came to the Mission on numerous occasions was one of those belonging to the clan and privileged to use the camps. The chief requisite for using a camp, he told us, was cleanliness and the willingness and ability to forage for food during their stay.

One day, during one of Billie's visits at the Mission, I had occasion to drive Father Ambrose Goulet, a guest, to Gaviota to take a south-bound train which left in the early afternoon. Billie, learning of this, asked if I would mind taking him with us so that he could fish from a camp situated a short distance from Gaviota near the ocean. It was in the horse and buggy days and Billie knew that we would be taking a lunch and be at Gaviota long enough to afford him time to fish.

So off we went, the Father and myself occupying the front seat and Billie with fishing rod and tackle, the lunch basket, coffee pot and a few pieces of fire wood in the back seat of the two seated buggy.

"Wouldn't you like to come to my camp to eat your lunch?" Billie suggested as we neared the station. It was a cold, drab raw day, and the Gaviota station seemed so uninviting for a picnic lunch that we acquisced.

We drove along some little distance south of Gaviota, then veered off the highway towards the ocean between clumps of sage and low brush until we came to a sheltered, wooded nook completely hidden from view of the highway. A grand sweep of sapphire blue sea and a gurgling stream of fresh water greeted us as we stepped down from the buggy and proceeded to prepare our lunch.

Billie was all excitement. "See Miss, I have a garden planted here," he said as he pointed to a patch of onions growing on the bank of the stream. "I planted these onions with some spinach and radishes last spring," he continued.

After building the fire for our coffee, he gathered a few of the onions and washed them in the running stream so that we could have them with our sandwiches.

All this was new to the visiting Father, and while Billie and I prepared the meal he entertained us by telling stories, quoting poetry and singing Irish ditties. The meal over, we crossed the stream by means of a few boulders and pieces of driftwood, and led by Billie were taken to the camp's cabin, made of odd boards of various dimensions, pieces of corrugated iron and old canvas. This six by eight shack contained a cupboard made from a dry-goods box which held a few tin cans, coffee pot and tin cup. There was also a shelf with dusty periodicals and a bunk bed on which, at the moment, a brother tramp was stretched out enjoying his pipe. Billie greeted him warmly and remained to have a chat before going fishing. The Father and I proceeded back to the station to await the train and Billie's return.

Extremely neat and respectful, of a rollicking, sunny disposition, Billie's carefree life radiated good humor and laughter. All day long as he worked he whistled, sang and philosophized. He never permitted the clouds of gloom to penetrate the atmosphere around him and having been at the Mission so many times, he was granted many privileges not usually extended the tramp.

Interesting are the marks, signs and other identification symbols these hoboes leave along their route of travel. During our earlier years at the Mission when the mail came by stage and was left at the road side mailbox, we invariably found chalk marks of various types on the box. Now and then Padre would take a wet cloth and wash them off, but always they would reappear.

After some persuasion, I prevailed on some of the "boys" to let me in on some of their mysterious sign language, and I will now bring to light a few that have been stored away these many years. Those done in chalk were usually in the form of a spear. A spear pointed upward indicated to the wayfarer to keep on traveling. If found on a water tank near a town it meant "bad police." A spear parallel with the gate rail meant it was safe to stop there. A method which is not so discernable is the placing of rocks to indicate various things. For instance, the placing of three rocks in a row parallel with the gate tells you that you should keep on going. A good sized rock placed next to the post on the right side of the gate meant a good place to stop. Two rocks placed there meant the owner of the place was generous. Four rocks in a square formation told you the owner was good but demanded work in return for food and lodging. A rock in the shape of a half circle indicated that it was a bad place, or a bad dog resided there. Small rocks placed in a spear formation pointed out the owner was very good in giving food but usually had work to be done. Another method was the cutting of notches in the gate rail or post. One notch meaning a good place to eat, two notches, very good and generous. Two notches, a space, then another notch revealed a good place to eat but work to do. The last of these that memory yields is a groove cut along the gate rail which marks the place as no good and a waste of time to stop.

We soon learned to classify the tramp by the language he used. The "hard boiled" veteran of the road had a vocabulary all his own, not very ennobling, to say the least, but with a flare of being expressive. This type seldom called anything by its proper name and used the language fluently. His brethren of lesser experience affected an air of know-it-all as he used the few expressions he had already acquired, while the novice who had not as yet become affiliated with the veteran did not use the spurious language.

Set forth are a few examples of the hobo language and their meanings. A tramp to them was a "blanket stiff", a freight train they called a "rattler" and a passenger train "the cushions." To ride a freight train was to ride the "rods" and to get a pas-senger train was to "ride the cushions." To get a meal was to get "junk", baking powder biscuits "dyspepsia tablets" and hot cakes "chest protectors." Money to them was "scratch, shiners, or bullets." A jail was a "can" and a policeman a "bull", "mug" or "elbows." To "throw out your feet" meant to hunt for food and "hit the stem" to strike someone for a dime, or beg along the street. "Picking huckleberries" indicated the stealing of a shirt or other pieces of clothing from a clothes line, and "hunt a flop" was looking for a place to spend the night.

A "house with a crooked stick" to the hobo meant a church and a "Buck" a clergyman. Cigar butts picked up on the street when they lacked money to purchase them were called "sidewalk brand" or "stoopovers." And so on ran their jargon. When put together it ran something like this : "When the rattler stopped to slop, I threw out my feet to make the rods; at the main stem I looked for the house with the crooked stick, the Buck gave me a shiner and dodging the elbows, I rushed the growler till it was time to hunt a flop."

The veteran was apt to think up some way of getting his meals without too much manual effort and resorted to all sorts of schemes. One of these told me how, on a hot day, he lay on the beach idly and aimlessly picked up the fine white sand and let it slip through his fingers. Suddenly an idea came to him, and immediately he went into the village. From a restaurant proprietor he begged a few sheets of writing paper. With these he returned to the beach, cut the papers into neat squares with his pocket knife. Into each square he put a pinch of the fine white sand and folded them in the manner the old fashioned country doctor folded his medical powders. He then proceeded to make a house to house sale of the unsuspecting housewife, of what he termed a powder to prevent kerosene oil lamps from exploding. "At ten cents apiece, they sold like hot cakes, but I never made the mistake of going to the same place a second time," he said, and his face brightened at the recollection.

Another "knight" told of how he had mixed shoe blacking with coal oil, put it into a gallon jug and sold it to farmers along his road of travel as something to put on their razor strops before stropping their razors. He would sell small quantities from the jug at from five to twenty-five cent's worth, the farmer supplying the small bottle or another container. As there was nothing to either improve or injure the razor strop, it was left to the farmer to judge the merits of the razor strop oil.

When the frame building was constructed back of the Mission, a place was provided for lodging the tramps. A room with two beds and a couple of chairs made them comfortable. Later, as their number increased, the storeroom next to it was converted into a lodging and two more beds were added. These we named "Hobo Villa" and they were cared for by the tramps themselves. Padre insisted on cleanliness and provided broom, mop, water bucket and soap for use in cleaning. At the start the beds were furnished with mattresses, pillows and a blanket apiece. The blankets, unfortunately for the beds, soon disappeared, and we did not replenish them except in rare cases. When an old man appeared not carrying a blanket and the weather was cold, I would manage to find one from the house's supply. Always, that too would disappear, oftimes taken by the man for whom I had provided it. The higher type of these road walkers preferred to carry his own blanket. Sometimes the tramp would make an advantageous exchange, taking the fairly good blanket from the bed and leaving his own soiled and worn in its place.

I recall one instance when a young man was forced to stay several days owing to a prolonged rain storm. He carried no blanket with him, and it so happened that I had nothing to spare from the house at the time. Padre's generosity prevailed, and he gave him the horse blanket which was used on the horse when making outpost trips in inclement weather. On the morning of the tramp's departure he came to me and asked for a pair of scissors saying, "I want to do some mending on my clothes." Perhaps he did mend his clothes, but when Padre went to get the blanket he found that only the leather straps and buckles of it were left. The scissors, evidently, had cut off all the straps and buckles and the blanket had disappeared with the young man.

When it became generally known that Padre harbored the wayfarer, he sometimes received boxes of clothing and shoes to give to them through the generosity of some kind friend. When this occurred we would pick out the best articles and set them aside to give to those appearing most deserving and appreciative. The rest of the things we would place in the "Hobo Villa." It was interesting to note the way these things found their way to their new owners. A tramp never burdens himself with excessive baggage, and when he appropriated a new coat, trousers or pair of shoes, he always left his own behind. When not too badly worn, these would in turn be picked out and exchanged for some more disreputable and of lesser worth. Finally on the Villa's next cleaning day they became fuel for a bonfire.

Shoes for these travelers evoked a greater problem than clothing. The shoes that came in boxes were mostly from white collared business men whose feet usually did not cover as much territory as the man who walked the rough roads or railroad ties. At all events, nothing must go to waste. Padre, the ever resourceful, purchased a primitive shoemaker's outfit and placed it in the workshop for the use of those who could or cared to use it. In this way many of the shoes too small to wear were cut up and used in mending others.

To see a "knight" wearing an overcoat was a rarity, and not infrequently he wore no hat.

It was in the year 1907 that Padre started to keep a record of the tramps that came to the Mission. A sort of register where, if and when he obtained it, he entered the man's name, his age and nationality, where he came from and where bound for, his reason for being on the road and his own private remarks about the wayfarer.

According to this register, I find the startling facts and figures regarding the meals given to these migrators.

The year	Number of meals	The year	Number of meals
1907 and 1908	352	1915	311
1909	232	1916	180
1910	576	1917	143
1911	386	1919	61
1912	619	1920	161
1913	462	1921	44
1914	225	1922	28

As recollections gently lift the curtain of time, I can see many impressionable characters, big men, little men, strong men and weak men, some sane and others insane. Many strange and pathetic sights there were with others as ludicrous and amusing. There were Japs, Chinamen and Negroes. There were crystal gazers, prophets, philosophers and reformers. Some of these seeming unfortunates had plenty of tomorrows while others burned with that ever surging fever of restlessness. But these knights of the road possessed many endearing qualities, charm, geniality and kindness of heart. God's hand to them when they have reached the end of the road of life!

WEARY WILLIES

Ed. Cowey

One of our earliest interesting characters to ask for food and shelter was Ed. Cowey. A stocky man of medium height with strong hard muscles that were used to swinging the pick and shovel, he was not afraid of work and did it well.

In January 1907 Ed. came for the first time and stayed several days, during which time he dug up rocks, hauled away melted adobes and cleaned up generally. Born in Ireland sixty years ago, Ed. was reticent but genial, respectful and neat in appearance. When his day's work came to an end he would sit under the big pepper tree to enjoy his pipe. He looked the very picture of contentment.

Ed. traveled up and down the coast from San Francisco to San Diego. He would go north for the summer and south for the winter. Padre called him his barometer. If Ed. appeared in March an early summer was at hand. When he appeared in autumn, early or late, he predicted that the winter rains were due. Strangely enough the predictions were invariably true.

Somehow, Ed. seemed to have an especial liking for priests and Nuns and found pleasure in working for them. He knew them all and knew too, that Father so and so always had some wood to chop; that at such and such a Convent there was a garden to spade, a hedge to trim or a lawn to mow. He knew too, that the Fathers and good Sisters were kind and would give him tobacco and clothing besides a little money to help him on his way.

Ed. Cowey came to the Mission many times. Each time as the years crept over him he appeared more gray, more feeble, a bit more shabby and, the pity of it, more dissipated. We discovered that Ed. was getting fond of hard liquor and becoming a periodical drunkard. Invariably, on arriving he would greet

136

Padre with, "Fa-ather, I came to sh-ober up. Yes, to sh-ob-er up. I'll do sh-um work for yous tomorrow."

Padre, always compassionate, would say, "Yes Ed., you go to your old room and have a good long sleep." Then Ed. would trudge to the Hobo Villa to forget his troubles until the following morning. After this long sleep Ed. was ready to do a little work in compensation.

According to the Hobo Register, Ed. Cowey came to the Mission for the last time on April 29, 1921. At that time he was seventy-two years old and a sick man, so sick that we arranged to have him taken to the General Hospital in Santa Barbara for medical care. That was the last we ever saw of Ed. Cowey. If death came to him I pray the welcome of God met him at the end of his earthly road.

Out of the many characters who knocked at our door, perhaps five or six others should have special mention: Mike Corbett, an Irishman; Joe Bosler, an Alsation; Anton Reineck, a Hungarian; Maximilian Morocutti, an Austrian; Fritz Walker, American; and the poor mad Mexican boy, Maximinio Martinez.

MIKE CORBET

Mike Corbet, a tall, large, raw-boned wily individual who knew how to plead his case and evoke sympathy, made his first appearance at the Mission in April 1905. Padre at that time had very little experience in dealing with the craftiness of some of these "knights" and was an easy mark. In pleading his case Mike mentioned the Father at this place and the Father at that place, and the good Nuns at such and such a place in the most familiar terms. All this he did in an effort to make an impression and to create an atmosphere of importance to himself. He was poorly dressed and wanted most of all, so he said, a place to work for his keep during the rainy season.

"It will be helpful to have someone to care for the horse and chickens, to milk the cow and to drive me to Lompoc,"

Padre said to me after he had taken Mike about the place and assigned him to his duties.

The following day Padre had Mike hitch the horse to the buggy and drive him to Santa Ynez. There Padre took him to the general merchandise store and outfitted him with a pair of overalls, a jumper, two shirts, two suits of underwear, two pairs of socks and a pair of shoes. Mike beamed approval. Padre felt benevolent and thought of the help he was to have.

Alas, he soon discovered that Mike was hard of hearing and often used that affliction to his benefit. Too, he discovered that he did not like to get wet and if the heavens wept he neglected to feed the stock. Instead, he begged for old magazines, made himself comfortable in his room and spent the day in reading. Very often he brought his magazine to the kitchen table and propped it up against the coffee pot and continued his reading while enjoying his meal. Another discovery was that Mike, though not a musician, liked to steal away into the church choir and lose himself in fingering the organ ivories. In every way he affected an air of a man with a life of ease and nothing Padre said made any impression.

When the Saturday came for Padre to make his regular trip to Lompoc he did not have Mike drive him there. The weather was cold and rainy and he thought it best for Mike to remain and do the chores. The result was that during the three days of his absence Mike scarcely left his room except to come to his meals. I spent most of my time preparing the three hearty meals, a much more irksome task than to have fed the chickens and milked the cow.

My rule for these men was to place their meal on the kitchen table and leave the room. On the third day of Padre's absence when Mike came in for his noonday meal he found that I had omitted or forgotten something in his fare. He pounded his cup with his knife until I came to see what it was all about.

"What is it, Mike?" I asked. I saw that he was in an angry mood. I do not, at the moment, recall what it was that was missing but I got it and then made sure that everything else was on the table. For some inexplicable reason I suddenly became alarmed at being alone on the place with Mike. As I went through the door and out of the kitchen, I quietly turned the key in the lock.

In a few minutes I again heard the pounding of the knife on the cup. This time it was I who found it convenient to affect deafness and I did not heed the call. I remained in my room until Padre's return late that afternoon.

When Padre returned he found Mike very wrathful, disgruntled and complaining. Before leaving home and unknown to me, Padre had locked the side door of the church, the door Mike used in going to play the organ. He complained of this and blamed me for it. When he was in the kitchen he happened to see Padre's memorandum list of instructions to me, which was hanging on the kitchen wall. Among other things on the list, and more for a joke than to be serious, was: "Close the Hobo Villa." It was understood that the "Villa" was to be closed when not occupied so as not to permit any one using it without our knowledge. Mike took offense at this and accused me of calling him a "hobo", and said that he had no time for me anyway. Padre listened quietly without comment and walked away.

The truth of the matter and reason for Mike's discontent was that he had remained long enough to get the creases of hunger out of his skin and was eager to be on the move. To accomplish this he was trying to create a legitimate excuse for leaving.

The following morning when Mike had had his breakfast and returned to his room without making any move to do the chores, Padre went to his room to tell him that since he was not happy at the Mission it would be better for him to leave. Whereupon he became very angry. If he had ideas of leaving he did not want to be told. He became abusive, saying, "I will leave when I am good and ready!" Picking up one of the new shoes, he was about to strike Padre. Padre left him and returned to the house.

During all this commotion I had been standing in the kitchen door trembling with fright. "We can force him to leave by not giving him anything to eat," I said as Padre came through the kitchen.

Sure enough, at noon, when Mike was not called for his meal he decked himself out in all the new clothes and, straight as a soldier, proudly walked past the front of the Mission and disappeared.

Two years later in November Padre, late one evening, answered the door bell. "Kin I git a bite to eat and a place to sleep?" came a thin voice from outside.

"Is that you Mike?" said Padre, recognizing the voice.

"Yis, I didn't think you would know me. I'm sorry for last time, that I am," said Mike.

The night was dark, the rain pouring and Padre did not have the heart to refuse him. I prepared a little supper which he ate heartily and then, apparently very glad to do so, went to the "Hobo Villa" for the night.

After breakfast the next morning he dillie-dallied around until almost noon, but on receiving no encouragement to prolong his stay, he left again.

In the Hobo Register, on the occasion of Mike's first visit Padre wrote "Dangerous man." On the occasion of this visit he wrote, "Nothing doing—Black list."

JOE BOSLER

An outstanding character was Joe Bosler, an Alsation by birth and an engraver by trade. For many years he worked for Tiffany's nationally known jewelry concern in New York City; here he commanded big wages and lived accordingly. Finally, owing to the very fine, intricate nature of the work his eyes gave out and he lost his position. Like a fish out of water, Joe floundered around trying to adjust himself to a new condition

of life. His meager savings soon dwindled away and he was
forced to accept work of a menial nature. It was then that he
took a position as waiter in a prominent restuarant. From this
he worked himself up to being the head waiter at the Waldorf
Astoria.

Everybody that was anybody socially or politically partook
of the hospitality of the Waldorf Astoria in that heyday of its
prominence. Many were the stories Joe told of the life of a
head waiter. It was an intricate life dominated by politics and
favoritism. As head waiter Joe collected a percent of all the
tips. The patrons, if they failed to tip the waiter as he felt
he should be tipped, were not treated with undue cordiality.
Joe told us of the case of a customer who invariably found
fault with whatever was brought to him, making a display of the
waiter's supposed negligence and his own importance. On a
particular occasion when some hot cakes were brought to him
he loudly complained that they were not hot. The waiter
obligingly took them to the kitchen to reheat. One by one he
lifted them from the plate and spat on them before placing them
on the griddle. For good measure he spat on them again as he
put them back on the man's plate.

It was during the presidency of Theodore Roosevelt at the
White House in Washington that Joe was head waiter at the
Waldorf Astoria, and he delighted in relating the eccentricities
of that President and of the many high officials from Washington.

Joe, reminiscing about President Roosevelt, told me how he
would stalk into the dining room to his favorite table. Very
often he would order a dove cocktail.

"But what is a dove cocktail?" I asked.

Joe then told me how during the dove hunting season the
chef would, with a press for the purpose, squeeze the blood from
the breast of doves and store it on ice until used. This liquid
delicacy was served in a tiny glass not much larger than a big
thimble with a cheese wafer or two. "Teddy had no table
manners but he got away with it," Joe continued. Then suiting

actions to the words he told of how "Teddy" would, at the end of dinner, "stick his fist in his mouth to pick his big teeth."

Joe also spoke of those connected with Tammany Hall and others who made the Waldorf Astoria their favorite rendezvous.

When Joe had grown weary of the clatter of dishes, of bowing and scraping and of playing the role of "Mine Host", he decided to come to California. With ever a song in his heart he was affable and kind. He still spoke with an accent. He did not indulge in intoxicating liquors. His one vice was that of gambling. If he had dollars he gambled dollars, and if he had nickels he gambled nickels. But gamble he must. The fact that he would from time to time lose his all in one fell swoop did not dim his exuberant cheerful nature, but rather spurred him on to greater effort in acquiring funds for the next big stake. In California he soon gambled away his hard earnings, and since he was well on in years it was not easy for him to find suitable work to do. The balminess of the climate, too, was partly responsible for his undoing. He began, like so many of his brethren, by walking from place to place in search of employment. Then the vagabonding became a permanent urge. He confided to me that he had kept company with a young lady for nine years and had broken off with her as well as broken her heart when coming to California. In retrospect, he regretted this act and blamed much of his unsettled state to the fact that he had no one to share life with him.

A number of visits were made to the Mission by Joe Bosler. He would stay several days and was always willing to work for his keep. Impetuous, scrupulously neat, he would chop wood, hoe weeds, wash dishes or mop the kitchen floor with equal ease.

Joe was ingenious, too; he related how he had spent two winters in San Diego, California, supporting himself by making and selling paper umbrellas. With a bunch of old newspapers which he procured from a printer, the purchase of some colored bordered paper napkins, a sheet of gold paper, a paper of pins and a bottle of glue he fashioned the umbrellas. He would roll a sheet of newspaper into a long tight cylinder to use as the stem, or stock, of the umbrella. Then cutting a small hole in the center of the napkin he inserted one end of the stiff roll into it. This was held in place by gluing it to the stock with a narrow band of gold paper. Then pinning the corners, or points, of the napkin down to the roll, he had, to all appearances, a fancy umbrella. Joe's face lighted as he said, "Of course the umbrellas would not open but what fond mother could refuse her child the pleasure of carrying a pretty umbrella?"

After making from fifty to perhaps a hundred of these umbrellas Joe would study the social columns of the daily newspaper and plan to be in the neighborhood of some social gathering to display his wares. These he sold for ten to twenty-five cents apiece, depending on the locality and affluence of the neighborhood. In this very ingenious way he supported himself in a state of comparative ease. A man of some education he would, when not occupied with his umbrella business, spend most of his time in the public library.

In another adventure of easy living, Joe confessed he did not fare so well. In a small town he joined the Salvation Army, then became so enthusiastic and displayed so much concern for the organization that in a short time he was elected to the Captaincy. In that capacity he moved around freely, led the singing of hymns by his little band and handled all the Army's funds.

His downfall came when, after the evening meetings and street singing Joe would invite a pal to the Army's headquarters for a friendly game and a bit of beer.

"You know I'm not a drinking man," he remarked as he related his story. "But one evening just as my pal and I were sitting with our feet on the table and a pail of beer between us, two Salvation Army dames came walking in!" Joe hung his head and said, "The jig was up and I left town before daylight the next morning."

ANTON REINECK

Anton Reineck, a Hungarian by birth and a butcher by trade, was the only person of all the "knights" to make a return visit to the Mission without appearing in a more dilapidated condition than before. Tony, as we called him, was ambitious, a hard worker and he made good.

On April 4th, 1910, he came to the Mission for the first time. He remained eight days. He was at that time thirty years old, neat, willing and respectful. In his Hobo Register Padre made this comment: "A good man, would like to keep him always."

In January 1912 Tony came again, this time staying three months. The weather was inclement most of the time. He was grateful for a place to stay and we were glad to have him to do the many odd jobs about the Mission. In fact we began to think of him as a permanent fixture. But alas, when the balmy days of spring brought forth the budding of the trees, the green carpet on the hills and the song of the birds, Tony could not resist the call of the road. He must be on his way and in search of that something to satisfy the longing in his breast. He bade us a grateful farewell and was gone.

We did not hear from Tony again until five years later, on May 5th, 1917, to be exact. Coming on the Gaviota-Los Olivos stage, all dressed up in new clothes and shining shoes, smiling broadly, was Tony. He was visiting the old Mission in grand style.

Padre greeted him warmly. Then at first opportunity, in an aside to me, he said, "We cannot ask Tony to sleep in the Hobo Villa with those new smart clothes!"

The same thought had flashed through my mind. "O, no— no," I replied, "I will make up one of the guest rooms for him."

Tony stayed three days and gave a glowing account of how he had worked, saved and managed to put something by for a future day. He was at the time taking a little vacation and decided to visit the Mission. He related that when he left us in 1912 he went to the Imperial Valley where he found employment at his trade. All day he worked in the butcher shop and lived an abstemious life in every way. When he had saved enough money he bought a farm wagon which he covered over with canvas. Then he purchased a cot and blankets, a small cooking stove, some cooking utensils and dishes. He saved his rent by installing himself in the covered wagon.

After some little time he purchased six acres of land and moved his house-wagon onto it. It was interesting to hear him tell of the way he managed to make six acres of land earn money for him. In the first place he fenced it off into two sections and seeded it into alfalfa. He then purchased a few little pigs and some young turkeys. These he turned loose into the alfalfa fields, first into one section until it was eaten down and then transferred them into the other section. In this way each section had a chance to be irrigated and grow up again. In the course of time nature took care of the multiplication of the pigs and turkeys. Tony took the fattened animals to the market.

He related that he purchased an old horse and built a two-wheel cart on which he arranged a seat and a place to hold a large garbage can. Each morning he hitched the old horse to the cart, drove into town and collected garbage from hotels and restaurants. This he fed to the pigs and turkeys as a relishing tidbit to their constant alfalfa fare.

"And how they did thrive," Tony ejaculated. "There were no pens or coops to keep clean," he beamed.

To his dismay, but later to his benefit, a new enterprise developed from his gathering of garbage. It soon turned out that he was taking home numerous pieces of silver and china along with the garbage. These he cleaned carefully and taking them back to town tried to locate their rightful owners. This created trouble for the hirelings in the kitchen. Their "boss" reprimanded them for their carelessness in dumping his wares into the garbage can. Next time Tony appeared for the garbage he was greeted with a good tongue lashing from the irate dish-washers. He was told to keep the silver and to keep his mouth shut. But lo, so many knives, forks, spoons and butter chips continued to appear in the garbage that good, honest Tony pondered over the situation. Finally, an idea came to him. A man who possessed more courage than means was opening a sort of third rate eating place; perhaps he could use the collection of silver and china. Tony lost no time in contacting this enterprising proprietor. After some dickering it was agreed that the man would take the odd collection and in exchange give Tony his noonday meal as long as the garbage continued to produce silver and china. Sometimes he had but one spoon, knife or butter chip to give in exchange while at other times the can yielded considerable. In this unique way Tony saved himself the trouble of preparing his nooday meal as well as the price thereof.

When Tony bade us "good bye" he affected the affluent tourist by insisting upon giving Padre something for the courtesies received during his visit. Thus it was that another interesting character passed through the portals of Santa Ines and out of our lives never to be heard from again.

Maximilian Morocutti

At eight o'clock the morning of May 11th, 1915, an unusual character found his way to our big front door. Padre answered the door bell. "Good morning, man, I think you must be ready for breakfast!" he humourously greeted his visitor as he gazed on a man with crumpled clothes and disheveled hair. The telltale signs of having slept in some hay-loft or stable manger were plainly in evidence.

"I am not asking for food," the man replied a bit indignantly. "The Lord provides for that and takes care of me," he continued.

Padre noticed that the man carried several bundles of papers under his arm and was curious to learn more of this unique stranger. He invited him to sit down on one of the benches that adorned the veranda and seated himself in a chair opposite. For some time he listened to the man talking excitedly and disconnectedly, then, excusing himself for a moment, he came to the kitchen to say, "Do get something on a tray for that man's breakfast so that he may go on his way."

I arranged a tray and set it on the Poor Sinner's table out there on the veranda. The man turned to it as the flowers turn to the sun. His enjoyment of the meal was immense. The Lord had provided, indeed, and the man radiated contentment as he ate every morsel of food placed on the tray and emptied the coffee pot.

What Padre learned about this wayfarer is copied from the comments he made in the Hobo Register and reads as follows:

"Maximilian Morocutti. Born in 1873, May 3, in Portschach nur WorsterSee, Karnthen, Austria. Ancestors came from Italy. The grandparents were well-to-do Jews: emigrated to Austria. He joined the Austrian navy when sixteen years old and deserted three years later. He was pardoned by Emperor Franz Joseph.

He is twenty-two years in America, lived in New York, joined the Socialists and Anarchists, drifted west, and is ten years in California. Calls himself literate and itinerant. Studierender der Philosophie. Cannot work for he says he must write Revelations, prophesies and philosophy. He is Christ the 2nd, imitating his example, no money, no baggage. He gets enough to eat and finds clothes (he wore three coats). 'I am a Bettler' (a beggar).

"He writes continually, says he left two large bundles of manuscript with the Austrian consul, Ruiz de Rojar in San Francisco, California, several bundles with a friend and he left one big bundle containing about thirty packages here at the Mission, which I should read and keep for him until he calls for them or send them to the Austrian consul.

"He carried another package with him also, the Book of Morman and an Oxford New Testament. Talks sensibly on every subject but religion. Is or was a Catholic, now a believer in Christ only, although the Catholic Church as he says when purged of her errors, like keeping Sunday instead of Saturday, will triumph.

"He saw his mother about a year ago standing before him telling him to spend forty days in the desert and starve himself. He did, he says, and returned a skeleton, but Christ gave him the spirit and he wanders from North and South and vice versa writing revelations.

"The world is near the end: the whole world will fight and Christ will win,' he said."

After having his breakfast he departed saying, "With praiseworthy thanks of the glory that surrounds us praise be Jesus Christ for ever and ever. Amen."

Padre laid the bundle of papers on a shelf in his study. Days passed and the man did not return. Then one day he untied the string that held the papers together and tried to read the closely written pages. The words done in a cramped handwriting didn't make sense. Carrying his curiosity a step farther, he wrote to the Austrian Consul in San Francisco, telling him about Maximilian Morocutti and his manuscript. Padre asked if he would like said manuscript sent him. The Austrian Consul's reply follows:

K. und K. Oesterreichisch-Hungarisches Konsulat
Cs. es Kir. Osztrak-Magyar Konzulatus
J. & R. Austro-Hungarian Consulate
No. 2284   San Francisco on May 18th, 1915

Mr. Alexander Buckler,
  Old Mission Santa Ines,
    Solvang, California.

Dear Sir:

      I hereby beg to thank you for your kind letter of 14th, inst. and in reply to inform you that Maximilian Morocutti is unknown at this office and that I am not desirous of receiving his manuscript.

                  Very truly your
                  (Signed)
                  Consul General of Austria Hungary

Some times later on a chilly morning Padre made a fire in the fireplace with the manuscripts and watched them ascend in flames while he breathed a prayer for Maximilian Morocutti.

FRITZ WALKER

Late in the afternoon on the eve of Ascension Thursday Padre sat on the veranda, enjoying the loveliness and balminess of Spring which comes at that hour. As he gazed through the arch towards the highway, he saw a gaunt, lank figure wearily coming towards the Mission.

"Good evening," Padre called, as the man reached the garden gate.

"Good evening," the man replied, his face breaking into a smile at Padre's cheery greeting.

"Come in and rest here on the bench," Padre invited.

Then came the same time-worn story of the "Weary Willies." He was coming from somewhere and going some place else. He had had a turn of ill luck, but was optimistic and knew that something good was in the offing. At the moment he was weary, foot sore, and hungry—would be only too grateful for something to eat and a place to sleep.

I prepared a tray and placed it on the "Poor Sinners'" table. The man ate heartily, but finding no sugar to sweeten his tea asked if he might have some. "I'm sorry I haven't any to give you," I told him.

In preparing meals for the wayfarer I often omitted sugar as something not altogether necessary, especially when the household funds were low and permitted only the purchase of bare necessities.

However, Fritz expressed his gratitude for the refreshing food and retired to the Hobo Villa to put away his cares for the night.

The following morning he was up early and although not of the Catholic faith he attended the Ascension Day Mass; then tramped all around the Mission, viewing it from all angles.

When he came for his breakfast he was all enthusiasm over the "beauty, grandeur, and stateliness" of the Mission's structure. No tourist ever appreciated it more. He then asked for some writing material, saying, "I want to ask a friend of mine in Santa Barbara for the loan of his camera that I may take some pictures of this Mission."

I gave the man some paper, a couple of envelopes and stamps, and dismissed the incident as just another item in the quirk of the brain of these wanderers.

"I'll come back to take the pictures," was the man's parting remark as he slipped through the garden onto the road and on his way.

In the Hobo Register Padre wrote: "May 20, 1914. Fritz Walker. Age forty years. Native of Illinois. Trade (?)." His private remark, "Screw loose."

Two days later a post card marked Santa Barbara came from Fritz informing us, in flowery language, that he was at the moment having lunch on the green lawn of a beautiful estate in the cool shade of a large spreading oak tree, and that he was thinking of the Mission and would soon be retracing his steps to it.

On reading the card Padre gave expression to what he had written in his Hobo Register by saying aloud, "Screw loose!"

To our great surprise, three days later at dusk, Fritz Walker again appeared at the Mission gate. With a good-sized camera under his arm he displayed it with that air of "I told you so;" then apologized for being very tired and asked to retire immediately.

All forenoon the following day Fritz was busy getting sights and taking pictures. Sometimes he piled up benches, dry-goods boxes, pieces of lumber or anything that was loose and could be used to get the proper position and angle for his camera and himself.

At noon, when I had prepared a tray and called him, he was nowhere to be seen. Finally he appeared, all excited and breathless. His films had given out and he had walked to Santa Ynez and back to purchase more, a distance of four and a half miles.

He apologized for being late, but before sitting down to enjoy his meal he handed me his camera, saying, "I'd like to have you take a picture of me under this arch." He picked up the tray I had placed on the "Poor Sinners' table", sat on the ledge of the veranda with it and posed for a snap-shot of himself.

It was late that afternoon when Fritz again made his adieus to be on his way.

When I went to the kitchen to prepare the evening meal I was quite touched, and felt a little remorseful on finding a small bag of sugar! On his trip to Santa Ynez for the extra films Fritz had thoughtfully bought the bag of sugar.

The incident of these visits of Fritz Walker, like those of so many of his fellow travelers, had been at least temporarily forgotten until one day a postal card addressed to "Padre Alejandro Buckler," and postmarked "Monrovia, California" was fished out of the mail sack. It bore this message:

"I have not as yet been able to fix up the pictures, but expect to before long. I hope you are again enjoying good health. Visited San Gabriel Mission the other day, but my heart is at Santa Ines. (signed) Fritz Walker."

The next word from Fritz came from Colorado, a small parcel containing twelve post-card views of the Mission — the most artistic and beautiful photos of the Mission we had ever seen. Enclosed with the photos was a small piece of paper with these remarks, written in a characteristic hand. "Hello, Padre Buckler. Greetings from Colorado. October is a fine month here. What proof have you of immortality beside faith? Adios. Fritz Walker. Oct. 12, '21."

Some times before Christmas another packet of photos came to the Mission, and with them Fritz had enclosed the negatives, saying that he wished the pictures to be sold to tourists and others, should Padre care to have any more printed. This was his contribution to Santa Ines.

Then came a Christmas greeting-card to "A. B.," with this notation: "To you and the provider of food, the milker of the cow, the charm of a nature finer than that of Man." Later from time to time, Fritz sent other pictures of his taking. A squirrel eating out of his hand, a lake scene, with himself sitting on a huge rock silhouetted in the foreground, and other bits of artistry that took his fancy in photography, all fine, friendly, and thoughtful gestures from a man who wished to express appreciation.

We discovered later that the camera Fritz used in taking the pictures of the Mission was borrowed from no less a personage than the late Alexander Harmer, nationally-known artist living in Santa Barbara, California.

It was the little incidents such as this that taught us to be patient, charitable and kind, and always to look for the good in these human derelicts.

MAXIMINIO MARTINEZ

Stenciled indelibly on my memory is the week end of the National Holiday July 4th, 1921. On the morning of the first, there was great activity, scrubbing, cleaning, baking and cooking and a dozen other tasks awaiting their turn.

"I'll lend a hand and help you a bit," Padre announced, as he came into the kitchen and found me almost buried under pots and pans and cleaning powders and cleaning rags. He then proceeded to fill the twenty odd coal oil lamps and clean their chimneys, put fresh candles in the candlesticks used in the dining room and in the bed chambers and gave a touch here and there with the dust cloth.

Yes, there was great activity. Mr. and Mrs. Edward Elliott of Los Angeles were to be our guests over the week end and for the National Holiday. There was considerable excitement as well as activity in making ready for our house guests. Mrs.

Elliott was none other than the former Margaret Randolph Axson, a sister of President Woodrow Wilson's first wife and aunt of President Wilson's daughters, Margaret Wilson, Eleanor Wilson McAdoo and Jessie Wilson Sayre.

The Elliotts had made previous visits to the Mission but on this occasion were to be our house guests and apparently were as excited over it as we were.

We were so busy that when, nearing the noon hour, the door bell rang we did not wish to take the time to answer it. Finally Padre thought he could best be spared from the duties at hand and went to meet the caller. A young man in his middle teens, dressed in blue jeans, was kneeling on the other edge of the veranda and facing the front door. His hands were outstretched and he was praying excitedly and fervently in his Mexican tongue.

Padre put his hand on the boy's shoulder, spoke to him gently, then taking him by the hand asked him to be seated on the bench while he talked and tried to discover by what turn of events this young man was brought to this mental state.

"What is your name and where are you from?" Padre asked.

"My name, Maximinio Martinez. I from Mejico," he replied.

He spoke little English or Spanish and Padre did his best to make himself understood and to console the distraught young man, but without much success for suddenly the boy was on his knees and again praying disconnectedly. After some time he had spent himself and was calm. Padre offered to give him food but he said he was not hungry. Padre advised him to go to Santa Ynez to a certain Mexican family where he could converse in his own tongue.

The boy started down the road and Padre returned to his tasks. "The boy is mentally unbalanced," Padre said, more to himself than to me. "He is respectful and seems well bred," he continued.

In the hustle and bustle of the day the incident was forgotten until mid afternoon, when I answered the door bell. The boy was standing in his bare feet, his shoes in one hand and the other cupped over his eyes as he peered in through the screen door.

"Op'th' door," he said in his broken English.

Not wishing to admit the boy into the house, I ignored his command and smiling, I said, "Won't you let me make a nice cup of coffee and something to eat for you?"

"No. No," he cried out and started on the run through the garden gate and on through the pasture fence into the field, dropping his shoes in the middle of the road as he fled.

The afternoon wore on and again the young man was temporarily forgotten. At five or thereabouts our guests arrived. They came by automobile. We went out to the garden gate to greet them. Then, as we turned to face the house we saw our young man, rubbing his eyes and looking puzzled, as he came from the far end of the garden. He had returned from his chase and evidently found a place among the bushes to take a nap. After greeting our guests, seeing that their suit-cases were brought in and they were made comfortable, Padre excused himself saying, "I'll go out and see what I can do for the boy." Our guests became interested and begged to go with him. While they talked and questioned, I made some coffee and arranged a tray of food for the unfortunate boy. He ate sparingly but drank the coffee. Padre then escorted him to the Villa and advised him to go to bed.

Later when going to the kitchen to prepare the evening meal and looking out of the window, I saw the boy again running out in the field. Through the dusk I could see that his hands were outstretched. He was evidently praying and just as unbalanced as he was on arrival in the morning.

Quite late in the evening as we sat in the large reception room enjoying our friends, a loud rap was heard on the back door.

"What is it, my boy?" Padre asked, seeing that he had returned.

"I want t' see the Lady," he replied.

"Here I am," I said as I squeezed through the door between Padre and Mr. Elliott, Mrs. Elliott following closely behind me. The case was becoming interesting and nobody wanted to miss any of it.

"I want 'dring water," the boy said when I had reached him.

"All right, you shall have it," I said, and put as much cheer in the words as I possibly could.

"I'll get the flash light and help you find the way to your room," I told him as he handed me back the empty water glass.

"You cannot do that alone," called Mr. Elliott, as I slipped my hand through the boy's arm and proceeded towards the Villa. "I'll go with you."

In the Villa I lit a candle, arranged the bedclothes and with a "good night" left our charge, apparently quite content.

Padre and Mr. Elliott retired for the night. Mrs. Elliott and I remained to have a little chat by ourselves. When we finally decided to retire, I took a look out of the back door and found that the light was still burning in the Villa.

"I think I'll go out and take a peek at our friend," I said.

"Señorita," said Mrs. Elliott (that is what Margaret Elliott always called me.) "I have some mild sleeping powder in my bag. Do you suppose the boy would take one?"

I thought he would. So with the sleeping powder and a glass of water we went to the Villa. Through the open door we saw the boy standing beside the bed looking puzzled. On hearing our footsteps on the gravel he got into bed.

"What is the trouble?" I asked as we walked into the room and towards the bed.

"I lost my money," he replied and put his head out over the edge of the bed to peer around.

Taking the candle from the small table, I set it down on the floor, then getting down on my knees and, amidst dusty cobwebs, pushed my head and shoulders under the bed to retrieve the lost coin.

"You ke-ep it, I want you ke-ep it" as I held the coin to him.

"O, no, no, I'll put it here on the table and in the morning you can put it in your trouser pocket. I will put out the light and you can have a good long sleep," I continued, after he had taken the powder and glass of water. And once more bidding our charge "good night" we left him to his dreams.

Late the following morning when the boy did not appear I went to his room to see what was happening. I found him kneeling in the middle of the bed, clothed only in his blue denim shirt, with his arms outstretched in cruciform position and his eyes fixed heavenward. He was silent and did not answer my questions of solicitations nor did he change his position. It was Sunday, Mass would begin in a few minutes and I could not tarry. However, the picture of the boy in cruciform posture remained in mind and, as soon as the service of the Mass was over, Mrs. Elliott joined me and we made another trip to the Villa. We found the boy in the same posture in which I had left him, and just as silent. I put my hand on his shoulder and patted his cheek, and rubbed his brow in an effort to get some response, all to no avail.

"Señorita, señorita, this is a very pathetic case, and you are so kind," Mrs. Elliott kept repeating as she stood at the foot of the bed and looked on.

"It is a case for medical care," I said as we left the room.

Later, Padre telephoned the sheriff at Santa Ynez to get information as to what procedure to take in caring for the boy. He advised that a warrant would have to be signed before Judge Lyons, at Ballard, a small village four miles away, as to the boy's sanity; then he, the sheriff, would take him to Santa Barbara to be examined and taken care of.

Immediately after lunch Mr. and Mrs. Elliott took me in their car to Ballard where I signed the necessary paper, Mr. Elliott signing as my voucher. Later the sheriff came to take the emaciated, pathetic looking figure to Santa Barbara and thus closed another interesting but depressing episode in our dealing with the Wayfarer.

In a letter written to me from Los Angeles, when the Elliotts reached home, Mrs. Elliott wrote in part:

"When we reached Santa Barbara on our way home, we drove to the County Hospital to inquire for the Mexican boy. He was not there, and the nurse, a very nice woman, became interested and began telephoning to get trace of him. He was found at the jail. They reported that he was quiet, but had not eaten or drunk anything and had not had any medical attention. When we left she was trying to get hold of the official physician, in order to have him transferred to her. If she succeeds she will take good care of him.

"She said, by the way, that your doctor could have sent him direct to the hospital without the need of a warrant sworn out as to insanity or mental aberration. Wasn't it funny that the sheriff did not know that?"

A few days later we read in the Santa Barbara newspaper the account of one Maximinio Martinez being sent to an insane institution. That perhaps is where the boy ended his mortal days in this busy world of ours.

On previous visits to the Mission, Padre had related much about the "Knights of the Road" to Mr. and Mrs. Elliott, hence their keen interest in this case. Too, I have gone into detail in this episode in order to bring out some of the high lights of what we sometimes encountered and the method of dealing with these cases or situations.

DESTRUCTION AND CONSTRUCTION

It was in March 1911, just six years after the first big destructive storm, that the Mission was almost lost to posterity. The winter rains, most of which came in February and March, reached a total of 40.05 inches. The ruinous storm started on February 25th. For twelve days and nights it rained incessantly. The total precipitation was 18.51 inches. These figures were taken from a Government rain gauge which Padre had at the Mission. Padre also kept a log of rainfall and I am quoting from that log.

For the most part the rain fell gently and soaked well into the ground but, to the detriment of the Mission, it also soaked into the adobe walls.

These were tense days as we kept watch, and from time to time heard the rumbling of tumbling bricks and adobe. One day one of the huge six-by-six foot buttresses supporting the north wall of the chapel crumbled and fell to the ground. Later, during the night, another buttress slithered into a huge pile of mud. By the end of the storm four buttresses had been reduced to heaps of soft adobe mud, three on the north side and one on the south wall of the chapel, leaving gaping cavities in the thick walls. The abutment at the end of the colonnade which Capitán had labored so ardently to erect, after the first storm also collapsed.

All day long Padre and my brother Henry, who was spending the winter with us, decked in rubber coats, hats and boots, would walk about the premises to view the destruction and sadly anticipate further devastations. When night came we were afraid to go to bed for fear that the whole building would crumble and bury us alive.

On the seventh of March the rain came down in such torrents and the wind was so terrific that Padre was very much worried for the safety of the chapel. The roof was in bad condition and the lower part of the north wall was so water-soaked that he was afraid it would crumble.

At three o'clock that day Padre and Henry came in to say they thought the chapel wall could not hold out much longer. "We really should remove the articles from the side altar, but I'm afraid it isn't safe to go into the chapel," Padre said.

"Shall I go over and see what I can do?" I asked.

"No, don't!" Padre shot back over his shoulder as he and Henry were again going out to keep vigil.

Disregarding the warning, I donned rubbers and a heavy coat and went to the chapel. Going through the south door, I peered around. It was as quiet and peaceful as the grave; the thick walls completely shut out the fury of the storm. I hesitated a brief moment, then with bated breath hurried across the chapel to the altar on the opposite side. Like the high, or main, altar this one was built of adobe and was a part of the wall itself. It was a huge protruding shelf with a platform at its base which extended some five or six feet in front of the altar. As I stepped onto this platform I found that it was already water-soaked and soft. I realized that it was no time to tarry. Quickly as possible I removed candlesticks, tabernacle (which was portable), altar stone and linens and placed them on the altar on the opposite side of the chapel. Without stopping to look around I hurried back into the house. There was a certain feeling of safety in that part of the house which had been reroofed, and it was that which kept us from deserting the building altogether.

At the hour of five Padre came in to take a short respite from the vigil while Henry proceeded to do the evening chores. We were standing in the middle of the living room trying to decide what to do, when we heard prolonged rumblings, followed by a heavy thud that seemed to shake the whole building, and the tinkling of bells.

We all ran towards the front door. Our nerves were jittery, almost beyond control from the constant strain and uncertainty.

"The bell tower has fallen," Padre exclaimed, as he looked down the veranda and saw the huge mound of debris. The bell tower had fallen forward leaving the bells protruding here and there among the stones, brick and adobe.

"I did not expect the bell tower to fall," Padre said as we walked to the end of the corridor to view the ruin. His face had become pale and drawn and his eyes were moist as he fully realized what had happened. Turning towards me, almost in a whisper, he repeated, "The bell tower has fallen."

When Padre had regained his composure we walked around what was left of the once proud, picturesque and commanding bell tower, then on to inspect the north wall of the chapel. To our great surprise it had withstood the shock caused by the falling of the bell tower and was still intact.

Presently Henry, who, up to this time had been forgotten, appeared on the scene. "Did you hear the bell tower fall?" I asked. Then with a second glance I noticed that he was covered with mud far above his knees and his face spattered almost beyond recognition. "Why Henry, what is the matter?"

"I heard some noise but could not say what it was," he answered, disregarding my last question.

"But what happened to you?" I repeated.

"Oh, I was having a little trouble of my own. Mascot (the horse) was bogged down to his belly in the mud and I had a hard time digging him out."

Mascot, on pasture, had wandered to a spot where the water-soaked adobe soil did not carry his weight and got bogged down in such a way that he could not extricate himself without help. Only Californians or those who have lived in the state can understand the treachery of its adobe soil when it becomes water-soaked.

By the end of this day we were all in such a state of nerves that, had the rain abated sufficiently, I fear we would have abandoned the Mission. As it was, all we could do was sit tight and listen to the fury of the storm. The true story of how we managed to live through those trying days and nights will ever remain among the hidden secrets within the ancient walls of the historic structure.

The total rainfall for that fateful day in which the bell tower was destroyed and the preceding night was more than seven inches. Finally, on the tenth day of the storm, the weather cleared. We were the most forlorn, dejected and disheartened individuals one could possibly conceive.

Immediately Padre reported the catastrophe to his Bishop. When difficulties occurred they must be overcome. Padre was making plans to do just that. I admired his courage but could not become enthusiastic over the prospects of the turmoil and hardship of more building. But then, my feelings were too insignificant to have any bearing on the matter. The Mission must be restored at all costs.

In time the newspapers of Santa Barbara and Los Angeles carried the news of the catastrophe. Appeals were made for financial aid. The late Bishop Conaty pledged his help from dioceasan funds as far as was expedient.

Padre, realizing that the task of restoration would be exceedingly costly, since the isolation of the place made the transporting of materials an added burden, appealed to the Santa Barbara Parlor of Native Sons of the Golden West for assistance.

But, alas, much to his surprise and dismay the appeal was not very well received. At a subsequent meeting of the Parlor the officiating President, Mr. L. H. Roseberry, was not in sympathy with contributing to what he termed, "a religious institution."

There were many Native Sons of the Parlor visiting the Mission in those days, many of them not of the Catholic faith, but what matter? To Padre's liberal mind religious prejudice was no excuse for the abandonment of one of California's historical structures. Consequently he did not hesitate to say what he thought of Native Sons who seemed to have no love for the very cradle of their birth, the California Missions.

Eventually, Mr. Roseberry's statement was brought to the notice of the State's Grand President, Mr. Herman C. Lichtenberger. As a consequence, one bright morning I answered the door bell to admit two portly gentlemen who asked to see "Father Buckler" and handed me their cards. One card bore the name of H. C. Lichtenberger, Grand President N.S.G.W., the other of J. R. Knowland, N.S.G.W. Landmarks Committee.

"Two gentlemen to see you," I announced as I handed the cards to Padre.

"I don't want to see them," he said, after a quick glance at the cards.

"I told them you were here, and they are waiting."

"Tell them I am coming."

"Father Buckler, we came to apologize in person," I overheard one of the gentlemen say as Padre walked into the reception room.

The men were very apologetic for what they termed the unfortunate attitude and statement of Mr. Roseberry. They wished to make it clear that the statement did not reflect the sentiment of the Grand Parlor. They would be glad to help so worthy a cause and begged to be allowed, as their part, to contribute towards the rebuilding of the bell tower.

The Santa Barbara Parlor, evidently piqued at the turn of events, wished to contribute but imposed conditions to their giving assistance. One of the conditions, as I recall, was that they wanted to place a bronze plaque on the reconstructed tower proclaiming to the world that the Santa Barbara Parlor of Native Sons had rebuilt the bell tower. Padre argued that if the Parlor contributed sufficiently to cover the cost of the tower's rebuilding they would be entitled to the honor of the plaque. But if they contributed only a portion of the necessary funds, it would be unfair to the rest of the contributors to give them all the credit and he could not in justice permit the erection of such a plaque.

The Native Sons evidently sent their offer to the Bishop, with stipulations, as a newspaper article revealed. On July 26th "The Independent" of Santa Barbara published the following, with heavy head lines:

BISHOP WILL RESTORE SANTA INES MISSION."

"Grateful to Native Sons, but cannot accept conditions imposed."

"Rt. Rev. Bishop Conaty is prepared to go ahead and restore historic Santa Ines Mission, damaged by the storm last winter, thus, undoubtedly, ending the controversy which has arisen between the church authorities and the Native Sons.

"The Native Sons appropriated a sum towards the restoration of the Mission, but there were certain stipulations which the Church authorities could not accept. There has been correspondence between State Senator L. H. Roseberry and the Rt. Rev. Bishop Conaty in the matter.

"The following is the Bishop's letter to Senator Roseberry, just made public, which probably closes the incident:

" 'Los Angeles, Cal., June 10, 1911.

" 'My Dear Mr. Roseberry:

" 'Your letter of June 6. relative to the preservation and restoration of the Santa Ines Mission has been received. I am deeply grately for the interest taken by the local parlor of the Native Sons, but cannot accept the conditions under which their cooperation is given.

" 'In the last seven years I have spent in the neighborhood of $7,000.00 in restoring that Mission and have already arranged to see to the repairing made necessary by the recent storm. I think you will readily see that I cannot, in justice to myself and to the position I hold, abdicate in favor of any committee in the work which becomes necessary for any Church building.

" 'You may not be aware of how much has been done for that Mission during the past few years and how little assistance has come from any direction towards it. I am quite certain what will be done for it in the future will be done along the best possible lines. For myself, I am thoroughly interested in the maintenance of these landmarks and I am prepared to see to it that the necessary funds be raised for their repairs. I would appreciate any assistance that might be given in the matter, but if the assistance is subject to the conditions laid down in your letter, I must respectfully decline to accept it.

" 'One thing is certain, the Santa Ines Mission will be restored and preserved, and I have already in hand money sufficient for the work. I am exceedingly grateful to you for the kindness of your communication and feel that you will appreciate the justice of my position in the matter.' "

The final outcome was that the Grand Parlor of Native Sons contributed $900 towards the rebuilding of the bell tower. Nothing more was said about the erection of a bronze plaque, or other stipulations.

The big job of restoration was given to Magnus Johnson, a contractor at Santa Barbara. The contract called for the rebuilding of the bell tower and buttresses, the taking down of the tile from the church roof and putting on a board and tar paper roofing, then replacing the tile, placing a concrete foundation along the cemetery side of the church to keep it from further decay from winter rains, and putting on gutters all around the church and convento roofs. The contract also included the reconstruction of the south end of the convento which was down and had become the haunts of reptiles, and reroofing that part of the convento which was not covered in 1905, also whitewashing the whole structure.

It was Padre's wish to have the tile, which had been on the convento, but for many years lying around, put back on the roof. He also wanted a cistern built in the back yard and have the water from the roofs run into it. Furthermore, the reservoir in front of the Mission to be re-surfaced in concrete and roofed over so as to catch the water from the front part of the Mission's roof. Too, his heart was set on having concrete floors laid under both front and back arches; but the Bishop did not think all these things were absolutely necessary at the time and asked him to wait awhile.

Knowing how very expensive it would be to bring all the tools and machinery from Santa Barbara to do the work, and how difficult it would be to hunt up workmen again, Padre was rather disappointed. Undaunted, however, and feeling that it would be such a saving to have all this work done while the paraphernalia was on the ground, he took up the matter with the contractor, Mr. Johnson, and an agreement was reached whereby the work was to be done immediately after the contracted work was completed. Padre was to assume the responsibility of the expense with the privilege of making payment at his own convenience.

So it was that the concrete floors were laid under the arches both in front and back of the convento, the cistern in the back garden built and the reservoir re-surfaced and covered over with a corrugated tin roofing. Padre paid for this part of the construction from his own fund as his contribution towards the Mission.

When the contractor had finished his work Padre bought the so called second lumber, which had been used as the mould for the bell tower and numerous tools which had been used on the job, as the following, copied from Mr. Johnson's bill reveals:

"To build cistern	$147.00
Rebuild and covering reservoir	175.00
Gutters, down spouts, and drain pipes from Dormitory to cistern and reservoir	145.50
Cement floors, front and back corridors	351.00
Building cross in cemetery	77.50
Blacksmithing, haw, rope, and labor on bells	37.50
Approximately 4,000 ft. of second lumber	40.00
2 Wheelbarrows, 5 shovels, 5 picks, one and one half barrels lime, 2 gallons linseed oil	20.00
Total	$994.50

Mr. Johnson very graciously donated $75.00 towards this bill, leaving a balance of $919.50. This bill, being a personal one to Padre, is now in my possession. Other bills for the restoration work were left at the Mission.

As for laying the tile on the convento, Mr. Johnson donated a half day's work of his men towards that, and Padre appealed to the Danish people of the new settlement of Solvang, as a civic gesture, to lend assistance, which they did. One morning there came nine or ten men, who with the force at hand gathered all the usable tile that were scattered about the place and covered all of the front part of the roof and a portion of the roof in the back.

Like busy bees the men worked, chatted, joked, some sang while others whistled as they pushed wheelbarrows, carried tile up the ladder or carfully laid the tile in place on the roof. No doubt each felt quite philanthropic in his contribution to the Mission and expressed it with a song in his heart.

Mr. Johnson's foreman on the job, Mr. A. M. Bidgood, erected a tent under a lone, large oak tree across the road back of the Mission, and there, with his wife and six year old son, lived during the four months he was working on the huge task of rebuilding the Mission. Two and some times more men, who were employed and housed in the Mission, took their meals with the Bidgoods.

As the men contributed their time for the laying of the tile, Mrs. Bidgood did her bit by assisting me in preparing a sumptuous meal for the workmen. With carpenter's horses and some loose boards, a table and benches were hastily set up under the back corridor, and the generous appetites of the kindly laborers were appeased.

Once again the picturesque tiles, so characteristic of these monuments, were in their rightful place.

It was not all clear sailing for the Padre with his great work, however. When it became known that good Bishop Conaty was lending a hand and ready to help, an enterprising busybody came to Padre and wanted him to turn over the work of supervising the reconstruction to him. Padre refused to do so. This seemed to greatly displease this man, and, after going about trying to create dissension among Padre's people and others, he went to Los Angeles to see the Bishop, but failed to get an audience, as the letter from the Bishop to Padre clearly shows. It follows:

"Chancery Office,
114 East Second Street, Los Angeles.
April 15, 1911.

"Rev. A. Buckler,
Santa Inez, Cal.
My dear Father Buckler:

"Mr. ————called here last night with reference to the Santa Ines Mission rebuilding, seeking authority to have him rebuild it. I did not see him as he came while I was engaged in other business, and I understood he went home today. Had I seen him I would have referred him to you because all that relates to the Mission rebuilding I wish to place in your hands. If they wish to help in the work we will be very much pleased, but it is our intention to have it all placed in your hands.

"With best wishes for the Easter time, I am yours very sincerely,

Thomas J. Conaty."

When the work of rebuilding was well under way, and this same individual learned of Padre's intention of putting the tile on the convento roof, he again made himself obnoxious. Going about among the workmen he tried to persuade them and the contractor that the beams under the roof of the convento were too decayed and weak to stand the weight of the tile. Failing to impress them, he wrote to the Bishop. The Bishop in turn sent his letter to Padre, and added that he should use his own discretion in the matter. I remember quite clearly seeing this letter, but for the moment fail to find it among Padre's papers.

To take care of the situation Padre secured the services of an expert who came up from Santa Barbara to examine and test the beams. It meant an added expense, but since the expert not only found the beams were sufficiently strong, but pronounced them superior to any new timber that could be used in their place, it settled the matter.

In rebuilding, as in painting and other arts, the modern artisan making copies often fails in his work to get the feeling of the old Masters. So it was in rebuilding the bell tower. Padre had been explicit, and most insistent, that the tower should be an exact duplicate of the old one. But when the heavy planks, making the form for the tower were removed, exposing the concrete structure, Padre was indeed sorely disappointed. For some reason or other the contractor and his foreman did not grasp the meaning of, nor did they follow the descriptive specifications written in the contract.

The old tower was built as a solid wall with openings for the bells. The new tower had the outline of the old, but was left hollow. Through this error it had lost its appearance of massiveness which was outstanding and picturesque in the old tower.

There was a slight change made in the new tower. Instead of three openings in the façade, it was built with four openings. This was done to accommodate a new bell which Padre purchased for the uppermost opening.

The old bells were sounded by means of clappers and did not swing. Padre's idea was to have a swinging bell that could be heard at a greater distance. The two bells which hung in the side openings, (these openings were not in the original tower) were from the Purisima Mission and had formerly hung on a wooden structure built back of the tower to take care of the bells.

May I pause to say that it was Father Buckler's idea and he who placed the present inscription, "EX ILLIS UNA EXIT," on the bell tower, not one of the early Padres, as Maria Walsh erroneously states in her book, "Mission Bells." The lettering, done on a wooden plaque, was painted by one of the many tramps when he was a "house guest" at the Mission.

A few days after the catastrophe that befell the bell tower, before Padre had found time to secure men to extricate the bells from the debris, the abominable characteristics of the curio seeker had appeared. To Padre's surprise and consternation, as he walked down the driveway to the mail box he came upon the smallest bell half way down the drive. On close examination he discovered that the eye inside the bell, cast to hold the clapper, was broken off. The vandal, or vandals, must have found the bell too cumbersome and heavy and so abandoned their intention of carrying it off, not, however, without taking a souvenir of their vandalism. The bells were immediately dug out of the debris and placed in the vestibule of the church until the new tower was ready for their placement.

Although the congregation was at times inconvenienced by the placing of scaffolding in the church, the services were in no way unpleasantly affected by the long procedure of reconstruction.

In restoring the south end of the convento a wall was built across the front room facing the corridor. Then a wall was extended to the west far enough to make an end to a large room and an added bedroom. This bedroom, at the south end of the back corridor, was constructed to strengthen and support the last arch of the corridor. The large room was used later as a recreation center for parochial activities. These new walls were built of lumber and plastered inside.

What a gigantic and long drawn procedure the job of reconstruction proved to be, and what a tumultuous state of confusion, dirt and dust there was everywhere. The work was so different from that of ordinary building that the workmen were often at a loss to know how to cope with the unusual situations that arose. Accordingly many discussions with suggestions and arguments occurred before a final solution could be achieved. The place being so large the men invariably took short cuts through the house, leaving tools, pieces of lumber, ladders and other paraphernalia strewn all over the place. Housekeeping was anything but a joy and there was no privacy!

For New Year's Eve, which came during the never ending months of rebuilding, Padre was most desirous that the time old custom of ringing in the New Year with the Mission bells should not be broken. Towards this end the men worked feverishly through the last week of the old year. Happily, the tower was finished sufficiently to permit the hanging of the bells.

Mrs. Frank Dudley Dean, (wife of the noted General of Spanish-American war fame serving under President McKinley) and Miss Frances Robertson (a newspaper correspondent who had walked from San Diego to San Francisco as a publicity stunt for the ground breaking of the International Exposition in 1915) were invited to spend the week end of New Year's day at the Mission. What took place on that New Year's Eve can best be told by quoting, in part, from Miss Robertson's article to the official diocesan paper, "The Tidings:"

"Just at sunset of the day that we arrived at Santa Ines, the last of the woodwork that held the concrete of the tower in place was removed, and the bells placed in their respective positions therein. Upon our arrival at the Mission Padre Alejandro informed us that Mrs. Dean, Miss Goulet and myself were to have the honor of being the first persons to ring the bells in the new tower, and that we were to have the unique distinction and rare privilege of heralding the dawn of a new year through the medium of the sacred old bells of Santa Ines. To say the three of us were 'enthusiastic' over the prospect is a mild expression. Surely, loving California as you undoubtedly do, and deeply interested in the romance and nameless charm which hangs about her beloved Missions, as you probably are, wouldn't you, girls of California, take delight in ringing in the New Year with one of the old Mission bells? Looking down the dim vista of receding years what phantoms promenade before these self same bells. It is the day of the Lotus-eater and the

Mission bell rings at dawn for Mass, which the Padre says while the Indians recite their prayers. The bells ring again and they go to their breakfast, and single men and women to their pozolera, the married to their own homes. A third time the bells ring and they go about their daily tasks. Then again, further in the day the bells ring and no matter what is being done, the neophyte pauses in his work with uncovered head and murmers a prayer to God. Thus we see them as they pass in review before the bells with which we are to welcome little 1912. One could write volumes on the many shifting scenes of life which the Mission bells have witnessed, but that is another story.

"Isolated as the Mission is, the great news that the bells of Santa Ines were in place in the new tower spread like the proverbial wildfire, and the country folk for miles around walked, rode, or drove to the Mission that wondrous New Year's Eve to hear once more the sweet-toned bells, for well they knew Padre Alejandro's time honored custom of ringing in the New Year.

"The ropes had not been attached to the bells as yet, and it was necessary for us to go up into the tower to perform the feat expected of us. Therefore, a few minutes before twelve o'clock midnight, we left the cozy livingroom of the Mission and with the assistance of Mr. B. H. Hopkins, who was at work on the restoration, and by the aid of lanterns which we carried, ascended two flights of ladders leading to the bells in the tower. Scarcely had we attained our coveted positions in the tower when far to the north of the Mission a good-natured voice sang out:

'All right: let her go, Padre!'

And Padre 'let her go' to the tune of twelve blank cartridges from his six shooter. To me the sound of those warning shots, clear and resonant in the blandness of the midnight air, marking the death of the old year, were extremely solemn.

"After Padre Alejandro's gun play, there was silence for a minute or two, then, for the first time in many months, there rang out in the transparent atmosphere of that New Year's dawning three beloved bells of old Santa Ines. Softly at first, with a touch as light as love's first kiss, then sweetly, tenderly, triumphantly; we rang them individually and collectively, joyously and happily and with devout thanksgiving, while the country folk were reverently and singularly impressed. There was no hilarity, no loud harrahs, yet everyone seemed ecstatically happy. And why not? Was it not in truth a glad New Year?

"The keen stars beaming with their eternal quiet looked down on that strange scene, and, mayhap, the shade of many zealous Franciscans hovered near, benign and content that La Mission de Santa Ines, Virgen y Martir, will stand forevermore on the King's Highway."

When the contractor and his men finally pulled up stakes to go back to Santa Barbara, there was still much work to be done. The broken bricks and adobe blocks and clots which had been scattered and spread all over the ground in front of the Mission and down the driveway, had to be crushed and leveled off. It was a sorry sight, and little could be done until the following winter when the rains moistened the clots and facilitated the progress of the work. When the rains did come many a tramp earned his meal, lodging and sometimes a little coin, breaking adobe clots and leveling the dirt.

In the house, too, there was much to be done. Doors in the unfinished rooms had to be hung, mop boards put in place and other odds and ends to be finished. For this work Padre kept Mr. Hopkins on the job until all was completed.

With so much patch work done throughout the house it was evident that the painting of woodwork and whitewashing of walls was sorely needed. Much of this, I foresaw, would be my spare time occupation.

In good time, as if in answer to my prayers, a tramp, a young fellow of twenty-three years, a lithographer by trade, Arthur Hendress by name, appeared at the Mission. Padre assigned him to tasks of general cleaning in the courtyard.

Observing that Arthur was adept, neat and thorough with his tasks, I asked Padre if I might have his help in the house.

"What do you want Arthur to do?" Padre asked.

"A lot of things, but principally, I would like to have him assist in whitewashing some of the rooms."

"Whitewashing rooms?   Why it takes a man to do that work."

"Yes, I know, that is the reason I am asking for Arthur's help."

Padre thoughtfully pondered a moment to fully take in the purport and extent of my request, then curtly, "Yes, you may have Arthur's help but you will have to ask him about it yourself."

The following days found Arthur and myself busy mixing lime and industriously wielding the whitewash brush.   The young fellow erected the scaffolding on which he climbed to reach the ceiling, and took care of that part of the rooms.   I did the walls, mounting the stepladder to reach the uppermost parts.   Following this method we whitewashed nine rooms.

Arthur related that he was one of two children of a widowed mother.   His sister having married early in life had left him to care for his aging mother.   "This is how I received my training in domestic work," he said, and beamed satisfaction at the accomplishment.   Like so many of his fellow foreigners he had left his homeland to escape the military training.   He was thoughtful and courteous and did many little things for me, such as keeping the wood box filled, starting fire in the cook stove in the morning and often helping with the dishes.   His request to stay a few days lengthened into two months.   Beyond that, he was one of a passing parade, and we never saw or heard from him again.

The work of painting was much more dilatory in progress, being strictly relegated to sparetime activity, or more strictly speaking, wedged into an already full schedule.   Not only was it necessary to paint the new woodwork but the old as well if harmony was to be maintained.

Owing to the thick walls and few windows the rooms were poorly lighted, and for that reason the walls were whitewashed and the woodwork painted in white paint. Eventually, my spare moments took care of the painting in all the rooms, except the newly erected large reception room and the added bedroom, these to await a more opportune time.

In March of the following year 1913, a Danish tramp, John Luna, who professed to be a painter, made his appearance. Padre engaged him for the sum of $1.50 a day with board and lodging. John stayed nineteen days. He not only painted the woodwork in the rooms but displayed the artistic side of his profession by painting and lettering a plaque, giving the names of all the Missions and the dates of their founding. This plaque was designed to be helpful to tourists in visiting the Missions. It was hung on the front wall of the convento under the arches. It was unusual to see a Dane tramping the road. Be it said in his favor, I doubt that John was a hobo in the strict sense of the word.

With its clean whitewashed bell tower and outside walls, its arches outlined in brick-red together with its weather softened tiled roof the Mission was now taking on some of its former grandeur and dignity. In its majestic silhouette against a background of ever green mountains and an azure-blue sky, it was the subject for an artist to paint.

Time consecrates. What is gray with age takes on the face of the Spirit. The story of the restoration will ever be a proud chapter in the history of the Santa Ines Mission.

THE DANISH COLONY

In the early part of 1911 a colony of Danes settled in the vicinity of the Mission. They called the settlement "Solvang", meaning sunny vale. The colony was founded by two ministers, Benedict Nordentoft and J. M. Gregersen, and Messrs. Mads Freese, Lawrence Pedersen and Professor P.P. Hornsyld. Mads Freese was a real estate agent and instrumental in selling the greater portion of the ten thousand acre tract of land. The sales were made mostly to middle west Danish Americans.

Among the first settlers were Mr. and Mrs. Hans Peter Jensen and three children. They built the first dwelling in the community. Pioneers were Afred Gorgensen, Marcus Neilsen, Peter Madsen and others.

The relationship between the Colony and the Mission was most cordial and friendly. At an early date Mr. Gregersen, the officiating minister, paid his respects to the Mission and to Padre by a friendly call. Incidentally, he had a favor to ask. He was having communion Sunday in his improvised church and had no wine. Would Padre be so kind as to let him have some? It was during the days of prohibition and wine was difficult to procure even for sacramental purpose.

"I will give you this bottle of wine as a token of my friendship for you and your people," I heard Padre say as he handed the bottle of wine to the Minister.

Almost immediately the Danes built a College, the Atter-Dag, where students came for higher learning, principally for theological studies. One of its assembly rooms was used for Sunday worship until some time later when a church was built.

The College, painted white and built on a hill overlooking the village, was imposing. The church was across the road that led to the College and it, too, was painted white. They called it the Bethania Lutheran Church. Following the Mission's pattern they reserved a plot of ground adjoining the church as

175

"God's Acre" to take care of their departed members. Stores of all kinds sprang up to fulfill the needs of the community. On May 8th, 1913, a bank was incorporated to do commercial banking and was open for business on August 25th of that year. It occupied temporary quarters until May of 1926, when it moved into its own new and modern building.

The Danish people were industrious, neat, home loving and thrifty. They developed a water system from the Santa Ynez river and in a short time had revolutionized and transformed the drab, unproductive, dry land into a beautiful green and fertile farming country, all of which spelled the well being and contentment of the community.

VISITS OF RT. REV. BISHOP THOMAS
JACOBUS CONATY, D.D.

It was on July 18, 1907, that the Rt. Rev. Bishop Thomas Jacobus Conaty D.D. chose to make his first visit to the Santa Ines Mission. It happened on one of those days when we were extremely busy about many things. Padre was dressed in soiled trousers and a khaki jumper that gave all the evidence of belonging to a working man. As for myself, I was portraying all the characteristics of a charwoman. In mid-afternoon we were suddenly distracted by the noise of an automobile driving up in front of the Mission. Automobiles made lots of noise in those days and were not to be mistaken.

"It's the Bishop," Padre announced as he looked out the window and recognized the tall handsome man getting out of the car. "It's the Bishop," he repeated, as he excitedly walked over to the front door.

"The Bishop," I gasped, looking down at my attire. My impulse was to run for cover; but it was too late.

With the Bishop was his friend Mr. Dan Murphy who was taking him on this trip. Padre greeted them warmly, made a feeble apology for his appearance, then introduced me.

To have a visit from the Bishop should have been quite an event but somehow coming as he did unannounced and finding us unprepared left us stunned and aghast.

The Bishop had all the information regarding the privations, inconveniences and handicaps Padre encountered when coming to the Mission, together with all the details of the destruction caused by the storm of March 1905, also of the laying of the new roof on part of the convento to keep us from being drowned out. He was keenly interested and eager to examine the premises. His Excellency was generous in his praise of Padre's enthusiasm for the restoration of the Mission but said nothing as to the desolation and ruin that met his eye at every turn.

177

On returning to the house the Bishop asked Padre to join Mr. Murphy and himself on a tour of what was then known as the Bishop's Ranch some three or four miles east of the Mission. Padre accepted the invitation and, changing from his work clothes to clericals, accompanied the men. Later, when they let him off at the Mission and proceeded on their way to Los Angeles, Padre was radiant with excitement. The pleasure of talking with his understanding visitors and the encouragement the Bishop had giving him had indeed given Padre new strength.

Three years later on July 28, 1910, when the Bishop with Rev. Francis Conaty, his nephew, and Harry, the chauffeur, were traveling through the valley they stopped to pay their respects to Padre and the Mission. This was another unannounced visit. By now we had overcome some of our primitive living. An unannounced guest did not have the terror that it did when our housekeeping was but a poor imitation of outdoor camping.

It was late afternoon when the visitors arrived and their stay was brief. Padre took them through the chapel and over the grounds to show the Bishop the work accomplished since his last visit. This consisted mostly of cleaning the debris within the ruined walls and in the courtyard, putting glass panes in windows, locks on doors in the rooms we occupied, mending broken furniture and otherwise making our existence more tolerable.

On returning to the house, Padre asked me into the living room to meet his distinguished guest. After paying my respects to his Reverence, the Bishop, I was introduced to the strikingly handsome young Father Francis Conaty. Clasping my hand firmly he made this comment: "You are a very significant person to be living in a Mission." I wondered!

The shadows were lengthening and the men had to be on their way. With an au revoir and God bless you they climbed into their car and sped away.

The Rt. Rev. Bishop Conaty, of pleasant memories, paid his third and last visit to Santa Ines Mission on August 2nd, 1911.

This time he came to appraise the amount of damage the Mission suffered from the big storm in March of that year. Accompanying him were Rev. Simon A. Ryan S.J. of Chicago, Illinois, Patrick J. O'Reilly S.J., Portland, Oregon, and Mr. Dan Murphy of Los Angeles. On this trip the Bishop did not come unannounced. He and his party came to spend the night and made his plans known in good time.

It was a momentous visit. There was so much to talk over with Padre, many things to decide, and plans to be made for the future of the Mission. It was a busy afternoon with inspection of the destruction and discussions of how best to remedy the situation. Long after the accompanying Fathers had retired the Bishop and Padre continued their talks. They sat in the living room dimly lighted with a coal-oil lamp. Much of the time was given to serious deliberations but they did have their moments of hearty laughter as one or the other related a humorous story.

Whether it was from the cares of his high office or other causes the Bishop did not appear in good health. He had lost weight and much of the verve which he displayed on former visits was lacking. He was the same sweet, genteel, lovable character that so endeared him to all with whom he came in contact. We were truly concerned about him.

The following morning the Bishop and the Fathers were up early, and going to the chapel they read their masses. After a hearty country breakfast and taking Padre with them, they drove to the Bishop's ranch; there his Reverence wished to consult with the agent in charge. On returning they sat out on the front porch under the shade of the arches to have a last minute conference and to get relief from the summer's heat.

During the absence of the clergy I had churned butter. Now it occured to me that perhaps the Bishop would like a glass of buttermilk. He did not take liquor in any form and hospitality could not be extended by offering a glass of wine. With some trepidity I went out on the porch to ask him, explaining that it was freshly churned and would be sweet. "That would be most acceptable," was the Bishop's reply.

"That sounds very inviting," came from the Fathers.

Arranging a tray with glasses filled to the brim, I returned to the porch where everybody partook of the foamy, sweet buttermilk. The men now refreshed made their adieus. The Bishop gave us his blessing; and with arms waving their farewell the men entered their car and were soon out of sight.

Padre's eyes were moist as he stood at the gate until the car had completely disappeared. However he was in a happy state of mind as he turned about and asked me to sit a while on the porch with him. He was in a talkative mood and related much of the conversation he had with his Bishop: of the promise of financial help in the restoration of the Mission; and of the plans they had discussed for the work to be done. He was elated over the Bishop's visit and the opportunity of consulting with him personally.

It was a long time that we sat there on the porch, long past the lunch hour, so absorbing was our conversation. Padre talked excitedly and seemed quite happy, but somehow, I thought I detected, or sensed, a note of discouragement as every now and then he made this comment, "Mamie, it is going to be a tremendous undertaking and will call for a lot of courage from both of us. It will mean hard work." I listened attentively and I was sorry that I could not offer encouragement. After seven critical years of self sacrifice and long hours of hard work we now found ourselves in a more deplorable state than ever. Padre's sobering comment, "It will call for a lot of courage. It will mean hard work," stayed with me in the long full days and months that followed.

From time to time following the Bishop's visit we learned of his failing health, until the final summons came four years later. Quotations from the Official Diocesan weekly "The Tidings" read as follows:

"The career of Bishop Conaty was one notable in the story of the American Church. His was a magnetic figure. He saw deeply into the hearts of people. Non-Catholic public men were deeply impressed by his sincerity and patriotism. President Taft was his friend. His death in San Diego on September 18, 1915, was a blow felt keenly throughout California and the Eastern States where so many years of his life were spent."

ALTAR SOCIETY ORGANIZED

For a long time the idea of organizing an Altar Society lurked in the back of my mind. On a few occasions I had voiced this idea to Padre, but he was slow in adopting it. His plea was that the women did well to come to Mass on Sundays when their husbands could take them.

With the coming of more and more tourists and having more house guests, household duties became heavier, and with the care of the Altar, Altar linens and the church in general it was getting to be more than I could handle alone. I reasoned that an Altar Society could take some of the burden.

The Santa Ynez Valley Argus, a weekly newspaper, was full of small town social items, of organizations being formed, organizations of both church and civic groups. It was spring time and the urge to be doing things was strong. Some of the valley folk were coming to the fore by purchasing automobiles and the women were learning to drive them. The ranch women in particular were broadening out, so to speak, and looked for an outlet to express themselves; they wanted to dress up and go places in their new cars; most of all they wanted social intercourse. All this I pointed out to Padre as I made my plea for organizing an Altar Society.

It was on Sunday, May 16, 1916, that Padre, when making his usual Sunday announcements, appealed to the women of the parish to get together and organize an Altar Society. He elaborated by pointing out the benefits, also the prestige and social aspect such an organization could have in the parish. In conclusion he asked the women of the congregation to remain after the service to meet in the recreation hall and talk the matter over.

This was indeed news, exciting news for the women. There was no organization of any kind in the parish. It seemed that at some time in the past an Altar Society had existed but had not functioned since Padre's coming to the Mission.

182

"Will you attend the meeting?" I asked Padre as I served him breakfast after Mass.

"That is your project, Mamie; I'll leave it all in your hands" was his reply.

Padre's appeal struck a responsive note in the minds and hearts of the women present. As they left the church and filed into the recreation hall for their deliberations all wore happy smiles of keen interest.

There were the Madames Will Fabing, Peter Montanaro, Eduardo de la Cuesta, Alonzo Crabb, Peter Flannigan, Mary Donahue, McCartney and Ward. Also the Misses Katie and Nellie Donahue, Miguela de la Cuesta, Mary Campbell and Miss McCarthy, to mention a few of the ladies.

It was a momentous meeting. The women stood in a circle and all eyes were focussed in my direction as they waited for me to make the first move.

In simple words I explained the purpose, what the functions would be and what benefits the members could derive spiritually and socially from an Altar Society, then called for a vote on whether the ladies approved or disapproved of organizing.

At first the women were shy and slow to express themselves. This was all so new and unexpected. Then like an avalanche, "Yes, we want an Altar Society," they chorused.

The restraint now broken, everybody was talking at once, submitting suggestions, giving advice and debating on possible candidates for the various offices of the organization. Soon ballots were cast and the Altar Society of Santa Ines Mission came into being.

Officers elected were:

President ....Mamie Goulet
Vice President ....Miss McCarthy
     (a teacher in the Santa Ynez school)
Treasurer ....Mary Campbell
     (a teacher in the Santa Ynez school)
Secretary ....Nellie Donahue

Membership dues were voted the very modest sum of 10 cents per month. The meetings were to be held once a month in the Mission's recreation hall. However in time some of the meetings were held in one of the reception rooms of the College Hotel in the village of Santa Ynez. Serving of refreshments at the conclusion of meetings was also voted upon.

The Altar Society meetings proved interesting. The women were enthusiastic and in a short time they were planning a Harvest Ball as a means of raising funds to take care of the hiring of someone to sweep and dust the church, to clean the altars, and help in the decorating of them for special occasions, etc. Also they wanted to help finance the purchase of candles and other necessities for the altar.

For some reason or other the women kept shy of doing anything about the altar linens, such as washing or ironing. But it was understandable since the various pieces required folding and creasing according to certain patterns. The women did not feel qualified to do it. Thus it was that the care of the altar linens remained my happy labor of love to Santa Ines for all the days it was my privilege to be in her good company.

PICNICKERS

The begoggled men and auto-veiled women of primitive automobile days who picnicked en route added another phase to the many interesting events which took place in the Mission's front yard. There, too, we were impelled to make a comparison between the propitious and the not so favorable.

It was always "So romantic," to picnic in the sheltered security of a picturesque old Mission. It did not matter whether the grass in the yard was spring green or an autumn brown, romance always lurked in the background. Surely the Padre would have no aversion to parties partaking of their lunch in the open space in front of the Mission. Not at all. The Padre was most obliging. There one could get "The grand panoramic view of the valley and mountain ranges" and enjoy the peaceful quietude of the place. Alas! the shock to us occurred when the picnic broke up and the party climbed into the automobile and departed. For what could be more disillusioning than to find a lot of tin cans, cartons, waste paper and perhaps a discarded car tire in one's front yard left by a party of picnickers. Certainly, there was no romance in the task of cleaning up the discarded leftovers. However, in all fairness credit must be given to the many thoughtful and appreciative picnic parties; they far outnumbered the less polite and did much to compensate for and to soften adverse comparisons.

Now and then, if the day was hot, perchance the travelers would be invited to partake of their lunch under the arches in the cool of the veranda. There were benches to sit on and others that could be improvised as tables. This privilege always brought an appreciative response and oftimes these kindly souls would invite us to partake of their prepared lunch. If the time was propitious and the Mission's larder had anything appropriate to contribute to the repast, we would accept the invitation and join the party. These very informal meetings, like so many in our

185

contacts with new and interesting people, were as bright lamp posts on the road of time.

The visit of Mr. Lorimor Johnson, the motion picture producer, is still fresh in memory as an example of the pleasures derived from these simple courtesies. It happened during the days of the Flying A Film Studios in Santa Barbara. On this hot October Sunday in the year 1913, Mr. Johnson and party of several motion picture actors and actresses motored to the valley and the Mission. Padre escorted the party through the Chapel and they were about to depart when some one asked him if he could direct them to a shady spot where they could eat their picnic lunch. "Why yes," Padre replied, "You may picnic right here on the veranda where it is cool if you like." All were delighted and they invited Padre to join them. Food baskets from the cars were brought in; benches were pulled together to form a table, and in a short time the picnic was on.

Meeting motion picture people was a new experience for Padre and almost immediately he began to ask questions about moving pictures, moving picture actors and actresses. The moving picture folk were surprised and filled with wonder to think that anywhere there could be anyone who had never seen a motion picture projected on a screen. The outcome of it all was that when the party broke up Mr. Johnson persuaded Padre to accompany him to Santa Barbara, where on the following morning he took him to the Flying A Studio and there reeled off film after film of moving pictures for Padre's pleasure. It was a great revelation and he was very much impressed with the wonders of modern methods in entertainment.

From the time of this first meeting with Mr. Lorimor Johnson until Padre passed away seventeen years later, many a cherished letter passed between the two men.

There were a few instances when the picnic party was invited to bring their lunch basket inside and eat in the Mission's dining room. These usually occurred when the party, or some member of the party, was known either by name, through correspondence or by recommendation. As an example there was the instance of Mr. John Steven McGroarty's first visit to the Mission and his being invited to share our dining room. It was on a Sunday, May 16, 1916, to be exact. Mr. and Mrs. McGroarty, Mr. Lou Lubrecht, brother of Mrs. McGroarty, and his wife, and several others who were connected in some way with Mr. McGroarty's Mission Play at San Gabriel, all arrived at the Mission in time for the 10:30 o'clock Mass. People, including myself, were gathering in little groups in front of the church, and were exchanging greetings and pleasantries when the party arrived.

"At what time does the Mass begin," one of the men of the party asked.

"In just a few minutes," I answered. "Will you remain for it?"

"Yes," the man answered, and, turning towards the man standing at his side he introduced me to Mr. John Steven McGroarty.

I expressed my pleasure at meeting so distinguished a person and added, "I am sure Padre will want to meet you; will you promise not to leave after the church service without seeing him?"

"We do not wish to impose on the Padre's time" said Mr. McGroarty.

"You will not be imposing, and I assure you Padre would be very disappointed if he learned you were here and did not call on him." It was time to go into the church. The men and women of the party who had lingered in the background now came forward and we all entered the chapel together.

When the church service was over Mr. McGroarty and party were invited to the house where presently Padre made his appearance. Very formally, introductions, handshakings and greetings took place. Then suddenly all formality and restraint vanished when Padre asked, "Where are you going to eat your lunch?"

The women of the party looked at each other; the men looked at the women. Then all laughed together as Mr. Mc-Groarty explained they were out for country air and had taken a picnic lunch with them which they planned to eat under the shade of an oak tree somewhere by the roadside.

"Wouldn't you like to stay right here and eat your lunch in the Mission's dining room?" Padre asked.

"That would be an imposition," from Mr. McGroarty.

"That would be wonderful," came from the women enthusiastically as they looked at me for approval.

"Oh, do stay," was my answer, "Our own lunch is ready to serve and we can enjoy our meal together."

In less time than it takes to tell it, boxes and baskets of all sizes and shapes were brought in and placed on the kitchen table. There the women unpacked and arranged food on plates, platters and deep dishes. The wood range was hot and soon the aroma of coffee was everywhere. Padre and the men gathered chairs from the various rooms and placed them around the long dining table; as they did so they talked, laughed and joked, apparently having a good time. The meal, in the atmosphere of such congenial company, proved to be another of those never-to-be-forgotten events in our book of memories.

Mr. and Mrs. McGroarty and Mr. and Mrs. Lubrecht repeated their visit to the Mission on several occasions. When Padre retired from active duty to live in Santa Barbara the visits between us were frequent. Thus the ties of friendship grew more intimate as the years moved on.

On March 10, 1930, when Padre was laid away, Mr. McGroarty in company with Mr. Lubrecht and wife, Grace, made the trip to Santa Barbara to attend the funeral and to be one of the pall bearers.

Some time later, for his Sunday column in the Los Angeles Times, Mr. McGroarty wrote about his trip to Santa Barbara and Padre's funeral. The following is a quotation from that article:

"There a while back—a couple of weeks ago, or maybe three—we made a sad journey to Santa Barbara. It was to attend the funeral of an old friend who has been our friend this long and many a year, and who also was a friend to many who had few friends in the world. Many of them had no friends at all, save him.

"We started out upon the high road before the break of day in order to be in time for the funeral at the Old Mission Church of Santa Barbara. It was a thrilling experience to speed upon the King's Highway and along the shores of the sunset sea as dawn was breaking. But our heart was heavy as lead within us notwithstanding all the splendor that Nature was showering upon us. We could not help but know our friend whom we mourned would never behold again the dawn of a new day upon this good earth which he loved so long and so well.

"It is about Alexander Buckler that we are talking this blessed Sabbath morning in the Synagogue. The Synagogue in which he himself sat every Sabbath day, having been also a member of the congregation of the faithful, saying his prayers every night and morning and many a time between. For long years he had been the Padre at the Old Franciscan Mission of Santa Ines which stands still, altho in ruins, upon a sunlit mesa between Santa Barbara and San Luis Obispo.

"When Padre Alexander was first sent to the Mission Santa Ines the roof had fallen and the floor was littered with the debris that the vandal years had flung upon it. With him was a devoted niece who kept his house. Together they cleaned away the litter of the years and rescued from dust and decay sacred old vestments of priceless value, and many another relic that museums might well quarrel over today. They cleared the place and made it clean and holy again. They lighted candles on the old altars where the old candles had burned away. They struck again the listening ear of the morning and of the evening the music of the Angelus from the rusted Mission bell. The house that was fallen was reared anew.

"This was a great thing that Padre Alexander had done with the help of his devoted kinswoman. But Padre Alexander afterward did a far greater thing than all that.

"It came to pass that the derelicts of the world sought him out in his quiet retreat. Tramps and hobos, outcasts and outlaws came to him for shelter and for food, year after year in endless companies.

"Not one of these homeless, shelterless, hungry men was ever turned away from the ancient doorways of Santa Ines while Padre Alexander held sway in that place. It is reckoned that through the years he was there not less than the number of three thousand tramps and hobos sought him out to give them lodging for the night and food to strengthen them on their friendless wanderings. What he did was to fully restore that traditional hospitality of the Missions in the days of their glory when their doors were never closed against the stranger.

"When Padre Alexander grew old and his health had failed him, he retired to a quiet little home at Santa Barbara where old friends were wont to seek him and spend a happy hour with him. And now all that, and the other things that we have told you about him, will come to an end. Padre Alexander has gone upon that long journey that has no turning trails, no bends in its road. His serene and loving soul is upon flight through the tracery of the stars where He who was a wanderer in Galilee awaits to welcome him.

"Perhaps some day there will be a monument builded in memory of this wonderful man, but it will not matter whether a monument be builded or not. He builded his own monument in the remembering heart of God, Who knows and sees all things, even to the sparrow's fall. The life of a man so generous, so charitable, so forgiving and so good constitutes a monument greater than any that can be builded of bronze or hewn of stone.

"In the Old Mission Church of Santa Barbara he was given, as he lay silent in his coffin, the greatest honors that his church

is able to bestow upon any man. Had he been a Cardinal in
scarlet robes he could not have been more honored.

"We shall miss him and others who loved, too, shall miss
him also. But the wanderer shall miss him most—the outcasts,
it will be they who shall miss him most. They will seek now for
shelter and his kindness in vain.

"God be with him, and may his rest be sweet.
                                    John Steven McGroarty."

In the days before the Gibraltar Dam was built to conserve
water for the city of Santa Barbara, the Santa Ynez river flowed
deep and wide. Well stocked with mountain trout, its banks were
a veritable camping and picnic ground. Campers came from all
parts of the State to indulge in the sport of trout fishing.

We, too, found it delightful and relaxing to spend a late
afternoon and evening near the silvery stream on the river.
Also, it proved an ideal way to entertain house guests. Shoulder-
ing our fishing rods and with a frying pan, coffee pot, a loaf
of bread and some bacon in a basket we would invite our guests
to join us in a walk down to the river a quarter of a mile away.

On arrival we baited our fish hooks and cast our lines until
dusk overtook us. Usually two or three members of the party
did the fishing and they averaged from twenty to forty trout.
There were no limits placed on the size or number of fish to a
person in those good old carefree days. Those of the party
who did not fish were assigned to the task of gathering drift
wood for the fire and to preparing the meal. With the willow
trees for a background, the river beach sand a place to spread
our table cloth, and an improvised fireplace, built of river
bed rocks on which to fry our bacon and fish and to boil our
coffee, we enjoyed our picnics to the full.

Dr. George R. Luton, the valley's physician, was a great
trout fishing enthusiast. One summer when my sisters Emma
and Louise were with us at the Mission, the Lutons and ourselves
had many a delightful river picnic party. Dr. Luton, Louise and

myself would cast our fishing lines while Emma, Mrs. Luton and small son Billie paddled in the water's edge and gathered drift wood for the fire. Always we had the same menu, bacon, fish, bread and coffee. The poignant aroma of frying bacon and boiling coffee was ever alluring. The tinkling of water over the rocks and pebbles, the symphonies of the frog's choir and the occasional hoot of an owl were gentle reminders of the supreme splendor of the evening.

During the days of good fishing in the Santa Ynez river many prominent business men from Santa Barbara came annually for their week-end fishing. Many partook of the Mission's hospitality for their short stay. Mr. John F. Diehl, owner and manager of the then Diehl's grocery store, Mr. Thomas M. Storke, owner and editor of the Santa Barbara Independent, Mr. A. S. Petterson, editorial writer, Mr. Mark Bradley, county recorder and Mr. Steve Nichols, hardware man, to mention a few who with their wives, were our guests.

With the building of the Gibraltar Dam the water in the river was reduced to a mere trickle and fishing along its banks became a memory of the past.

HOUSE GUESTS AND TOURISTS

An interesting phase of life at the Mission was its house guests and tourists. During the first years of Padre's pastorate there, there were few so called tourists coming to the Mission. For the most part they were local people from the neighboring villages and surrounding country, who, when having house guests whom they wished to entertain, would take them to see the Mission. Rarely did anyone come from a greater distance.

The clergy from the parishes of Arroyo Grande, San Luis Obispo and Santa Barbara made up the greater part of our early day house guests. Later, when parishes were established at Santa Maria and Lompoc, their respective pastors were frequent visitors.

At times even Protestant ministers came to partake of our hospitality, as for instance, the Rev. M. M. Moore, the Episcopal rector of the church of "All Saints by the Sea" in Montecito, who came to the valley on several occasions in connection with his ministerial duties and asked if he might stop at the Mission during his stays of two or three days. I distinctly recall the first occasion of his being with us. It was late afternoon when he arrived, having made the trip by train as far as Gaviota and then on to the Mission by the Gaviota-Los Olivos stage.

I had no idea how I should address a Protestant clergyman. When Padre introduced him as Rev. Moore I took the cue. Shaking hands with our guest I said, "I'm glad to know Rev.

Moore." The Rev. Moore held my hand firmly and with an appealing smile said, "Call me Father."

An elderly man, tall, stately, with snow white hair, rotund of figure and very genial, the Rev. Moore had been asked to christen a new arrival in the home of one of our neighbors a half a mile away. But since the christening would not take place until the following day the Reverend was to be our guest for the time being.

After lunch the following afternoon Rev. Moore very carefully arranged his white, lace trimmed, linen surplice and elaborately embroidered white satin stole on his left arm. Then, with long strides, he walked across the sun-parched stubble field south of the Mission to the home of Mr. and Mrs. Francis M. Shaw to christen their new offspring.

The Rev. Moore was invited to remain for the christening dinner that evening but returned to the Mission for the night. The next morning he again took the Gaviota-Los Olivos stage and was on his way back to Montecito and his little church "All Saints by the Sea."

From this and subsequent visits to the Mission a bond of friendship was established that lasted until the passing of Rev. Moore some years later. During the interval many amicable letters passed between the pastor of Santa Ines Mission and the pastor of "All Saints by the Sea."

On the occasion of the death of Rev. Moore a touching letter came from Mrs. Moore telling us how much her husband had enjoyed his friendship with Padre. He had cherished the memory of his visits to the Mission of Santa Ines.

Also, there was the incident of the Presbyterian minister and his wife, the Rev. and Mrs. Lawrence S. Sherman from Pennsylvania. They were touring California by automobile and were en route from Los Angeles to San Francisco. They had negotiated the Nojoqui grade over the mountain range and had reached a point a mile south of the Mission when something went wrong with their car. The nature of the trouble was such that they could not repair it on the spot and there was nothing to do but walk to the little village of Solvang, which at that time consisted of eight or nine buildings fringing the Mission grounds. Here an enterprising mechanic had set up a primitive garage and repair shop.

It was late afternoon. The couple were informed that the car would have to be towed in and that it was not likely they could have it repaired that day. The genial mechanic, taking in the situation, assured them that under the circumstances they could find asylum for the night at the Mission.

What mental reaction took place in the minds of the Presbyterian couple at the thought of spending the night in a Catholic Mission was not revealed. They read the sign, "Notice to Visitors" and probably using that as an approach to meeting the priest, they rang the door bell.

"We would like to see the Mission," the man said, as Padre opened the door.

"Oh, very well," Padre answered, and reached for the huge key of the church door which hung on the wall next to the door frame.

"And where are you from may I ask," I heard Padre say as they sauntered down the corridor towards the church. Padre had that charming gift of putting strangers at their ease and I feel sure that this question was an appropriate one for the distraught couple.

On their return from the church Padre advised me of the couple staying for the night. Two more plates were added for the evening meal.

The Reverend and Mrs. Sherman proved to be congenial company and we had a delightful evening as we sat and chatted in the large reception room. Like so many strangers who were guests at the Mission, they wished to keep alive that indescribable, intangible something which they had experienced by writing to us. A number of interesting letters passed between

Rev. Sherman and Padre while others passed between Mrs. Sherman and myself.

Several years later when our correspondence had all but ceased I received a lengthy letter from Rev. Sherman telling me of the long illness and death of Mrs. Sherman and how, to the end of her days, she had cherished and relived her visit to the Mission.

The fact that living conditions were very primitive and the meals necessarily extremely simple at times did not seem to matter. Guests took it all in good part. Usually they looked upon their stay as a great privilege, a rare adventure, and often waxed romantic as they enjoyed the quiet and peacefulness of the place. Padre was a genial host and, as the Mission itself was a great attraction, we soon found ourselves having guests frequently. Yes, and I might add, in later years we had house guests almost continuously.

A middle aged, affable and charming couple who delighted in visiting the Mission were Mr. and Mrs. August Vollmer of San Luis Obispo. They were always welcome and frequently received a special invitation to join us for Christmas, New Year's or Easter Sunday dinner and week end. Their first visit was in 1910 from May 21 to 30th. Making the trip in a small one-seat buggy drawn by one horse they were two days on the road, and enjoyed every mile of it. They often referred to the trip as their second honeymoon.

Mr. Vollmer was a fishing enthusiast. During their stay he would get up at dawn, take his fishing rod and creel and tip-toe out of the house to walk down to the river, there to cast his rod for a couple of hours. His keenest delight on returning was to empty his creel on the kitchen table and, with a twinkle in his eyes, would pleadingly say, "Please, Mamie, fry these for our breakfast." Sometimes he would have two or three good sized trout and at other times his creel produced from one to a dozen small fish. But always his genial smile and pleading were the same.

Mr. and Mrs. Vollmer were numbered among the closest friends we had in California. Our first meeting was on the occasion that Padre and myself made the trip to San Luis Obispo to do some shopping. We wished to lay in a supply of staple groceries such as flour, sugar, cereals, tea, coffee, etc. along with other commodities. Especially did we plan on getting a supply of coal oil for the coming winter. During the heavy rains of the previous winter, 1906, the narrow gauge railway, running between Los Olivos and San Luis Obispo, went out of commission and many supplies in the valley's stores ran out. This was true with coal oil lamps. Electricity did not extend to the valley at that time. People came to the Mission and asked for candles and candle ends left over from those used in the church that they might have some light in their homes. It was some time before the railroad resumed operation and the Mission's supply was well nigh exhausted. We had learned a valuable lesson and coal oil now headed our shopping list.

We had been advised that a Mr. Vollmer had the leading grocery store in that town and we made the trip via the S. P. Narrow Gauge R. R. from Los Olivos to do our shopping. Early in the morning Mr. Confaglia, a neighbor, took us to the station.

It was a long list that we had with us; it contained a lot of things besides groceries. To our surprise we found that the store had dishes, lamps, cooking utensils, brooms, all sorts of garden tools and many other items for good housekeeping. As we moved about making our selections our list grew longer and longer; we saw so many things we could use and hadn't thought about. Mr. Vollmer was most genial and proved a good salesman as the number of boxes indicated when they arrived at the Mission. These boxes were shipped by rail as far as Los Olivos, then brought to the Mission by Mr. Confaglia in his light spring wagon.

Before we left the store Mrs. Vollmer came in to do her morning's shopping. We were introduced and, on learning that we came from Santa Ines Mission and were in San Luis just for the day, she invited us to have lunch at their home. We demurred, saying that it would be an imposition. Padre wished to see the San Luis Mission and pay his respects to Father Valentine Aguilera, the pastor. So we compromised; Padre went to the Mission and I walked home with Mrs. Vollmer some four or five blocks from the store.

Housemaids were then in vogue in the so-called middle class families, so Mrs. Vollmer had the leisure to take me through the garden. She was a small woman with ruddy complexion, a foreign accent and a ready smile that made me feel at ease. The garden was a hobby with Mr. Vollmer and herself, she explained with justifiable pride. I felt as if transplanted into a fairyland as she pointed out and named the rare shrubs and plants imported from many lands.

Mr. Vollmer joined us for lunch and after the meal I rode back to the store with him, sitting on the high seat of his one horse delivery wagon. It was all so simple, informal and gracious.

At the store Padre was waiting. We immediately retraced our steps to the station to board the train for Los Olivos where Mr. Confaglia met us and drove us back to the Mission. In due time our groceries and gadgets arrived. It was fun to unpack the boxes and distribute their contents to the various places assigned to them.

In looking back into the misty past, time revealed that we had done more than purchase groceries. Unconsciously, we had planted the seed of a friendship that grew and flowered into full bloom with the passing of the years. When Padre passed away Mr. Vollmer, now aged and slow of step, came to Santa Barbara to attend the funeral service and to be one of the pall bearers. He came to place the flower of his long and cherished friendship on Padre's grave.

The first party of "tourists" to visit the Mission after my arrival left an indelible mark on my memory. It was at that period of the Mission's history when doors were all but useless and everything was open to any one who cared to walk in, as well as the elements.

It was a party of high school boys and girls chaperoned by the mothers of two of the girls. They were on a vacation trip and seeing the Missions that lay in their path of travel.

The party went through every room in the building. Giving no heed to my protests, they went so far as to trespass even into my own sleeping rooms. They laughed, snickered, and made wise-cracks about evrything they saw and otherwise displayed their lack of ordinary common decency.

Coming back to the big front room through which the party had entered one of the women offered me a small piece of money. "I do not wish to take anything," I said. But she insisted, saying, "I want to make a donation for the Mission."

On a shelf below the mirror near the front door was a small box. In it was kept some small change with which to purchase meat and vegetables from vendors who came every so often with their products. I pointed to the box and said, "You may leave your donation here if you wish to give it."

The woman dropped her small coin into the box and we walked out on the veranda. Then one of the boys said that he, too, would like to make a contribution. With that statement he stepped back into the room.

When the party had departed I was curious to see what the contribution might be. I counted, and recounted the contents of the box. The results were always the same. There was considerably less money in it than there was before the party made their contributions. In a way it was a small matter but for me it was a new experience. I was gullible and the party made the most of the situation. As a tourist guide, I had learned my first lesson.

In the years 1907 and 1908 the automobiles began to make their appearances. Under the supervision of Mr. Charles Fuller Gates a cavalcade of seven automobiles stopped at the Mission. It was an endurance run to test the performance and capabilities of the cars. They called it "El Pismo Run," and stopped at this point to register time and mileage. The main highway had not as yet been diverted to its present location and all traffic passed by the Mission.

Through the publicity, in the year of the storm, 1910, devastation and construction, the heretofore almost unknown Mission, as far as the general public was concerned, became a focus of interest. Even Mr. John Steven McGroarty, writer of Mission history and author of the "Mission Play," knew little of the Santa Ines Mission at that time and thought it an uninhabited and abandoned ruin.

Tourists seeing California by automobile seldom passed up the Mission. Its quaint, bold Spanish architecture against the mountain background was ever alluring. Most of these tourists were out-of-state people and the Missions fascinated them.

Not infrequently automobile parties whose cars were unfortunately crippled on the road through the giving out of a part, or parts, sought shelter at the Mission.

Cars coming from the South often found it difficult to negotiate the primitive rough and narrow road through the mountain pass between Gaviota and the Santa Ynez valley. Their occupants, forced to get out and walk, invariably made their way to the Mission. Feeling confident of finding asylum they usually took their mishaps cheerfully. The length of time they were forced to stay at the Mission depended on the nature of the mishap. If an integral part was crippled and had to be sent for at Los Angeles the delay extended to two days or more. At other times when the motorist encountered only a slight mishap the chauffeur would remain to do the mending while the rest of the party walked as far as the Mission.

Of course we made no pretense of going into the rooming and boarding house business. True to its tradition the Mission harbored all who sought food and shelter regardless of what their color or religious belief might be. If the traveler, or

travelers, were in need of food and shelter the Mission gave un-
stintingly.

As a rule the touring visitors were charming, intellectual and
appreciative people. There were times when the Mission, and we,
too, would have been in a sorry state had it not been for the
goodwill and generous contributions of these benevolent people.
The tourists that always found approbation and brought delight
and gratification to the guide were those who displayed no
haste; were interested and eager to see and learn all there
was about the Mission. Not infrequently these charming people
came again and again, oftimes bringing or sending others
just as interested and congenial. Through the recurrence of
informal visits of affable and appreciative tourists many staunch
friends were made for ourselves and for the Mission. Kindly
and thoughtful, many expressed their appreciation of the
courtesies extended them by sending the latest in books or
magazines or some other token of their friendliness, thereby
keeping in close touch with us both in spirit and in remembrance.
These friendly gestures contributed so much towards making our
isolated lives pleasant and, in after years, gave grace to lingering
memories.

There was a very human and oftimes a humorous side to
the tourist. One of these laughable occasions took place when
a big car drove up the lane and stopped in front of the Mission.
Two elderly women got out and walked about in the front yard.
Occasionally they peered over the picket fence to admire the
flower garden. As they walked along the veranda they paused
at the windows, cupped their dainty hands and pressed them
along with their noses against the window panes. The window
of the reception room being higher than the rest was beyond
the reach of the women and from this vantage point Padre
humorously observed, through the thin curtain, the women and
their determination not to pass up anything. On finding their
height only measured up to the window sill they pulled up one of
the old morticed benches. One of the women climbed onto

it, cupped her hands and, pressing them and her nose to the window pane, came face to face with Padre. Enjoying the situation, Padre did not move away. But evidently the woman's curiosity was satisfied. At least her exploration ended there. She motioned her companion and they went on their way.

Another episode, and one that Padre enjoyed immensely and often related, took place one late afternoon when he was sitting on the veranda reading. His attention was attracted to a glistening limousine which had driven up the lane. The obliging chauffeur was holding open the car door while four well dressed women were stepping out. The women then leisurely walked up and down along the garden fence uttering their "oh's" and "ah's" as they admired the architecture of the building, the panoramic view and the flower garden. Now and then they cast furtive glances at the white haired Padre who sat quietly reading. Finally one of the ladies, in a thin falsetto voice, ventured conversation by asking, "When was this Mission founded?"

"In 1804," Padre replied.

The lady walked a few paces, thoughtfully, then suddenly returned. Looking at Padre in all seriousness she said, "And you have been here ever since."

Padre did not consider himself young but a long way from being a centenarian; however he was enjoying the joke and, affecting a deep sepulchral tone, answered "Ye-es, I've been here ever since," and continued his reading.

Apparently the women felt enlightened and pleased. They had learned something of the Mission's history and were content as they went back to their limousine and were off.

In keeping with the tradition of the Mission there was no charge or fixed fee imposed on those who wished to be escorted through the place with a guide. All visitors were welcome and every courtesy possible was extended to them. Usually visitors who were used to traveling and sightseeing gave what they considered a sum equivalent to the worth of the guide's time.

Others with generosity exceeding their means would manifest their appreciation by small donations. Now and then a public spirited individual would, for sentimental or other reasons, make a substantial gift. Donations towards the restoration and upkeep of the Mission were always appreciatively accepted.

An amusing incident took place when I was sweeping the church. To sweep the rough, uneven tile of the church floor was no small task; one had to dress for the part. So here I was a towel wound around my head, old dusty shoes, a big apron and loose cotten gloves, industriously raising the dust with a big broom when Padre walked in with a party of tourists, a man with the appearance and manner of affluence, and his son, who apparently was in his twenties. Giving them no heed other than trying to taper down the volume of dust, I kept right on with my sweeping. When the men had completed their tour of the chapel and were registering in the big book near the front entrance, the young man asked Padre if he might give the women sweeping the church a little donation. Padre, somewhat surprised, said, "As you like."

The young man walked up the long aisle to the front part of the church where I was and, extending his hand in a flourish said, "I want to give you something."

"Oh, no, no!" I demurred. Whereupon he dropped his offering in my apron pocket and was off.

When the big front door clanged shut and I knew I was alone, I fished out twenty-five cents from my apron pocket.

Mr. J. Smeaton Chase, author of "California Coast Trails," "California Desert Trails," "Yosemite Trails" and "Cone Bearing Trees of California Mountains," came to the Mission on several occasions. On his first visit Mr. Chase was traveling with a horse, starting from San Gabriel he was going North with the Oregon State line as his goal. The matters of principal concern to him in making the trip were the facts and beauties in nature and the humane and historical elements in life. He wished to preserve, through writing, something which was distinctively Western in life and manners.

The episode of Mr. Chase's visit to the Mission on this occasion and recorded in "California Coast Trails" follows in part:

"At Mission Santa Ines I proved for myself one virtue for which the Catholic Church has always been famed, its hospitality to travelers. The Mission is under the charge of Father Alexander Buckler, a whole-souled Teuton from the Lower Rhine. His extensive parish keeps him much on the move, but, luckily for the Mission, the Father is a man of taste, and has chosen for headquarters this lonely old church, where he has fitted up a suite of dusky, cell-like rooms for his dwelling. I found him among the roses of the tiled corridor, explained my presence, and asked permission to camp for the night in the meadow near by. 'Camp!' he echoed; 'Why can't you sleep in a bed?' and straightway led me off to a plainly but comfortably fitted room, and detailed Chino to the stable and a well-filled manger. Then he was sure I must be hungry, so, his housekeeper being away, he ransacked the larder to find me a meal. Whether I were a Catholic, Protestant, or Mohammedan, Quaker, Shaker, Supra-lapsarian, was all one to him: I was a traveler, and a guest of Santa Ines I must be.

"I learned that the room assigned to me had once been the quarters of the 'commandante', when, after the secularization of the Mission, one half of the then remaining building had been taken by civil authorities and put to the use of jail, blacksmith-shop, or whatever purpose it would serve. I heard also that in my bed an Indian who was murdered a few years ago near by had breathed his last. But no ghost disturbed my sleep, and I awoke next morning to the strains of the 'Romance in F', played by the good Father out of compliment, because I had happened to mention a special liking for Schumann. (The Father is an enthusiast in music. He played the organ when four years of age, and performed in public at twelve; and often his piano is heard by the owls of Santa Ines at the most abnormal hours).

"I was able to be of some service to the Father in photographic matters, and spent three days in his cheerful society . . .

"My departure from Santa Ines was in the operatic manner, for I rode away to the imposing strains of the 'Pilgrims' Chorus,' which the Father thought an appropriate valedictory."

Another author with a love for the great out-of-door life was Mr. Charles Francis Saunders, author of "The Southern Sierras of California," "The Indians of the Terraced Houses," "Under the Sky in California," and others. He too, made several visits to the Mission when on his jaunts through regions of the back country.

"Padre Alejandro is the present rector at the Mission Santa Ines, an elderly man of comfortable rotundity of figure and known the countryside over.

". . . . . About this Mission of Santa Ines there is a home-like atmosphere that cannot escape you, for the niece is a rare housekeeper, and the feminine touch is over all. The south corridor, which runs the length of the convento's front, and which is bright with sunshine the greater part of the day, is less a cloistered walk than an out-door living room, cheerful with potted plants and fragrant with perfumes from the strip of garden along the front where roses and wall-flowers, stocks and poppies, lift dear, old fashioned faces to the sky. Through the great arches is an unobstructed view up the quiet, pastoral valley and across the river to the mountains that look down on Santa Barbara where Santa Barbara looks on the sea. In all Southern California I know no more charming spot for respite from the world's cark and care than this lovely open corridor of Santa Ines Mission."

Through the visits of Mr. Chase and Mr. Saunders to the Santa Ines Mission the men met, became well acquainted and close friends. Both being writers and with similar tastes, they soon got together and in the year 1915 became co-authors of

a book entitled, "The California Padres and Their Missions."
A chapter is devoted to each of the Missions, and each is divided
into two sections. In the first section, the historical facts most
likely to interest the general reader are discursively woven into
a personal narrative, together with matters pertaining to the
present-day condition and activities of the establishment. Following upon this, and forming a second section of the chapter,
is an essay or story, designed to portray some feature of Mission
life or history, a very delightful and informative book if one is
interested in California's colorful past.

"The Caifornia Padres and Their Missions" was published by
Houghton Mifflin Co. of Boston and New York. The book was
so well received that a few "deluxe" copies were made. For
these Miss Jean Woolman Kirkbride of Camden, New Jersey,
was sent out to California to take on-the-scene photographs,
which she hand painted in their original coloring, to illustrate
the book. While on the tour through California she also took
pictures for Helen Hunt Jackson's "Ramona," and a few copies
of that well known book, too, were illustrated.

On reaching Santa Ines Mission Miss Kirkbride took a respite
from her travels and remained for a couple of days. So appreciative was she of Santa Ines' hospitality that Padre became the
proud recipient of an illustrated copy of "California Padres and
their Missions." I was presented with an illustrated and autographed copy of "Ramona."

We were always very happy to welcome Mrs. William
Thilenius. The first time she came to the valley she was a guest
at Mattei's Tavern for a week's vacation. During that time
she made several visits to the Mission. She came to sit on the
veranda to enjoy the panoramic view through the arches, and
to have a chat with Padre and me. But on subsequent visits to
the valley she was a guest of the Mission. Mrs. Thilenius had
the most responsible position of private secretary to General Otis,
owner and publisher of the Los Angeles Times.

These visits of Mrs. Thilenius occurred shortly after the notorious bombing of the Times building. Mrs. Thilenius told interesting stories of the exciting moments in the General's office following that incident. The arrival of the mail was a dramatic moment each day. Some of the letters received by General Otis were actually written in human blood. Mrs. Thilenius would go to the General's house to receive her directions from the General, and it was there on one memorable day she was met by the Japanese house boy who was in a state of fearful excitement. The postman had just given to him a small square box. Apparently the devoted house boy had an extremely active sixth sense. Holding it up he kept saying over and over again: "Mrs. Thilen' me no lik-ee, you call police, me no lik-ee."

"What's the matter with it?" she asked.

"Me no lik-ee." And putting the parcel to his nose and sniffing he repeated, "Me no lik-ee, you call police."

General Otis was fearless, and when Mrs. Thilenius took up the matter of the parcel with him he tried to laugh it off, but she thought it best to let the police open the parcel. They took it to a vacant lot for investigation and there discovered the box filled with explosives. The cover of the box was so arranged that in slipping it out of its groove it would scratch a match and immediately set off the bomb. It contained enough explosives to wreck a good part of the building.

Mr. and Mrs. Frank A. Miller, of the Mission Inn at Riverside, California, were delightful and interesting guests of Santa Ines "en tiempos pasados." Mr. Miller as Master of the Inn was a man of vision and made his hostelry one of three or four best known hotels in the world. He filled it with all sorts of priceless treasures from all parts of the globe. Brought up as a Quaker, most humble and mild of manner, Mr. Miller's world fame did not dim his interest and unselfish devotion to his city and state.

On the occasion of Mr. and Mrs. Miller's spending the night as our guests they were surprised to find the Mission in such good order and were lavish in their approbation of the work Padre and I had accomplished in making it attractive as well as comfortable. In this enthusiasm Mr. Miller rose and coming towards me, curtsied. He took my hand, kissed it, saying, "In appreciation I do thee honor." Imagine my surprise and embarrassment! It was one of those "moments you never forget!"

Some time later it was my good fortune to be a guest at the Mission Inn. On my arrival Mr. Miller assigned me to what he called St. Francis' room, — a very spacious room overlooking the front entrance and garden. It was nicely furnished and in a niche in one corner was an almost life-sized statue of St. Francis. To do me honor Mr. Miller, evidently, had designated St. Francis to be my guardian during my visit.

Another innkeeper worthy of mention and a staunch friend of Santa Ines was Mr. Frank McCoy of Santa Maria. Our first meeting with Mr. McCoy was during the years he spent as secretary for the sugar-beet plant at Betteravia in the Santa Maria Valley. Later, when he bought the Blockman dwelling and converted it into a small hotel, which he named the Santa Maria Inn, his visits were very frequent. He delighted in driving some hotel guest or guests the thirty or so miles to show them the Mission and to see that they were introduced to the "unique" occupants of the historical structure.

Mr. McCoy, like Mr. Miller, was a visionary and created a hotel of distinction. A man of integrity and good taste and a lover of flowers, he put his ingenuity into practice. Soon the Santa Maria Inn gained prominence through the use of flowers as well as good beds and good food. At all times throughout the year the dining room and lobbies were a veritable flower show, with flowers grown for the purpose. The original building has had many additions and its fame now stretches far beyond the borders of the continent and across the waters to other lands.

Other visitors of prominence who at one time or another partook of the Mission's hospitality were the actress, Miss Nance O'Neill who came in July, 1908; El Señor Juan Riaus, Spanish

Minister to the United States, with Fabian de la Puenta, Washington, D. C. in October, 1913; Governor and Mrs. Hiram Johnson of California chose April of 1911; Mrs. Grover Cleveland Preston, wife of ex-president Grover Cleveland of the United States, made her visit in April, 1917; and Mr. Louis Hill of St. Paul, Minnesota, son of James J. Hill, builder of the Great Northern Railway, came in January, 1919. John Barrymore, the actor, Alexander Harmer and John Gamble, artists, and many others found their way to the Mission.

THE DABNEYS AND LUCY IN PARTICULAR

In the years between 1912 and 1924 Mr. and Mrs. Charles W. Dabney with their young sons, Charles and Samuel, spent much time at Mattei's Tavern in Los Olivos and at the Manzana on Figueroa mountain. The Dabneys built a log cabin at the Manzana and camped there during the hunting and fishing seasons and during their sons' vacations from school.

It was on one of their week-ends at the Tavern that Mrs. Dabney and Samuel rode their ponies to the Mission. "We'd like to see the Mission if you will take us through," Mrs. Dabney said, when, late one afternoon, I answered the door bell.

It so happened that I had nothing pressing to do and took plenty of time in taking my visitors through the chapel and the large recreation room where many objects of interest were temporarily placed. So interested were the visitors that it grew almost too dark to see before they took their leave. Mrs. Dabney apologized profusely for taking so much of my time and, thanking me, asked if she might come again and bring friends. It was from this small beginning and subsequent visits to the Mission that our friendship with the Dabneys originated and became deep rooted.

In coming to the valley from Santa Barbara Mr. Dabney and the boys often came on horseback by way of the San Marcos Pass, practically an all day ride. Mrs. Dabney chose to ride in their big Pierce Arrow car and came by way of the coast and through the Gaviota Pass and into the valley. Chauffeured by Patrick Lennon the Pierce Arrow would, if the Manzana was their destination, be loaded with all sorts of provisions for the sojourn at the cabin. From Los Olivos, however, all the provisions had to be taken up the mountain trail by pack mule. The party, too, had to make the trip to and from the cabin on horseback. Such were the only means of transportation to the rugged, remote and almost inaccessible regions in those "mañana" days of carefree living. The Mattei boys, Frank, Charles and Clarence, were often included in these expeditions.

May I digress at this point to relate a most amazing incident which took place on one of these expeditions when Clarence was one of the party and rode his own small horse. All went well until the morning they were breaking camp to return home, Clarence could not find his horse. A search was started. Mr. Dabney and the boys rode their horses over all the rideable trails, peering down deep canyons and scanning the landscape in quest of the lost pony. Eventually, peering down a precipice into a deep canyon far below, they spied the pony all crumpled in a heap and motionless. It had evidently lost its footing and tumbled over the precipice.

Some three months later when the incident was all but forgotten, Clarence early one morning was "flabbergasted" to see his pony standing in front of the stable door. Blinking his eyes to make sure of what he saw, he laid his hand on the pony and received a grateful and familiar whinney. On closer scrutiny he discovered that the pony carried his head on one side. His neck had been broken in the fall, and when he had recovered sufficiently had found his way back to the stable. From that time on he was named "Crook-neck." One day Mr. Mattei offered the pony to Padre, and Padre accepted him. For more than a year Crook-neck decorated the valley's landscape by taking me on all my errands to Los Olivos and Santa Inez or on my visits to the neighbors. He was a very gentle horse and always evoked my sympathies when driving him. Later Padre sold him to a Danish boy who wanted a pony to ride to school at Santa Ynez.

It was late one afternoon when Mr. John Libeu and his aged father sat on the veranda with Padre and myself, giving us a vivid picture of Zaca Lake, its setting and their home on the water's edge way up on the top of Figueroa mountain. It sounded so unreal and fantastic that a longing to some day visit that fairyland and hidden lake was ever with me. The wheels of time ground slowly in those tranquil days and it was years later that one day while visiting with Lucy Dabney, she suddenly said, "Mamie, would you like to join me on a trip and a week's stay at Zaca Lake?"

"Would I like it? I'd love it!" The invitation was so unexpected and I was so pleased that I almost jumped out of my chair.

The date and time were set and at the appointed hour, with Patrick at the wheel of the car, Lucy and I were on our way to the land of my dreams. We reached the foot of the grade at 11 a.m. and from a telephone installed in a box fastened to an oak tree we telephoned Mr. Mark Craven that we had arrived. In a short time we heard the rumbling of the big wagon drawn by four heavy horses, coming round the curve and down the grade. Lucy dismissed Patrick with instructions to return to Santa Barbara. We climbed onto the big wagon and onto the high seat with Mr. Craven.

The ascent was the longest and narrowest grade I have ever gone over. Suddenly we found ourselves in a huge bowl with the famous opaque Zaca Lake filling the bottom of it. On the lake's edge we were assigned to a log cabin on the opposite side from the main house where the Craven family lived and served meals to their guests. Our cabin, set high on a shelf, was spacious with living room, bedroom and large screened front porch that looked out over the lake. Here were two cot beds which we decided to occupy. The only means of lighting was with kerosene lamps and candles. All the furniture save the beds was made from branches of native pine trees. The small tables, chairs, dressers, shelving and what-nots were artistically fashioned and in some instances the small pine cones were ingeniously used and fitted into the setting of the place.

Incidentally there was a forest fire on the mountain range not too far away and the air was hot and blue with smoke. As the afternoon faded into evening we observed the deer noiselessly come down to the water's edge to refresh themselves, and

the quail in droves enjoyed the stillness and safety of their
sanctuary by strolling along the shore to feed on bugs and insects.
Later on owls could be heard making their "Hoot — hoot" calls
from the tree tops. All the while we were enjoying the majestic
beauty of the lake as it reflected the rising of a round full moon
and the red flames of the fire as they leaped above the crest
of the bowl. In the morning we shook the white ashes that
looked like snow flakes from our bed covers.

In going to our meals we either walked the half mile trail
bordering the lake or rowed ourselves across in a small boat.
The days of utter relaxation and quiet conversation amid the
indescribable stillness and poetic loveliness of Zaca Lake revealed
a deep understanding of a true friendship between Lucy Dabney
and myself. It was with great reluctance that we said good bye
to Zaca Lake, and the memory of it has never dimmed.

It was in 1926, after Padre and I had moved to Santa Barbara, that Lucy again invited me to join her on a trip, this
time to New York and to Connecticut. It was September and
Santa Barbara was still having settling earth shocks following
the severe earthquake in June of that year. A trip away from
home at this time was indeed most welcome. Lucy had that rare
gift of doing nice things in such a way it left you perfectly at
ease in accepting. This was one of the nicest things to come
to me, and Padre was just as pleased as I was.

The chauffeur drove us to Los Angeles where Mr. Dabney
saw us off on the Santa Fe train.

On arriving in New York we took rooms at the Commodore
Hotel where we staid for several days. We did some sightseeing,
visiting St. Patrick's Cathedral, the Cathedral of St. John the
Divine, (Episcopal), the Smithsonian Institute and other points
of interest. We attended an opera at the Metropolitan Opera
House and did some shopping.

Leaving the Commodore we proceeded to Middletown, Connecticut, where Lucy was a guest of her parents, the Honorable
and Mrs. Samuel M. Russell. I was the guest of her cousin

Maidie Jones and her sweet mother. We were lavishly entertained by Lucy's parents, and in the home of her brothers,
Thomas and Samuel Russell, and by the Jones'. All these people
lived in stately Colonial houses and the grace with which we
were entertained bespoke the traditional New England hospitality.

My last trip with Lucy was to the Yosemite Valley where we
spent a week at the Ahwahnee Hotel. It was in the month of
October, 1935. The scenery was captivating, not unlike an
oriental tapestry in its varied shades of reds, yellows, browns
and greens in the hills, valleys and trees.

Unfortunately, Lucy seemed frail. She lacked the exuber-
ance and enthusiasm displayed on former trips and I was truly
concerned. The long illness of her husband, which confined him
to his bed, was telling upon her. It made me sad. Not many
months later Mr. Dabney was laid away.

Lucy Dabney had a small cottage in Los Olivos near the
Mattei's Tavern where she and Mr. Dabney spent weekends
when they felt the urge to leave Santa Barbara for a few days. On
many an occasion Lucy would ask me to join her for weekends
at the cottage. Taking our needle work with us we would sit
quietly by the fireplace and visit or drive ourselves through the
valley, doing our shopping in the small country stores for groceries and making little calls on valley folk.

All my memories of Lucy Dabney are bright and happy ones.
That rare, sweet, generous and understanding soul will always
stand out as a memory that grows more brilliant with the passing
of the years. Deeply spiritual, and a membr of the Episcopal
Church, an Anglo-Catholic in spirit, she manifested tolerance
and wisdom which endeared her to all who had the good fortune
to know her.

In June of 1935, Mrs. Dabney, too, was called to answer the
last summons. The simple private funeral service was held in
the garden of the beautiful Dabney home. To this the family
very graciously included me. The remains were placed besides
that of her husband in the Santa Barbara Cemetery, which looks
out to the sea.

PIONEERS

What sturdy, ruddy and interesting characters dotted the valley and surrounding countryside. Courageous men and women who had settled down to a grim life of self-sacrifice and countless privations, rearing families under the most trying and destitute conditions. Yet withal, they were a most kindly, big, open-hearted people with no trace of bitterness or resentment. The men kept up their morale in keeping busy with their ever absorbing work of ranching or conducting a country store. The women, in their loneliness, dreamed of a better day for themselves and their children.

In visiting these homes, particularly the more remote and isolated in deep canyons or high up on mountain sides, one usually encountered a reticence which was hard to penetrate. The men usually held the floor as far as conversation was concerned while the women remained self-conscious, silent and inarticulate. As for the children, some would stand and stare at you in awed wonder; others, if they saw you coming, ran under cover of some out-building or into a clump of bushes and you never saw them again. Under the circumstances conversation with these kindly, detached people was of necessity very limited. After making your inquiries as to the general health of the family, the prospect they held for the coming yearly crop, or returns for the stock raised on the range, and showing some interest in the children and what they held in prospect for their future, conversation lagged and your visit was at an end. When you arose to take your leave it was generally the house-wife whose face lighted up and, beaming in her abashed way, would offer something of her limited store for the Padre. It might be a loaf of freshly baked bread, a roll of butter, a paper bag of dried beans or some vegetables from her garden. If the time was propitious it would be a nice piece of freshly butchered beef or pork; perhaps a live chicken tied up in a gunny sack. Always Padre must share in the choicest they had to offer. Whether the call was made by Padre and myself or just by me, there was always something to take home. The simple and modest way in which the offering was made was touching and sincere.

Our nearest neighbors were the Donahues to the south, Peter Hanly, James Troupe, Louis Janin to the east and Peter Confaglia to the northwest of the Mission. Although all lived within a mile their homes were built on low lands and could not be seen from the Mission. Visitors were always impressed with the vast expanse and the panoramic view of the valley and the mountain ranges on either side that stretched out and converged in the distance, not a sign of habitation anywhere. These mountain ranges, Santa Ynez to the right and San Rafael to the left of the Mission, were like huge walls shutting out the noise and confusion of the outside world. Ever changing with the seasons from bright green to Quaker brown and with the moods of the day from glowing rose tints of early morning to the deep purple of evening, they lazily kept their watch over the sleepy valley.

It was always refreshing to sit on the veranda at the end of an arduous day. We looked out over a bright moonlit valley and listened to the "Hoo-Hoot" of the owls, the howling of coyotes and the flitting back and forth of the bats. They had a friendly sound, these night prowlers, in the vastness of the night. It was often with reluctance that we returned to the dead silence of the adobe rooms.

Mrs. Mary Donahue was a widow, her husband having died three weeks previous to Padre's coming to the Mission. There were nine children. Three were married, James to Marianna Cordero of Las Cruces, then living in Santa Barbara; John married to Emma Foster of Santa Barbara, now living in the valley; and Mollie married to Frank Mahoney, son of the owner of the Mahoney ranch stretching along the river east of the Mission. Edward, Katie and Annie, the twins, Nellie and Lizzie were at home with their mother. Katie and Nellie took up teaching. Katie, we were told, started teaching in a small abandoned house a short distance west of the Mission. This was the start of a school district and was called the "Ynez" school. Katie taught the four or five and sometimes six or eight pupils for twelve consecutive years. Not until 1906 or 1907 was the old dilapidated and wind battered house torn down and a modest building erected. It was then, too, that a new teacher, Miss Luella Harriet from San Diego, was engaged. Nellie for many years taught the Refugio school at the top of Refugio Pass. While teaching she transported herself to and from her school by means of horse and cart. The road over the Pass being a mere trail, she was forced to remain on the mountain top for most of the rainy winter months. Life was taken philosophically in those colorful days and people made the most of existing conditions. When Nellie could not come home she would avail herself of the time by studying special subjects and preparing for examinations which she took each year in Santa Barbara.

Mrs. Donahue told us they came from Iowa in a covered wagon and landed at Gilroy, California, with scarcely anything of this world's goods except the clothes on their backs and little in their pockets. They called on the resident priest for help in locating a place to stay. The priest in turn solicited the help of Bishop Francis Mora. Santa Ines Mission at that time was unoccupied, though pretty much in ruin. The Bishop allowed the Donahue family to move into it. Thus it was that on November 1st, 1882, All Saints Day, the Donahues came to the Mission and for sixteen years it was home to them. They made themselves comfortable by making minor repairs to the rooms they occupied and raised what they could on the few acres of land surounding the Mission building. In 1898 the Donahues bought land along the river south of the Mission, and built a house on it. In September of that year they left to move into their new home.

Peter Confaglia was a shrewd Swiss-Italian who had migrated from his native land with, as the saying goes, all his worldly possessions in his red hankerchief. He had a great sense of humor and keen business acumen. Affable, quiet of manner, methodical in the least detail, he managed to have good returns from his rented land. Whether the year was a dry or wet one Peter always managed to produce a crop. Besides raising a crop he had a dairy of fifty or sixty cows. With the help of a hired man the milking, skimming of milk, making butter, washing pails and pans and taking the butter to Los Olivos every morning for shipping, was all done in clock like precision.

There were seven children in the Confaglia family, five girls, Edorina, Theresa, Adeline, Esther and Anna; two boys, Henry and Joseph. As soon as these children had reached the age and size when they could sit on a milk stool they were assigned to milking cows. Each child had his or her own milking stool. These hung in a row on the outside wall of the milk house. All the children were sturdy, healthy, strong and aglow with life. Their dark brown eyes, brown hair and ruddy complexion made them a joy to behold. In their simplicity and naturalness they were like pictures in Grandmother's album.

Mrs. Confaglia was a comely, sweet, submissive wife and mother. Self-sacrificing and hard working, she seldom left home except to go to church on Sunday. She was an excellent cook and had a vegetable garden. To be invited to the Confaglias' for a Sunday evening supper was always a treat. The menu was usually Italian menestra or polenta with stewed chicken.

Menestra was a soup made with milk, rice and grated cheese. Polenta was made of corn meal. In a big round iron kettle on a cast iron stove Mrs. Confaglia made the Polenta. Milk was heated to the boiling point then with a round stick made from a broom handle the corn was slowly added and stirred. The stirring continued during the whole time of cooking. When nearly done the meal began to adhere to the stick and continued to adhere until all the meal was on the stick, looking like a huge round loaf of bread. This loaf was placed on a long platter and the stick pulled out. With a sharp knife the Polenta loaf was cut in thick slices and stewed chicken in rich gravy poured over it. It makes my mouth water to think of it!

Mr. and Mrs. Louis Janin Sr., of Rancho Marceleno, had two sons, Louis and Charles. They lived in a charming adobe house with a long grape-vine covered pergola across its front entrance. Mr. Janin, a geologist and mineralogist with offices in San Francisco, was said to have had ex-president Herbert Hoover associated with him when that young man was starting out on his career.

Mrs. Janin was a sweet, genteel and friendly person. Her first visit to us is vivid in my memory. Her son Louis, driving two black ponies hitched to a shining black carriage, was accompanying her on a tour of neighborly calls. I can see her now, through the mist of years, very handsome in a large picture hat and black lace gloves. She was regal as she stepped down from the carriage. Her son carried a large basket of fruit, apricots and plums from their garden. Shortly after this visit Mrs. Janin's health became impaired and she seldom left home. When the fruit was in season she would send me a note by the gardener asking me to have lunch with her, then later would send me home with a box or large basket full of fruit. She was a sweet, thoughtful and delightful neighbor.

There were many staunch early settlers in the valley. Not the least among them were Mr. and Mrs. Felix Mattei, owners and managers of "Mattei's Tavern" in Los Olivos, that age mellowed hostelry of poetic loveliness and friendly atmosphere. The Matteis had five children, Frank, Fred, Charlie, Clarence and Albert. All contributed in making the Tavern a place to remember. Clarence became a portrait painter of renown and Albert distinguished himself as a geologist. For a number of years Mr. Mattei had charge of the U. S. mail and passenger route, making daily trips between Los Olivos, Santa Ynez and Gaviota. Not until a post office was established at Solvang was the stage route discontinued.

Another early settler was Mr. Peter Montanaro. Mr. Montanaro was a butcher who peddled meat twice a week to the housewives of the surrounding ranches, making the trips in a horse-drawn covered wagon equipped for the purpose. His supply of meat was in turn bought from the ranchers as the demand required. He was always affable, but his meat was not always tender! From experience you had the feeling that it was from an old cow that had outlived its usefulness, juiceless, and tasteless. Since he had a monopoly on his market, out of sheer desperation you bought the "very nice piece" of meat which he offered you.

Mr. and Mrs. Alden March Boyd and two daughters, Joan and Jessie, of Rancho Los Olivos, came from New York State in the 1880s'.

In 1882 Judge and Mrs. Samuel Lyons came to the valley from Pennsylvania. Judge Lyons was active as justice of the peace for almost half a century and lived to the good old age of ninety-four years. He was kindly and indulgent, and much beloved. He was one of the representative men of his day. At the time of his death, his wife having pre-deceased him, four children were left to mourn his passing, William M. Lyons of Cambria, Mrs. Grace Davison, Mrs. Alice Potter and Miss Jeanette Lyons, all of the valley.

Mrs. Caroline Lansing and son Alonzo came from Schenectady, New York, and lived in a small adobe house near Ballard. This house was said to have been a stable built by W. N. Ballard

as a part of the old stage station between Santa Barbara and San
Luis Obispo.

Mr. and Mrs. Patrick Murphy lived on the road between
Santa Ynez and Los Olivos. Their ranch was known simply
as the Murphy ranch. They were among the earliest settlers,
coming in 1879, and said to have been the first to raise wheat
in the valley. To dispose of the crop they hauled it to Gaviota
wharf where it was loaded on a steamer bound for San Francisco.
There were five children in the Murphy family, all boys, Edward,
John, Joseph, William and Thomas. John and Joseph for
many years were partners in a general merchandise store in the
village of Santa Ynez. The other boys remained at home to
manage the ranch and, since the mother was quite old, looked
after the house as well, cooking, baking bread, doing the laundry
and whatever else was to be done. This earned for them the
nickname of the "Murphy Sisters."

The names of Rufus and Linus Buell are closely and promin-
ently connected with the valley's pioneers. The large Buell
ranch remains in the hands of their descendants.

Other old timers were Mr. and Mrs. Alonzo Crabb and
daughter, Blanche; John Torrence, Cyril Gordon Lamb, Samuel
Coiner and the Eduardo and Gerardo de la Cuesta, to mention
a few.

The Eduardo de la Cuesta had five children, Samuel,
Micuela, Ines, Gerardo and Dulce. The Gerardo de la Cuesta
had two children.

Both families lived in charming adobe houses. A visit to
them always seemed to transplant one to an old world atmosphere. Eduardo named his Rancho La Vega, meaning river
bottom or low land; while Gerardo called his El Cerro, meaning
hilltop.

Padre's and my first visit to the Eduardo de la Cuesta home
I am not likely to forget. We were invited for Sunday evening
dinner. In a light spring wagon drawn by our small black
horse we started out. It was in "los tiempos viejos" before there

was a bridge across the river near the de la Cuestas. The stream was wide and deep and rapid. As we approached it the horse slowed his pace and pricked up his ears. Mr. de la Cuesta had cautioned me to give the horse the reins and that he would take us through. So with a "Gid-dap" and a tap of the whip on the horse's back we plunged into the river. As we proceeded the water kept rising higher and higher into the wagon until we had to put our feet on the dashboard to keep them from getting wet. Finally, with a sigh of relief we got out safely on the opposite side. The de la Cuesta's greeted us with true California hospitality, but somehow the thought of having to ford the river in the darkness had a dimming effect on the evening's pleasures.

FERNANDITO CARDENAS

Fernandito was so small. So small, and so very big. Fernandito who knew so much, did so much for his adopted brethren, the Indians and Mexicans. Was it not he who read their letters for them, wrote their letters for them, and gave them counsel? He interpreted their cases in the courts in Santa Barbara, and interceded for them in the courts when they found themselves entangled in the meshes of the law.

At the reservation, if a baby arrived Fernandito saw to it that it was brought to the church for christening. If a couple contemplated marriage he notified the priest and arranged for a church wedding. If an Indian or Mexican became ill, Fernandito could tell them what herb, root or seed to brew, or what mixture of roots and bark to crush and boil, and how to administer it. If there were none of these at hand Fernandito would hitch Nancy, his horse, to the cart and go into the mountains, along the Santa Ynez river, or Zanja de Cota creek, close by, to get them. He always knew where they grew and the season for picking them.

In the flower garden in front of the Mission, Fernandito always kept a plant of "Romero" for which he claimed so many uses. A familiar scene before the service on a Sunday was Fernandito with a watering pot in hand giving the "Romero" a good soaking.

He once brought me the branch of a shrub which, he explained, was very rare in these parts and which he was fortunate in finding on this occasion on the Refugio mountain. He called it "Fresno" and explained that the bark of its long slender branches was used to make a cooling drink. A small piece dropped into a glass of water turned it into a delicate jade green and gave it a mild biting taste similiar to that of lemonade, a favorite summer drink among the Indians.

In a case of death Fernandito was always on hand to recite and lead the prayers for the deceased and, on the day of burial, saw that the proper tomba on which to place the casket was in readiness. Of these, there were three of different heights and were used according to the social status of the person to be buried. He usually led the funeral cortege and arrived a bit ahead of the procession in order that he might toll one of the bells as the funeral came into sight of the Mission.

In the year 1837 Fernandito Cardenas was born at San Jose, Peru, nine miles from the sea port of Paita, Peru. His father, Rafael Cardenas, was a native of Ecuador, and his mother, Tomasa Arrata, a native of Mission Colon.

José Domingo Yndart, a sea captain, owned a sailing vessel and plied the seas between Peru and the Pacific coast. When his vessel touched port on the Peruvian coast he made his headquarters at the home of Fernandito's parents. During these visits he grew very fond of their unusually bright boy. In 1850 when Fernandito had attained the adventuresome age of thirteen years he persuaded the mother to let him take the boy to the Pacific coast with him, promising to return the following year.

The ship which they sailed had a cargo of shovels and nuts to be delivered at a port on the Mexican border. After many, many long days and weeks, Fernandito never knew how many, they landed in Mexico. There they stayed about three months, then set sail for San Diego, California. On this trip, José Domingo Yndart, captain and owner of the vessel, died and was buried at sea. His death, due to bad water, must have occurred in the month of August, since the solemn, very solemn exequia was held at the Plaza Church in Los Angeles reputedly soon after his demise and recorded in the Plaza Church register as of the month of August, 1850. Father Ancleto was, at that time, pastor of the Plaza Church.

The ship which Mr. Yndart owned, Fernandito informed us, cost $7,000.00 and was sold after his death in San Francisco, California, for $5,000.00.

Fernandito remained in Los Angeles until 1853 when he took a steamer at San Pedro for Santa Barbara where he lived until 1855. Then on horseback he went to Santa Inez, by way of Refugio Pass, to live with the Ulpiano Yndart family. Ulpiano Yndart was a nephew of José Domingo Yndart and owner of the Alisal rancho situated about three miles south of the Santa Ines Mission.

In 1865 when the rancho changed hands, Fernandito went to San Francisco where he took up the agency for religious books and magazines. He remained there until the death of Mr. Yndart at Los Angeles in 1865. After the funeral he remained in Los Angeles with Fathers Rubi, Asmuth and McGill. From these good Fathers he received many instructions both religious and secular.

Fernandito's heart, however, seems to have been in the Santa Inez valley, for, on Corpus Christi 1868, he returned and remained in and around the valley until he died in 1919.

For a number of years he followed the sheep shearing camps and was known as a good wool packer. When not otherwise occupied Fernandito spent much of his time with Father Juan Basso, the last of the Franciscans to remain at the Mission. He received further instructions in his religion and in turn imparted it to the Indians of the Zanja de Cota reservation.

Fernandito had a deep, pleasing voice for singing. In conversation his tones were low and musical. He hesitated a little in his speech. Until the last few years of his life, when his singing voice was practically gone, Fernandito would climb the creaking old staircase to the choir loft on a Sunday, and sing the Spanish hymns he loved so well.

During our earliest years at the Mission there were several other Indians who, from the body of the church, would join Fernandito in singing hymns. I recall Maria and Usebia Solaris and Marguerite Bernal as having especially sweet voices. Then there was Fernando Liberado, a Purisima Mission Indian, with a deep bass voice. Fernando was short and corpulent with a shock of snow white hair that stood straight up from his fore-head. On occasion, he too made the old staircase creak as he went to the choir loft to join Fernandito in singing.

To preserve some of the hymns Fernandito sang in his inimitable way Padre made records on the phonograph of some of them. At first Fernandito was reticent about "singing in the big horn" and several records were spoiled when, in the middle of a piece, he either coughed his habitual cough, or turned to Padre saying, "I cannot sing today." However, after several attempts four hymns were recorded—The Alabado, Santa Ines Hermosa, Santa Cruz and San Francisco, all of which are in possession of the writer.

When Padre took over the guardianship of the Mission, Fernandito was a veritable mine of information and proved a great help in clearing up a lot of data concerning the history of the early Indians and the Spanish speaking people. Knowing their customs and traditions, he was indispensable in giving Padre correct names. Many of them had nicknames, such as Yuyu, El Capitán, Mocho, Tuarto, Huero and Nieve and others, all of which was very confusing when a baptism or death certificate had to be looked up. Some of these people could not say under what name they had been baptized or registered as they had never heard their true names.

Another source of great help to Padre was Fernandito's marvelous memory for days and dates of birth, marriages and deaths of so many people. If he could not remember the exact date he would always remember some unusual incident that would lead up to it. Frequently when a birth or death certificate was required for legal purposes, Padre would hand over the old parchment register to Fernandito and say, "I want the day and date of such a person's birth or death" whichever the case might be. Fernandito would take the register, sit out on the front veranda, light his cigarette, take out his small reading glass, which was tied to a string that hung around his neck and tucked into the top pocket of his blue denim jumper, and holding it up to his right eye would peruse the finely written pages of the register until he had found that which the Padre wanted. Sometimes he found it very quickly, other times he smoked many a cigaretto before finding it.

Fernandito was never in a hurry. If he came in the morning and the lunch hour overtook him, he knew that the Señorita Mamie had a sandwich or two, perhaps some olives, and a glass of claret to refresh him.

The reading glass that Fernandito used was a small magnifying glass about one and a half inches in diameter with a heavy rim of onyx. When using it he would with his right hand hold it up to his right eye, and with his left hand hold the register, paper or whatever he wanted to read, close to the magnifying glass. In this uncomfortable and trying position he would sometimes sit for hours.

On several occasions he had consulted oculists, but none seemed to be able to fit him satisfactorily with eye glasses, so he clung tenaciously to his own little magnifying glass and prized it more than any of his small possessions.

Fernandito manifested superiority over his confreres of the Zanja de Cota and considered himself a few scales above them in the social status. In speaking of them he always referred to them as natives, never as Indians. He was fond of elaborate church ceremonies and liked to take part in them. He liked the way some of the ceremonies were carried out in the old days, especially the services in the cemetery on All Soul's Day and the procession on Corpus Christi.

On one occasion when Rt. Rev. Bishop Thomas Conaty visited the Mission, Fernandito, having been duly and properly introduced, and praised for his part in the ceremonies of the day, made this remark to his Lordship, the Bishop: "Sometimes Padre Alejandro forgets his rubrics." The genial Bishop gave a quick glance at the Padre and with a twinkling, scarcely perceptible wink answered, "That's right, Fernandito, you keep an eye on the Padre and should he forget anything let me know."

Notwithstanding his defective eyesight Fernandito had a keen sense for discerning a camera, and always when it clicked he was standing or sitting besides the most distinguished personage of the party.

Fernandito often told us many interesting stories about the Mission, the Indians of the Zanja de Cota and the people of the valley. On one particular occasion he told a good story on himself. Or was it on the Bishop?

In the primitive days when mail rarely came and the Bishop made his official visits to the Missions on horseback, Fernandito often found himself guardian at Santa Ines while its pastor was on duty at outlying posts. During one of these guardianships, his Reverence Bishop Thaddeus Amat unexpectedly arrived to visit the Mission. Fernandito greeted him warmly, extended a hearty welcome with explanations of the Father's absence, and invited him to enter the house while he took over the care of his horse.

"The good Bishop has traveled all the way from Santa Barbara in the heat of the day and must be weary and hungry." This Fernandito was turning over in his mind as he tied the horse in the stable and put a generous helping of hay in the manger. What was he to prepare for him as an evening meal? No meat of any kind on hand. He could make some tortillas and there was coffee, but that seemed a very meager meal to offer a Bishop who had ridden on horseback all the way from Santa Barbara, he thought.

"There were no neophytes to run errands in those days," mused Fernandito as he related his story. "But as I came back to the house, by way of the back corridor, I noticed an owl huddled in an opening of the crumbling wall under the arches. That would make a good stew, I thought, and creeping up silently I had no trouble in capturing it. When I had it all prepared and on the stove stewing, I put into it some romero, from a bush that grew in the garden, to give it flavor. The Bishop must have liked it or been very hungry for he helped himself generously a second time."

In 1907, or thereabouts, Fernandito was delegated to take Joseph Ortega, a half orphan of four years, to an orphanage in Los Angeles. This was his first trip on a railroad train and Nancy, his traveling companion, was left behind. On his return he spent most of an afternoon telling us of his experience in the big city. Poor Fernandito, after an absence of thirty-nine years could not visualize the changes that took place in Los Angeles and expected to find his way about as of yore. "I was bewildered," he told us, as he brushed his weathered hand across his wrinkled forehead in demonstration. "I was so bewildered I could not find my way, and there was so much noise."

Leaving the peace and quietude of the sleepy Santa Ynez valley to find oneself in the midst of the unaccustomed roar and din of a modern city must indeed have been bewildering to say the least.

During our early years of acquaintance with Fernandito, he had no permanent stopping place. Home to him was anywhere that he chanced to hang up his hat for the night. Whether it was at the Zanja de Cota, Las Cruces, Lompoc, a ranch house on the mountain top or Santa Barbara was immaterial to him. He was well known everywhere and always received most kindly. After a visit of a day or two, or perhaps a week, just as the spirit moved him, he would again hitch Nancy to the cart and with an "adios" and "Espero que le volveró a ver a v pronto" would be off.

At one time Padre offered him a room at the Mission, but he declined, saying, "I want to be a free man," meaning that he did not wish to be restricted to living in one spot or be obligated in any way. Later in 1912 Padre gave him the use of three acres of Mission land and some lumber that had been used in the erection of the concrete bell tower, to build him a little house. He then hired a carpenter, and, with the help of a couple of "tramps" that happened along at the time, they soon had a house of two rooms ready for occupancy. In one room they built a sort of "bunk" bed and some shelves for clothes, etc., in the other, shelves for dishes and a low deep shelf from which meals could be eaten.

Padre interested some of his friends in the project and they contributed twenty-five dollars with which he bought a cook stove, bedding, cooking utensils and dishes.

Fernandito gathered up his small worldly possessions that seemed to have been scattered in as many places as he had friends, and moved into the new house. Some days later, Padre called on him to see that all was satisfactory. It was not. Fernandito complained that there was no place provided where he could do his writing. He would like a table large enough on which to place his writing materials, also to be used as a dining table when he had a guest or two. Padre surmised that the main reason for a larger table was the accomodating of the guests, so he ordered some new lumber and had a nice looking thirty-by-forty inch table made for him.

After the death of Fernandito the table was brought to the Mission, and when Padre and I moved to Santa Barbara the table was among our belongings. It now graces the middle floor space of my kitchen and is used as a breakfast table.

Fernandito proved to be a good gardener. He dug a well some six or seven feet deep which supplied him with enough water for irrigating as well as his household needs. He raised all the small vegetables besides potatoes, tomatoes, chilli, cabbage, cauliflower, cantaloupe, Jerusalem artichokes, green and tamale corn. Rest assured that he had a place reserved for "Romero" and endless other treasured mints, sages and medicinal shrubs. He supplied the Mission with whatever vegetables were required and took great pride in bringing "El Primero" of things as they came into season. Each morning he filled his cart to overflowing and peddled his vegetables to the housewives of the valley. In the fall he shelled the tamale corn and, with their husks, which he would carefully remove and save, take it to

Santa Barbara where they were sold to Spanish restaurants or tamale parlors for a considerable sum.

Fernandito never married. One day as he sat on the front veranda he seemed to be in a particularly reminescent mood and related the story of his romance. He had fallen in love with a girl by the name of Samona Cordero, a vivacious and capricious girl many years younger than himself. After a short courtship they became engaged and the date was set for the wedding. Fernandito was affluent in those mañana days. A gallant, desirous of making a favorable impression on his enamorata and bride-to-be, he gave her fifty dollars with which to take a trip to Santa Barbara to purchase her bridal gown and accessories.

Immediately he took the glad tidings to his pastor, Father Lynch, and on the following Sunday the customary reading of the marriage bans took place. He also planned to have a big barbecue at Las Cruces after the church ceremony.

In good time Semona went to Santa Barbara to do her shopping. "But she stayed too long," Fernandito related.

As the wedding day approached Semona announced that she wanted to be married at Las Cruces, and not at the Mission as planned. "What was I to do but acquiesce?" Fernandito asked.

Las Cruces in those halcyon days was a place of great activity. The Southern Pacific Railway had not as yet been built through Gaviota and all shipping to and from Santa Ynez Valley was done by boat. A wharf at Gaviota accommodated the vessels.

On the main thoroughfare and half way between valley and port, Las Cruces was a rendezvous for vaqueros who drove cattle, horses, sheep and hogs to Gaviota for shipping and for cabelleros who delighted in horsemanship and the supervision of the transportation of their ranch products. A general store, a hotel, a blacksmith shop and a saloon made up the town. The distance from valley to port necessitated an all night's stop-over at Las Cruces, hence life was never dull in the little town.

When the news of a wedding and barbecue went abroad there was indeed great activity. The fatted beef was killed, large pots of frijoles and many dulces were prepared, and all looked forward to the feast and a happy time.

There had been much rain and the Santa Ynez river was high and wide. It required skill and courage to cross it. Father Lynch possessed both. He mounted Japola, his fleet horse, and, with a couple of men to accompany him, started out. At the river, however, he hesitated. The torrent was forbidding. Realizing the danger the men tied long ropes around his waist for safety's sake, and with Japola swimming under him, Father Lynch soon reached the opposite shore. There to his great indignation, he was met by a messenger with the news that Semona had changed her mind and broken the engagement.

"She stayed too long in Santa Barbara," Fernandito reiterated.

Two weeks later she married Philipi Serrano. Her wish to be married in Las Cruces was all a hoax. She thought Father Lynch incapable of crossing the river which would leave her free to enjoy the barbecue without getting married.

"I did not mind losing the fifty dollars," mused Fernandito philosophically. "It was worth fifty dollars to find her out and to get rid of her."

So ended Fernandito's story of disappointed love and never again did he permit himself to become entangled by Cupid.

One of the most delightful and cherished visits ever spent with Fernandito was on a rainy evening, January 25, 1911, to be exact, when Father William Hughes of Capitola came to the Mission for a few days visit. Padre invited him for an evening so that he too could have a visit with the Reverend Father. Father Hughes was very much interested in Indians and Indian affairs. Subsequently, in 1915, he was made Chaplain Corps O.R.C., Director of the Bureau of Catholic Indian Missions at Washington D. C. On April 17, 1930, according to the "Tidings," official paper of the diocese of Monterey and Los Angeles, he was made president of the Chaplains Association of the Army of the United States at the sixth annual meeting of the association held at Washington, D. C. He was Chaplain with the Eighty-Seventh Division in France during the World War, later with the First Division.

On this memorable evening, as we sat around the fireplace in the peace and stillness of the large reception room oblivious to the rain coming down in torrents, Padre and I had the pleasure of hearing some of the almost forgotten, rare old Indian songs that Fernandito knew.

"Do you know any of the old Indian songs?" Father Hughes asked Fernandito.

"Yes," Fernandito answered as his eyes beamed and a smile spread over his deeply wrinkled countenance.

"Let me hear some of them," said Father Hughes.

While Fernandito sang the songs Father Hughes joined in the chorus of those he knew. With their arms crossed in front of them, their bodies swaying from right to left rhythmically, their heads moving and eyes rolling, they sang their treasured songs of the Indian language.

What a rare treat: a never-to-be-forgotten evening!

In time as Fernandito grew old, his face took on the appearance of a wrinkled, blistered piece of parchment and his body became too feeble to do much gardening. Then it was that Padre secured county aid for him. During the winter's rainy season when the weather was disagreeable and he felt indisposed to do his own cooking, Fernandito would wander up the bluff to the Mission for a few days.

One day in January, 1919, the year of the influenza epidemic, Fernandito walked up the bluff to the Mission. He complained of a severe cold and cough and looked altogether miserable. Padre thought that he had better stay at the Mission for a few days or until he felt better. Without any urging he remained. I administered all sorts of home remedies for a cough and cold. But it was influenza that he had and we as yet did not know of the epidemic. At the end of two weeks he felt somewhat better and thought a trip to Santa Barbara and a change to a warmer climate would be beneficial. So he hitched "Nancy" to the cart and was off. We never saw him again.

When in Santa Barbara Fernandito stopped at the Borderre or French Hotel, an old adobe building facing the City Hall Plaza. The Borderres were very kindly and made Fernandito feel at home. According to Mrs. Borderre, whom I visited after Fernandito's death, on his arrival in Santa Barbara he heard of the death of a friend and went there that evening. As was customary, he led in reciting the Rosary in Spanish for his deceased friend. Later in the evening, he returned to the Borderre's and remained there until he died on February 7th, just a week from the day that he had led in the prayer for his friend.

He suffered a relapse of the influenza. On February 6th, feeling very miserable, he retired early. Mr. Borderre, who was at that time still living, brought him a hot drink, and later went into the room to find Fernandito sound asleep. Next morning the chambermaid found him dead in bed. Mr. Borderre said he lay in the same position as he had left him the night before, indicating that he had departed without a struggle.

On account of the influenza epidemic the body was not taken to the church but one of the Jesuit Fathers of Our Lady of Sorrows parish went out to Calvary Cemetery, recited the usual prayers and blessed the grave, it being in the large vault or mortuary, in the upper row, to the right as you enter, grave number 21. On the marble slab which seals the grave is this inscription:

Fernandito Cardenas
Died Feb. 7th, 1919
R. I. P.

Mrs. Borderre repeated what Fernandito had often told me, about having a lot and house in Santa Barbara which he was leaving to defray his funeral expense. This was sold by the attorney who had been entrusted with the transaction, for three hundred dollars. Mrs. Borderre furthermore related that the funeral expenses amounted to five hundred dollars, and that his friends had made up the deficiency. Also, that later they had a Requiem Mass celebrated for the repose of his soul because they all had been so fond of him. Fernandito loved life. I had often heard him say, "I don't want to die because I can't see when they put me under ground." Sometimes I have wondered if that accounted for his arrangement to be placed in a vault.

After the burial, Mrs. Borderre came to Fernandito's little cabin to see what might be left there. She found that the padlock which secured the door had been broken and most of the contents of the cabin had disappeared, among them the trunk which she told us contained some books and a few other things treasured by the little man. Padre tried to locate it but failed to find any clue as to who the perpetrator might be.

Thus it came to pass that one of the most unique, interesting, colorful and picturesque characters of the Santa Ynez valley passed to his eternal resting place.

CHURCH CELEBRATIONS

Five notable celebrations took place during Padre's pastorate at the Mission, the first being the event of the one-hundredth anniversary of the Mission. This celebration, because of the nature of things, was postponed from September 4th, 1904, until the same date in 1905. Even then, of necessity, it had to be very simple. It consisted of a High Mass with Rev. Joseph J. O'Keefe O.F.M. of San Luis Rey Mission as celebrant, Rev. Ludger Glauber O.F.M., Santa Barbara as Deacon, and Padre filling the role of Sub-deacon. Nellie, Lizzie and Anna Donahue with Fernandito made up the choir. A scattering of parishoners occupied pews for the event.

Drenched in the richness of the valley where dignity of nature reflected the hand of God everywhere, this simple scene enacted to the honor and commemoration of brave and heroic men who builded this once proud structure was most touching. In the tranquil coolness of the chapel, tapers burned on the altar while the Reverend Fathers, robed in the vestments of the church's more glamorous past, moved about in devout seriousness and chanted the prayers of the Mass.

The owls and bats, tired after their night of orgy, were unmindful of what was going on as they slept peacefully in the belfry and in the openings of the cracked and battered walls that gave them asylum. But we were intensely awake and felt that something tremendous and sacred was taking place. The simple scene reminded us of an old print found in grandmother's attic.

In May 1908 Padre was to celebrate the Silver Jubilee of his ordination to the Holy Priesthood. Although we were still living primitively he could not lightly pass over such an important event in his career. "Nothing very elaborate," he explained, as he formulated his plans.

A few printed invitations were sent out which read as follows:

Rev. Alexander Buckler
Rector of la Mission de Santa Ines
Santa Ynez, Cal.
will celebrate his Silver Jubilee of his
ordination to the Holy
Priesthood
Tuesday, May nineteenth,
nineteen hundred and eight.
High Mass at half-past ten, a. m.

You are cordially invited to be present.

The clergy arriving at the Mission the day previous and taking part in the ceremonies were Rev. A. Garriga, San Luis Obispo Mission, Rev. Fred Lack, Arroyo Grande, Rev. Mathias Ternes, Santa Maria, Rev. Candon S. J., Santa Barbara, and Rev. Julius O.F.M., Santa Barbara Mission. Padre, on this occasion, was celebrant of the Mass. Memory fails me as to which of the visiting Fathers were assigned to the parts of Deacon and Sub-deacon. The usual small church choir also took part.

The attendance at the church ceremony was gratifying. Many remained to await the clergy's coming out of the church to offer their congratulations to Padre and meet the visiting Fathers.

The festivities of the day closed with a dinner for the clergy in the Mission's dining room. All visiting Fathers remained until the following day when they returned to their respective parishes.

Padre, ever enthusiastic about church celebrations, never lost an opportunity to use events to that end. Now that the new bronze plaque had been placed in the church walls to commenorate the Padres who had at one time or another served at the Mission and whose remains now lay burried under the red brick floor of the church, he thought it fitting to have a little ceremonial in unveiling the plaques. And too, since it was the

thirtieth year of his priesthood, he could combine the two events
into one celebration.

At this point the work of restoration after the storm had
been accomplished and our facilities for taking care of house
guests was much improved.   May twentieth, 1913, was the date
set for the celebration.   This date was chosen because it fell on
a Sunday and gave greater opportunity for attendance.   The
invitations for this two-fold event read as follows:

> Your presence is kindly requested at Santa Ines Old Mission
> Tuesday, May 20th, 1913, to attend the two-fold function:
>
> The unveiling of monuments to the Old Franciscan Padres
>
> The 30th anniversary to the priesthood of Fr. Alexander Buckler.

Part 1.

9:30—The Mission Bells.

10:30—Procession, Cross Bearer,
Acolytes, Clergy Chant,
Miserere Mei Deus
Unveiling of Memorials
Solemn High Mass of
Requiem,
Padre Zephyrin O. F. M.
of Mission Santa Barbara,
Celebrant
Eulogy, Padre Fernando
Ortis, O.F.M.
Chant, Libers Me Domine
Absolution over graves.

Part 2.

On the same day will be cele-
brated the anniversary of the
ordination of the present pastor
of Mission Santa Ines, Father
Buckler, or, as he is known
among the Indians, — "Padre
Alejandro."
Sermon by that gifted orator,
Father Raley, of Lompoc.
After the sermon the Benediction
of the Blessed Sacrament will be
given by the Jubilarian, Father
Buckler, assisted by several
Priests.
The Clergy will return to the
house singing the Te Deum.

As in the former celebration Padre was celebrant of the Mass,
with Rev. J. D. Nevin of Mission San Miguel and Rev. Zephyrin,
O.F.M. assisting as Deacon and Sub-deacon respectively.   Be-
sides those taking part the visiting clergy were Rev. Alysius,
O.F.M., Rev. Octavius Villa, S. J. of Santa Barbara, and Rev.
J. Coen, Santa Maria.

Padre was becoming known far beyond the confines of the
valley and this occasion proved to be a big event; people came

from as far as Santa Margarita to the north and Los Angeles to the south. It seemed to us that almost everybody we knew came to help celebrate. The neighborly Danes from the newly founded village of Solvang manifested their appreciation for the Jubilarian by attending the church ceremonies and mingling with visitors afterward.

After the church ceremonies a sumptuous luncheon was spread on a long table set up under the arches along the east corridor to take care of all who participated in the morning's events. The ladies of the parish prepared the food and acted as hostesses. The newly finished recreation hall was used as dining room for the Clergy and other invited house guests.

When all was over and we had dismantled and put away tables, benches and everything else that had been brought out to take care of the throng, the Mission took on its usual serenity until four years later, when another event of considerable import loomed up — The 100th anniversary of the Dedication of the Mission. This event singularly enough fell on the 4th of July, 1917. That posed a question. Would people come to a church celebration on a national holiday? Padre gave the matter much thought and then decided to have a two-fold program, with the church service in the forenoon and an outline of public entertainment in the afternoon, with a barbecue in between.

This event, I think, can best be summarized by quoting, in part, from an article written for "The Tidings" (the official diocesan paper) entitled "By a Spectator." This person was at the Mission a few days previous to and during the celebration and his comments read as follows:

. . . . "It had been Padre's custom to give food and shelter to every wandering outcast who trudged the dusty road past the venerable mission, and it is likewise the custom for the "hobo" to help in the work of renovating grounds and buildings. We were no exception. We brought out tables and chairs, strung bunting, went to the river to cut boughs and foliage for decorations and we climbed up the campanario to fling Old Glory

to the breeze, in honor of the national holiday which was comb-
ined with the mission festival, for the blue-eyed Alsatian Padre
is neither French nor German but genuine and sincere American
through and through.

"At length the great day arrived. The bells were tolling,
the hour had come. Out from the old convent came the United
States flag and the papal flag borne side by side, followed by
little girls, American, Spanish, and Indian, dressed in white and
bearing flags and banners, then the torch bearers, altar boys
with candles, censer-bearer with incense boat, sub-deacon,
deacon, and celebrant.

"They marched across the path the saints have trod into the
house of God.

"Then came the solemn High Mass, celebrated by Padre
Alejandro Buckler, assisted by Father A. Goulet of Santa Bar-
bara, as deacon; Father A. Serra Montecito, as sub-deacon, and
Father C. N. Raley, Lompoc, as master of ceremonies; Father
M. Cordeiro of Guadalupe was cross-bearer and Messrs. Jos. J.
Herlihy and A. A. Koch, torch bearers.

"The choir, which consisted of Mrs. Abe Antiveros, soprano,
Miss Bennet, alto, Mr. O. Westfeld, tenor, Mr. A. Antiveros, bass,
and Mr. W. W. Stetson, bass and organist, rendered Conconc's
Mass in F. During the offertory Fernandito Cardinas sang in
the pure sweet Spanish of olden days 'Santa Ines Hermosa.'
(Beautiful Saint Agnes).

"After the Mass came the blessing of the graves of the Padres
who lie buried within the church.

"Then came the barbecue and fiesta attended and enjoyed
by all.

"In the afternoon on a platform erected in front of the
church, patriotic and historical addresses were given by Father
Raley, Serra, Cordeiro, and by Mr. W. Joseph Ford, District
Attorney of Los Angeles. Not the least interesting events were
the addresses of congratulation given by Dr. Brown, the Pres-

byterian minister of Santa Ynez, and by Rev. J. Hornsyld, Lutheran pastor of the little Danish town of Solvang. * * * *

"The exercises closed with Padre Alejandro singing the "Red, White and Blue," everybody joining in the chorus.

"The day was ended, the celebration was over and the tired Padre retired to rest and to dream of the next centenary which he will surely attend in spirit though his body may be laid to rest with the Mission Padres who have gone before."

The following year on May 14th, 1918, another church function of importance took place. On this occasion the Bishop, Rt. Rev. John Joseph Cantwell D. D. of Los Angeles, came to the Mission to administer the sacrament of confirmation. He was accompanied by his secretary, Rev. Henry Gross.

This was, strictly speaking, a parish event. The class had been instructed in their Christian Doctrine and were now ready for their confirmation.

On the morning of the 13th the Bishop administered the Sacrament of Confirmation to a class in Lompoc. Late that afternoon Father Raley drove the Bishop and his secretary to the Mission where they remained for the night.

The service on the following day started with a High Mass at ten o'clock, and immediately following the Mass, confirmation ceremonies took place. There was quite a large class considering the size of the parish. The parishioners filled the remaining church pews for the simple but inspiring ceremonies.

For a brief half hour after the services the Bishop and visiting clergy held a reception on the front veranda and chatted gaily with the congregation.

As was the custom for all gatherings of any consequence, the ladies of the parish served a picnic lunch on long tables in the cool of the corridor under the arches. This took care of the confirmation class as well as visitors and parishoners. This very informal way of entertaining enhanced a life of rare simplicity and charm.

THE ZANJA DE COTA INDIAN RESERVATION

When Padre came to the Mission the few remaining Indians were living on a strip of land west of the village of Santa Ynez. This strip of land compromised about 120 acres and had a creek, or small stream of water running all the way through its center. It was put aside from Mission lands expressly for the few remaining Indian families, and became known as the Zanja De Cota Reservation, so named for the late Ramon Cota who lived there.

The inhabitants were not particularly interesting as far as their arts were concerned. They did not spin, weave or make baskets or pottery. For the most part they lived an indolent, care-free existence and unless hunger for themselves or their horses forced them to seek employment they would be content to sit on a dry goods box on the sunny side of their casas and, as the farmer once said, "Sometimes I set and think, and sometime I just set." The Indians would "just set." The men usually worked out on the neighboring ranches. They would ride the ranges to round up the cattle, do some sheep shearing and such like jobs. The women took in washing, which they did out in the open, using the tub and washboard method.

For want of suitable conveyance very few Indians came to church on Sundays. Some of the men came on horseback, others brought their esposas in two wheel carts. Now and then one of their group came with a spring wagon filled to capacity with women and children. It was on All Soul's Day and on

Easter Sunday that they turned out all together. They loved the church ceremonies and exhibited great reverence.

In preparation for All Soul's Day men and women came a couple of days in advance to clean the weeds and dry grass in the Campo Santo. Bringing their lunch with them they would stay all day, working, laughing and apparently enjoying themselves. When the cleaning was accomplished they placed flowers and candles, mostly candles, on the graves of their loved ones. Then on All Soul's Day they would light them in readiness for the Padre's blessing.

The Mass of Requiem being concluded, the congregation formed in procession. They were headed by Padre in his robes and the altar boys in their black and white, bearing high a silver cross and tall standards with flaring candles, and carrying censer and aspergill. All marched chanting from the church to the cemetery. Here for an hour or more prayers were chanted at each lighted grave. Silently the congregation followed the Padre, the men with bowed impassive heads, the women sometimes sobbing. When the prayer at one grave was ended with the beseeching Kyrie Eleison, Christe Eleison, the crowd moved on to another. So the round was made until all were blessed.

During our early days at the Mission a few Indians with sweet voices would join Fernandito in singing their favorite hymns during the Mass. Fernandito would bring copies of his favorite hymns done in his own handwriting in letters half an inch high, with heavy pencil on brown wrapping paper. This he did to facilitate his defective eyesight. These were the Alabado (song of praise), Santa Ines Hermosa, Santa Cruz, Santo Dios and Viene El Alba (the dawn is coming).

Mariá Miranda, sister of Capitán José Dolores Solaris, and her daughter Clara would on occasion climb the creaking stairs to the choir to sing. Margarita, common-law wife of the late Ramon Cota and her son, Juan and daughter Rosa, delighted in blending their soft musical voices with that of Fernandito. "Old Margarita" as she was called, was short, round and fat and did not climb the stairs to the choir, but preferred to raise her voice from one of the old morticed pews in the rear of the church. After the demise of Ramon Cota, Margarita married Francisco Bernal. The marriage ceremony was performed by Father Lack at the Mission.

Another colorful Indian character and singer was Fernando Liberado, the medicine man, or herb doctor. Fernando was over a hundred years old. He laid claim to remembering, as a small lad, of being with his father while work was being done on the Purisima Mission at Lompoc. Fernando was very stout, with a protuberant stomach. He had snow white hair that stood straight up from his low forehead and an equally white long beard. He never wore a sombrero. He had received some education from the Mission Padres and, perhaps, the knowledge of how to use herbs and plants to alleviate the aches and pains of his people. He had a deep bass voice and would at times join the choir in singing the Spanish hymns, this much to the annoyance of Fernandito whose voice was soft and low.

Besides being a medicine man Fernando was a sheep herder and sheep shearer. He was for a number of years employed by the Dibblee family on the San Julian Rancho. When we knew him he was a viejito (old man) living in an oyo (cave) near Las Cruces on what had been a part of the San Julian Rancho.

It was during Teddy Roosevelt's campaign for the Presidency that Fernando startled Padre one day. While in quiet conversation he suddenly burst out with "Hur-r-ah for R-Roosevelt!" rolling all rs at length in his unmusical bass voice. The incident was so unexpected and so funny that Padre laughed over it for days.

Capitán José Dolores Solaris was one of the few Indians with whom we had any close contact. Having done considerable work around the Mission we learned to know him and admire him. Capitán was kindly and distinguished looking, with heavy black hair and full beard. His mild manner had a sensitiveness that set him apart from some of his rough and ready tribesmen.

We were told that José had a "past." A dark "past." But no one seemed to hold that against him. The incident as related was that José, on returning late one night found another man in his casa conducting himself in an improper manner. Whereupon José became incensed, got his gun and shot him. A trial was held in Santa Barbara and José was sentenced to life imprisonment. However, public sentiment proclaimed him justified in his deed and after a few years' imprisonment he was released.

It was with sincere regret that we learned of José's untimely death. It happened on a Sunday afternoon when he was returning to a neighboring rancho where he was employed. He was waylaid, knocked off his horse and beaten senseless, then robbed of $10.00 he was known to have on his person. As he did not recover, another bead in the long rosary that linked the days of the Padres with the present had slipped through the fingers of time.

A canny figure was Francisco Astrada, nicknamed "Mocho," meaning maimed. Francisco had but one arm. He was sometimes known as "the bad man." It seems that when Capitán died, Francisco inherited, or took over the captaincy of the Zanja De Cota. From all accounts Capitán José had ruled with kindness and a compassionate heart. Francisco ruled with a strong arm. A strong left arm. Hence the title "the bad man." Francisco was of the Yaqui Indian tribe. One day Padre asked him why he did not go to church. "Padre," he replied, "if I come to church I must do what you say, and Padre, I don't want to do that. I'm too young. Poco poco, cuando viejo." (By and by when I am old).

"I hope poco poco won't prove to be jamas (never)," said Padre.

They were like children in many respects, these quaint naive and simple souls, shy and reticent. Not until Padre had mastered the Spanish language sufficiently to converse with them did they become friendly and trusting. Like children they needed a guiding hand, and one could appreciate their love and devotion to the Padre. For was it not he who gave them sympathy, understanding and lent them ear to their small problems and difficulties?

The Indian though, could be very cunning and his reliance on the Padre carried to a profitable degree. He would ride or even walk all the way to the Mission "tomar prestado uno peso" (to borrow one dollar). Aways they had an alibi for needing the peso. I recall one instance when an Indian came with one side of his face all tied up in red bandanas, his large sombrero cocked on the opposite ear, saying that he had a very bad tooth ache and needed un peso to have it extracted. Some time later when Padre inquired of Ed. Dŏnahue about the Indian, Ed. threw his head back and laughed heartily. "Padre," he admonished, "you'd better ask the Indian to work for the peso before giving it to him."

In one of Padre's small memo. books labeled "Sick Calls" I find this entry covering one of its pages:

"Sept. 20. '05. To Theopista Pajuli, an old Indian woman near Santa Ynez, whose husband used to be cook of the old College. Very poor people, bed on the floor, terrible smell, box for a chair . . . She was ninety years old and died on Oct. 19 and was buried near her husband's grave at the Old Mission on Oct. 21. Heart disease. She was the wife of José Domingo Pajuli. Native of California."

It was in 1908 that the U. S. Government displayed interest in the Zanja De Cota Indians. On Nov. 10th a government agent, William H. Stanley, from the Cajui Reservation at San Jacinto, California, came to look over the Zanja De Cota Reservation. He had with him an Indian, William Pablo, whom he introduced as his policeman of the Banning Indian Reservation, and a Mr. R. B. Crevecoeur. On this occasion they stopped at the Mission to confer with Padre.

On discovering that some of the children did not attend school Mr. Stanley became quite concerned. Finding, on subsequent visits, that his admonishment to the parents to send their children to school went unheeded, he decided to have some of the older girls transferred to the Indian school at Banning. The parents listened to this plan in stoic silence. But when Mr. Stanley came prepared to take the young girls, they had taken to the hills, or hidden in the willows along the river.

Not wishing to be outwitted Mr. Stanley came again; this time he took the parents unaware and managed to take four or five girls to the Banning school. But alas! At the end of two weeks two of the older girls had found their way back to their Zanja De Cota.

This plan of transferring children having failed the Government authorized the building of a small one room school on the Reservation; also a small dwelling for the teacher, Mr. Carl Stevens, his wife and two small children. This was done under the direction of Mr. Stanley.

What yardstick of reasoning brought a Methodist from Oklahoma to teach the Mission's Indian children was hard to understand. Not that the school was a religious school, or do I wish to cast any reflections on the teacher, but it proved to be a mistake nevertheless. After two unsuccessful years the Stevenses returned to Oklahoma and the school was abandoned. Once more the Indian children were left to live their own sweet care-free indolent way. While the men rode the rancho's expansive lands and the women washed clothes, the children, like so many little brown chocolates, clustered at play around the few remaining huts that made up the Zanja De Cota Reservation. God's children, every one of them.

REVEREND FATHER ZEPHYRIN ENGELHARDT
Historian

Our association with California Missions' Historian, Rev. Zephyrin Engelhardt was most pleasant. During our early years at Santa Ines the Rev. Father was a frequent visitor; usually he would offer to assist Padre with Holy Week ceremonies. Arriving on the Gaviota-Los Olivos stage on Wednesday, he would remain a week, or, if he wished to peruse some of the Mission's records he remained several days longer.

A large, tall man of stately bearing, with piercing dark eyes, heavy graying hair and long patriarchal beard, the Father inspired a sense of awe and respect. He was a kindly and genial man. He adjusted himself admirably to the primitive conditions under which we were living. His words of encouragement and deep appreciation of the work being done to restore and preserve the Mission helped us over many a hard period. Later, in his history he was most generous in his appraisal of our work at Santa Ines.

Then came a time when the historian was too busy with his life's work to leave the monastery and we did not see him for several years.

It was on September 1st, 1931, that I received the following letter from our beloved Historian Father Engelhardt. It follows:

"Miss Mamie Goulet
1818 Bath Street, Cal.

Good Miss Goulet,

Could you find time some day or evening to visit the Mission. You need but give the Brother your name and that you had an appointment.

There is no better qualified to give the information I need concerning Father Buckler and yourself at Santa Ines. I must have exact dates, any incident that would interest historical readers.

Perhaps the late Father Buckler left some Notes which could be use to me. Anyway you would know best, and may have heard some things that I wish to clear up. You will know all about Fernandito. I did not learn anything about his death, nor where he was interred.

Perhaps you have some photos of the time or any other time. Whatever regards the history will be of use.

For me the best time would be after 4 p. m., and after 7 p. m. If a morning suits you better I have time from 9 to 11 a. m. You can also telephone at what time you can spare and will come up. I hope you are well enough, otherwise I must appear at your place, which is not easy, as I am so feeble in my feet.

Wishing you all the blessings of the Lord

    I am respectfully,

                        Fr. Zephyrin O.F.M."

There were many visits to the Santa Barbara Mission to see Father Zephyrin, and many letters passed between us following this first note. It was a long conversation that we had on my first visit. We talked of many things, the Father asked many questions, made comments and took notes. Then he gave me a list of questions, saying that he would like me to write the answers as well as I could, and make any comment or write additional information I might wish to give, then mail it to him.

That was a big order. I was scared. It was easy to give information in conversation but to put it into print would be something new. I realized that the information would have to be very accurate as to dates, places, etc. With great timidity, and going into minute detail, I answered the list of questions and mailed them to him. Then, keeping my fingers crossed, I eagerly awaited another letter.

It would seem my fears were groundless. My letter put the historian in a happy mood, as this quotation from his following note reveals:

"Your long yet altogether too short letter delighted me immensely. Here was something intelligent and rich in information. Just as I like it. Nothing superfluous, all useful to me.

So if you wish to gratify me some more, just let me have all you can think up during the two decades and more of your stay at the Mission Santa Ines" . . . .

This allayed some of the fears I had in writing my first letter and those following became a pleasure. There were times when the Father would send me a note, or telephone, asking me to come to the Mission to clarify some of the things I had written. Always he was most kind.

At one point he had mislaid some of the material I had given him and a note came saying: — "I am in real distress and you alone can help me out. . . . . The contents I remember though not in its entirety, otherwise I should not trouble you. If you retained a copy, it would be well. If you did not make a copy, you would know the facts related, and repeat all in your own words. It was all so graphic and touchingly beautiful, that I would print it as it was." Needless to say he got the missing link.

On my last visit to see the venerable Historian, I found him looking very frail as he came into the reception room where I sat awaiting for him. "I only want to clear up a couple of points," he said, as he shuffled his feet slowly on the uneven brick floor and groped for a chair to sit down at the side of a long table. Our meeting was brief and when it was over I took his arm to help him from his chair and led him into the adjoining room and to the door that took him beyond that part of the convento where women do not enter. "Thank you Mamie, I will be all right now," he said, as he disappeared through the door.

On coming down the steps of the front entrance I met Father Felix, who was at that time assigned to help the aged Historian with his work.

"What are you doing here?" he asked, looking surprised.

"I have just had a visit with Father Zephyrin," I explained.

"Father Zephyrin! Why he hasn't been down stairs for a month," and he seemed more puzzled than ever.

"He came down to see me," I said.

"You should be complimented."

"Oh, I am, I am," I said. "I thought he looked frail today."

"He is not well and I am surprised to hear that he came down stairs."

It was in January 1932 that I received the Historian's last letter, telling me that he now had all the materials together for Santa Ines. His letter follows in part:

"Brave Heroine of
Mission Santa Ines,

Miss Mamie Goulet,

Your letter must have tired you mentally and corporeally. I regret that I have caused you to lose valuable time. I hope you get along passably, at least. You have accumulated great merit with Our Lord and Saint Agnes. They will not forget. You might have had a happy life, speaking in the worldly sense. It was generous and in a measure heroic to agree to that hard life at Santa Ines; but you saved the Mission with your uncle. I want to make that stand out. It was well that I preceded you and Father Buckler several months, otherwise what I say would be interpreted as ungenerous boosting of you two at the expense of predecessors.

"I believe that I have all the facts now, and I can unravel all now that seemed puzzling, thanks to your interest.

"Your letter this morning came half an hour before 125 copies of books which were on contract to reach here two months and more ago. (Books on San Juan Bautista). Right off I put the first copy aside for you. Santa Ines will be longer and more interesting on another line. Every Mission has its own story.

Thanking you, brave heroine and beloved of Christ, for all this information,

I am in SS. Corde,

Fr. Zephyrin, O.F.M."

When the book on Santa Ines came from the press the good Father Historian sent his assistant, Father Felix, to my home to present me with twelve books on that number of Missions. Two of the books were autographed by the author. Santa Ines with this inscription: "As a mark of gratitude and esteem," and Santa Barbara with, "In recognition of much invaluable historical material ceded to the author." Something to treasure always.

In April of that same year the Santa Barbara newspaper had this head line on its front page:

"Fr. Zephyrin Engelhardt, Famous Historian of Old Mission, is dead."

Quoting the first two paragraphs, it read:

"Santa Barbara, Calif. (Special)—While America is on the eve of commemorating the 150th anniversary of the death of Junipero Serra, Father Zephyrin Engelhardt O.F.M., noted Historian of the Padres, died April 27 at the Old Mission Santa Barbara. Death came to the venerable Franciscan scholar in his 83rd year as a result of a pneumonia attack.

"Father Zephyrin for many years past stood in the first ranks of historians on the early Spanish and Mexican period in California. No less an authority on California than Dr. Herbert Bolton, Sather professor of history and director of the Bancroft Library of the University of California, holds his work to be 'Without a peer in the field, and doubtless he will long remain the standard authority * * * * *' "

PADRE ALEJANDRO

There are personalities that live after the persons themselves
have passed on. Padre is one of these. In life he radiated
personality. He was reared in an atmosphere of strictest order
and discipline by his father. This regime of severity was balanced
by the living kindness of his mother. Most certainly he was
endowed with the liberal heritage of both. His affable, genial
and sympathetic nature endeared him to his fellow man while
his strict, austere and unyielding moods often led him into
unpleasant situations and a misunderstanding of his truly lovable
and charitable character. His indomitable spirit and tenacity
of purpose served him well in his great desire to restore the
Santa Ines Mission and at no time would he allow himself
to be discouraged or swayed from that purpose.

In one of Padre's diaries I find this item, "Every man, who
has really lived, has had sometime in his life the Great Adventure. The Old Mission Santa Ines has been mine." This, I
think, explains his unflinching ambition and integrity in his
work to restore the Mission.

In meeting Padre you thought not of his intellect or dignity
or spiritual power but of how human he was. In accepting the
pastorate of Santa Ines Mission he was making a great sacrifice.
A man of aristocratic birth, reared amidst culture and refinement,
an accomplished musician, he now found himself buried, as
far as his talents were concerned. There were times when he
felt very lonely during those first years at the Mission. He
keenly missed not having a piano. At one time he bought an
inexpensive violin thinking that it would partly satisfy his longing for music. But with building fences, mixing adobe mud,
and the many other manual labors, he found his fingers had
lost their nimbleness and would not respond to the touch of the
violin strings. In despair he gave it to an Indian boy who
occasionally served him at Holy Mass.

In the years that followed a great change took place. The Bishop appointed the Rev. Mathias Ternes to build a church and parsonage in Santa Maria. The little church at Sisquoc then came under the jurisdiction of the new pastor. This relieved Padre of the long tedious trips of thirty miles with horse and buggy over roads that were for the most part only wagon trails. Some time in 1911 Rev. Charles N. Raley was appointed as resident pastor for the church at Lompoc. The little church at Los Alamos was then an outpost to be served from Lompoc. All this relieved Padre of much of his heavey burdens. In one of Padre's "Day-Books," under date of Feb. 27, 1910 I came upon this interesting notation: "To Lompoc; we carried our own blankets and slept in the church on the floor. Nothing to eat except the lunch we brought along. Cold and windy." Again under date of March 12, 1910: "To Lompoc with my horse and buggy, taking Francisco Arrellanes, (a Mexican boy). We took our lunch along and slept on the floor of the church. We had two blankets. I never since I am in California suffered so much from the cold as on that night. My hands were dead: black; no blood circulation." When making the trips to Lompoc Padre sometimes asked one of his altar boys to accompany him and do the driving. Usually the trip was made to and from the Mission on the same day.

When the rebuilding and repairing had been accomplished at the Mission, Padre was relieved of his charges at Sisquoc, Lompoc and Los Alamos. Then he found more time for leisure and recreation. He could relax by taking little trips away from home, by visiting other Missions and places of interest. It was then, too, that he gave way to the longing of his heart.

"If we do a little pinching here and there and sacrifice the things that are not absolutely necessary, I think we could manage to purchase a piano," he said to me one evening as we sat by the open fireplace.

Personally I didn't see where we could do any "pinching" beyond that which we were now doing, and as for self sacrifices,

that too had limits.   However, not wishing to dim the hopeful
enthusiasm Padre had put into words, I said I felt sure we could
find some means of getting a piano.

How pleasant the remembered scene of the coming of the
piano! How very excited Padre was! Being of an emotional
nature his joy knew no bounds as with eyes dimmed in happy
tears he sat and softly, sweetly caressed the piano keys, now and
then raising his tremulous tenor voice to sing his favorite songs.

It was during these more leisurely times, too, that Clarence
Mattei, the well known artist, offered to paint a portrait of
Padre.   Clarence, son of Felix Mattei, owner and manager of
Mattei's Tavern in Los Olivos, was a frequent visitor at the
Mission.

Early in the afternoon of Aug. 24, 1916, Clarence was again
paying us a visit.   This time he had with him his paint box,
easel, smock and a canvas neatly tacked on a large frame.   He
was ready to go to work.   Ever affable, he now was all smiles
as he arranged Padre, dressed in his cassock, surplice, stole and
beretta, in a comfortable chair in the recreation hall for posing.

All day long Padre sat and posed with only now and then
a little rest and a breathing spell to relieve the tenseness of his
features.   By five o'clock that afternoon, when the shadows were
changing, a very good likeness had been transmitted to canvas.
It was a long sitting and Padre was weary, but he expressed
pleasure at the results as he looked at the portrait, first at close
range and then from a distance.   He was very grateful to the
artist, Clarence Mattei.

Among Padre's hobbies was the collecting of rare coins and
postage stamps, the latter being a happy source of relaxation,
especially during the long winter evenings.   Padre was near-
sighted and wore eyeglasses since the age of seven when the
defect was discovered; otherwise his eyes were perfect and
remained so until the time of his death.   A characteristic of his
was to use a candle light when working at his desk; even after
coming to Santa Barbara where we had electricity, he continued

the use of candles. For hours at a time he would sit, pouring over and sorting out postage stamps and pasting them in his stamp album. A familiar gesture was the pushing back of his eyeglasses when he examined a stamp; he saw better without his glasses when he was examining a stamp at close range.

In the spring of 1922 Padre's health began to fail. He was losing much of his vigor and cheerfulness. The winter had been hard for him. He had had a siege of influenza and after that, and more painful still, pleurisy. It had left him in a weakened condition and without ambition or zest for anything. He now spent much of his time out on the veranda basking in the warm sunshine. It was hard for me to admit that Padre had become a pathetic figure but now that he was not in robust health, his worried and palid face brought a pang of alarm to my heart.

During the long days, which often extended far into the night, that I had spent in nursing Padre, I had occasion for some deep thinking. It was then I realized that sooner or later a difficult situation would have to be faced. Padre had papers from his Bishop stating he had been made irremovable pastor of Santa Ines Mission, and could remain as long as he himself did not ask for a change. Having been a part of Padre in his great dream for restoring the Mission and having shared in all of its hardships and privations through the long difficult years, I understood how difficult it would be and what it would mean to him now should he have to leave it. Yet I did not see how he could carry on under present conditions. On one of those delectable days when spring's sweet odors are everywhere I joined Padre on the veranda. He was in a talkative mood and, as we sat there, cautiously I ventured in voicing the anxiety I had for him and suggested that a change away from home might be beneficial.

"I think it would," was Padre's prompt comment, indicating that he too had done some thinking. "But where would I go?" he continued. "I could ask the Bishop for a six months' leave of absence, but where would I spend it?"

This was an opening I had hoped for. Quietly and at length I suggested we put our little savings together and purchase a house in Santa Barbara, where he could have heat and conveniences, and where he could spend his leave of absence in the comforts of his own house.

Padre listened attentively as I elaborated on the advantages of having a house in Santa Barbara, but made no comment. I excused myself and went to the kitchen to prepare our lunch. During our meal he seemed willing to continue the talk about getting a house and for several days we discussed plans towards that end.

Later in the summer Padre's health seemed to improve and the idea of a house in Santa Barbara was almost forgotten. Not until winter was approaching and the cold unheated rooms added to the discomfort did he petition his Bishop, the Most Rev. John J. Cantwell, D.D., for a leave of six months' absence.

Immediately I drove in my car to Santa Barbara. Stopping with our good friends, Dr. and Mrs. George Luton, I spent four days scouring the town for a house that would serve our requirements and be within our means. When I had found such a place I returned to the Mission to report to Padre and suggested that he make the trip to Santa Barbara to see the house before coming to a decision about it.

"Oh, I will leave it all to your good judgment," was his offhand reply. I wanted him to be satisfied and I insisted on his seeing the house, realizing that to buy or not to buy a house was, indeed, a difficult and momentous decision for Padre to make. He had debated with himself, and with me, whether it was the wise thing to do. Somehow, I wasn't fully convinced that he really wanted to buy a house.

Finally at breakfast one morning he announced that he was ready to go to Santa Barbara to look over the house I had selected as a possibility. "We can leave early tomorrow morning and be back before dark," he said with finality. Having made his decision he seemed anxious to be off.

In Santa Barbara I retraced my tracks to show him some of the houses I had previously looked at and then came to the one I thought best suited to our needs. There was a two-foot retaining wall next to the sidewalk; the lot had a fifty-foot frontage which extended two hundred and sixteen feet to the rear. The house set back about thirty feet from the sidewalk and had six concrete steps leading to a large front porch. The roof across the front slanted forward and in the middle was a gable, with four small windows, that jutted out to break the monotony of the long roof, all of which gave the house a distinctive air.

"It's not a bad looking house," Padre commented as he stepped out of the car and stood on the sidewalk for a moment to survey the place. The location and environment was good, being in what was known as the better part of the town before building took to the hills and dotted the mountain landscape.

The house was comfortably large, having a living room, dining room, den, two bedrooms, kitchen, storeroom and service porch. All rooms were large. Off from the dining room was a patio ten feet wide by twenty-two feet long; this had a red cement floor and a rose-covered arbor. There was a barn at the rear end of the lot and between it and the house were half a dozen or so fruit trees, some berry and guava bushes and flowering shrubs.

"What do you think of the place, Padre?" I ventured as we walked through the garden. "Do you like it?"

"Yes," was his instantaneous reply. "The house is well built and apparently in good condition. With some minor changes it could be made to meet our requirements." Thus it came to pass that Padre and I put our little earnings together and bought our home in Santa Barbara.

As was our custom when going anywhere in the car, we had taken with us a few sandwiches and a thermos bottle filled with hot coffee. On leaving the house we drove a few miles out of town and parked the car on the side of the road, where we ate our lunch. Like a small boy with a new toy, Padre was in high spirits; the thought of owning a house pleased him. "I never thought I'd ever own a home," he kept repeating, more to himself than to me, and before we had reached the Mission he had completely furnished the house with our small belongings, made the barn into a garage, and built a small chicken house for the few hens he planned to take there. He was enjoying himself.

On our return from Santa Barbara, Padre found a letter from the Chancery Office in his mail sack. It read in part, "The Right Reverend Bishop has written to Father Quinn, an elderly priest in Los Angeles, and requested that he go to Santa Ines as soon as possible. The Bishop would be pleased if you could postpone your departure until he arrives, so that you may instruct him in his duties."

Busy days followed in preparation for our going to Santa Barbara. Some of the furniture in the Mission was Padre's own, and from this we must choose what we would need in our new home.

On October 10th, 1922, Father P. A. Quinn arrived at the Mission and on the 15th Padre and I left for Santa Barbara in my car. It was fun getting adjusted to our new surroundings. Padre seemed to have taken a new lease on life; he was cheerful and busied himself doing little things about the place, changing and adjusting gate hinges, locks, screen door hinges and any other object that needed attention. For the most part the weather was balmy, and when not otherwise occupied he would take long walks, sometimes walking the eighteen blocks down to the beach. He would then take the street car back home.

For his daily Mass Padre went down to St. Vincent's Orphanage nine blocks away. Taking the street car down, he leisurely walked back. On Sundays the Jesuit Fathers at Our Lady of Sorrows church were always glad to have him read one of the Masses. Later, with days growing shorter and winter rains setting in, he found it a hardship to go to the Orphanage for daily Mass whereupon he wrote his Bishop, asking permission to read Mass in his own home. The Bishop's letter follows:

December 11, 1922

Rev. Alexander Buckler,
1818 Bath Street
Santa Barbara, Cal.

My dear Father Buckler:

I hereby grant permission for you to say Mass in your own home. I am sorry that you are not as well as we would desire, but the tone of your letter is very hopeful.

Father Quinn can take care of the Mission and he will be solicitous about the fabric until your return.

Very sincerely yours,

John J. Cantwell
Bishop of Los Angeles and San Diego

For the purpose of a suitable place to celebrate Mass Padre had the Patio enclosed, a roof put on and an altar built at one end of the room. He then held his week-day Mass in his own private chapel. This he named St. Gregory's Chapel. On Sundays he continued reading Mass at Our Lady of Sorrows.

The change proved beneficial for Padre and on April 21st 1923 he returned to the Santa Ines Mission to resume his duties. Incidentally, his returning to the Mission created a new problem. Should I return with him or remain in Santa Barbara? At all events I found myself going back and forth and looking after two places instead of one. This proved unwise. In preparing his own meals when left alone, Padre was not getting proper care. My trips to Santa Barbara were a hardship during the rainy season and cold winter months. This state of affairs continued until August 2nd, 1924, when Padre's health again made it necessary for him to ask for another leave of absence from his duties. This time he asked for three months only. The Rev. L. Bourke was sent to the Mission as temporary pastor. Once again I drove Padre to our Bath Street home.

This time in coming to Santa Barbara, Padre seemed to have lost much of the verve he had displayed on his previous vacation. As the end of his leave of absence drew near, and his broken health was not completely restored, he dreaded more than ever to return to the Mission and face the winter in cold damp rooms. So rather than go back, he, on November 2nd, 1924, sent in his resignation as pastor of Santa Ines to his Bishop.

Bishop Cantwell at once offered Mission Santa Ines to the Provincial of the Franciscans, very Rev. Hugolinus Storff. Father Hugolinus declined the offer. Whereupon the Bishop offered the Mission to the Capuchin Fathers who had recently come from Ireland. They took possession on November 20th, 1924.

After a year or so of Santa Barbara climate and a good rest, Padre's health improved and his cheerful sunny spirit returned. He readily adopted himself to his new life and environment and liked meeting his many Santa Barbara friends and making new acquaintances. We had a swing-seat put up under the shade of a tree in the garden, and Padre enjoyed sitting there to read his newspapers, entertain a guest or two, or just to sit and take in the ever-changing view of the mountains that formed Santa Barbara's background.

In 1926 Father Luke Dignan, pastor of Our Lady of Mount Carmel in Montecito, asked Padre to read one of the two Sunday Masses there so that he might attend the little church in Carpinteria. Padre obliged, and for more than two years he read the 10:30 o'clock Mass in the Montecito church. It being a distance of over five miles from our home, I took him there in my car, remained for the service and then brought him home.

On November 26th, 1929, I took Padre to St. Francis Hospital where Dr. C. Naglemann performed a minor operation. It was Padre's first experience in a hospital and he was not happy there. To ease matters I went every day from nine in the morning until nine or ten in the evening to wait on him. After a month in the hospital I took him home in my car. Although he seemed quite weak, looked pale and had lost weight, I had every hope for his recovery. But somehow, when the rains set in and the weather grew colder, he took to his bed and grew weaker all the time until the end came on March 7th, 1930.

In the Old Mission Church of Santa Barbara, as he lay silent in his coffin, Padre was given the greatest honors that his church is able to bestow upon any man. At the Requiem High Mass the Rev. Alexander Oyarzo, S.J., was the celebrant, Rev. Mathias Ternes, S.T.L., from Santa Maria, was deacon. The Rev. Ambrose Goulet, a retired priest who had often assisted Padre at the Mission, served as subdeacon. The Rev. Charles N. Raley preached the sermon. Others in the sanctuary were Rev. Augustine Hobrecht, O.F.M., Rev. J. B. Roura from San Diego, Rev. C. M. Turcotte from Simi. The pall-bearers were John Stevens McGroarty from Tajunga, Frank McCoy from Santa Maria, August Vollmer, San Luis Obispo, Peter Confaglia, Los Alamos, James M. Abbott and Theodore Meese of Santa Barbara. The funeral was intrusted to the care of Martin J. Haider Mortuary, and the remains were interred in Calvary Cemetery. It was the place of his own choosing which he had made a few years previously. When all was over, and in compliance with his wishes, a marble slab with the following inscription was placed over the grave:

REV. ALEXANDER BUCKLER
BORN MAY 23RD, 1855
ORDAINED MAY 19TH, 1883
DIED MARCH 7TH, 1930
R. I. P.

Having builded his monument in the rememberance of God who knows and sees all things, a monument greater than any that can be builded of bronze or hewn of stone, Padre, with a smile on his lips, a song in his heart, and the knowledge that the work he had begun would be perpetuated by his successors at the Santa Ines Mission, was going home to his eternal home, where all is sweetness and peace.